PLEASURE PAVILIONS AND FOLLIES

PLEASURE PAVILIONS AND FOLLIES

In the Gardens of the Ancien Régime

BERND H. DAMS & ANDREW ZEGA

Foreword by Charles Ryskamp

Flammarion

Paris – New York

Designed by Thomas Gravemaker, Studio X-Act, Paris
Picture Research: Sophy Thompson

Flammarion – 26, rue Racine, 75006 Paris

ISBN: 2-08013-561-9
Numéro d'édition: 1023
Dépôt légal: September 1995
Printed in Italy

CONTENTS

FOREWORD

*H*ours *of idleness, the pursuit of pleasure and love by per-sons royal, noble, or by other very rich, have in past centuries frequently resulted in astonishing buildings created for casual amusements. In France, these edifices are exemplified by a few surviving garden follies, and evoked in the letters and journals of those who built or visited such pavilions and pagodas, tem-ples and hermitages, nymphæums, grottoes, and ruins.*

In recent years, numerous books and articles have appeared on such buildings. The publications have either been photographic picture books of the follies that still exist through-out Europe, or essays in scholarly journals presenting sociologi-cal and architectural data discovered concerning the building processes and the completed structures.

This volume takes a unique approach to the subject. In a witty and delightful manner, it unites intensive architectural and biographical research with social and political history. These brief essays and their accompanying watercolors depict both surviving and vanished follies built in France over a two hundred year period, from the early 1600s to the outbreak of the Revolution. Nearly one half of the structures date from the reign of Louis XVI, "an age," the writers believe, "defined both by the fragile spirit of Reason and the restless search for meaning."

The paintings are brilliant and original. The author/artists, American and German, have captured the French genius of these buildings through the medium of water-color, which enables the rendition of various building materials and surfaces with remarkable versatility and sensitivity. The illustrations overcome the special problems of recreating the appearance of each building. The paintings are abstractions of the elevations of the main facades of each building; yet they are also informative of the architectural particularities of the entire structure. The resulting illustrations both document the archi-tectural past and are modern works of art in their own right.

The essays are models of succintness: the personalities behind the pleasure pavilions and the social and political back-grounds relative to the buildings are tied to architectural and garden history in a lively and amusing way. The authors' style emphasizes that these follies are lighthearted, charming, and essentially frivolous.

The investigations necessary to recreate these buildings were quite another thing. While buildings such as Retz and the Petit Trianon are well-known and carefully documented, the far more obscure Reuil, Crécy, Armainvilliers, Gennevilliers, and the menageries and pagodas demanded intensive original research. Determining the precedents and subsequent influences which have hitherto been overlooked was a formidable task.

I have been fortunate to have been involved with this work from its earliest moments. A source of the authors' inspi-ration has been The Frick Collection itself, which has within its collections the two greatest series of paintings existing from these French pavilions of pleasure: Fragonard's The Progress of Love, *and* The Arts and Sciences *by Boucher. The gates and gardens and architectural fragments which form the serene oasis adjoining the Collection on East Seventieth Street in New York City have similarly inspired our authors, as well as hundreds of thousands of visitors to the Collection. It is a plea-sure to introduce this book with its fascinating text and mar-velous architectural paintings.*

Charles Ryskamp
Director
The Frick Collection

INTRODUCTION

There is something I don't know;
I must write a book about it.
—Friar Claude Buffier of the Society of Jesus

FOLLIES AND PAVILIONS are able to charm us effortlessly, for it is all they were ever meant to do. They are one of life's great and simple pleasures, and like the faintly anachronistic word *charm* itself, they suggest a better, more refined and carefree world that probably never was. A few of the buildings that concern us here, such as the Hameau of Marie Antoinette at Trianon and the Petit Trianon itself, have become iconic places, redolent of the spirit and the preoccupations of their age, but inevitably these buildings have become the province of historians, who have usually examined them in the context of quite other concerns than those we find most compelling. Time has also obliterated many noteworthy pavilions and follies, and period representations can be impenetrable to the modern eye, leaving them in unjust obscurity. It seemed obvious to us that these architectural riches should not be marginalized but celebrated, as the buildings themselves celebrate pleasure, company, idleness, and amusement, and with these watercolors and this book we hope in some way we have succeeded in bringing this rich legacy to a wider public.

The replanting of Versailles in 1774–1775; detail of the painting by Hubert Robert, Designer of the King's Gardens. Musée de Versailles, Versailles.

The Watercolors

The watercolors illustrating this volume were begun with the intention of documenting a remarkable period in history—*ancien régime* France—through the garden follies and pleasure pavilions that in many ways are its most characteristic architecture. We formulated a few specific guidelines and goals: buildings would be chosen based upon our own æsthetic judgment, informed by the desire to present a broad spectrum of building types, and would be presented chronologically, beginning in the 1630s with the decades before the advent of Versailles and ending with the Revolution. We hoped that, by focusing upon individual structures and the lives that determined them, a larger architectural and social history would emerge.

The watercolors present the main facade of each building in architectural elevation, in which all points of a structure are brought to a picture plane without perspectival distortion. This mode of drawing is both abstract—one can never see a building in this way—and richly informative, for it depicts a building's true dimensions in scale, and with floor and roof plans and secondary elevations, these drawings document a building's outward appearance. However, we have taken some artistic liberties by omitting the confusing overlap of architectural elements, as would have occurred in the watercolors of Bagatelle if the peaked roof of the entry facade and the dome of the garden facade were drawn in alignment, and we have also eliminated purely functional elements never intended to be seen, such as the inelegant roofscapes hidden behind the balustrades of the Petit Trianon and the Music Pavilion at Louveciennes.

The process of drawing reconstructions effectively retraces the original architect's design process; all available information is first weighed and sifted, then synthesized in rough concept sketches; the plan is paramount, and elevations and roof plans are generated from it; the drawings are refined and detailed successively as various discrepancies in structure, materials, or proportion come to light and are explored. Once finalized, the elevation is drafted upon paper and painted solely in watercolor.

Visual Sources

Those buildings still extant are rather straightforward to record, but fully half of the follies and pavilions we have selected have been destroyed or altered severely, and three are unbuilt projects. Buildings commissioned by kings are usually well-documented, with plans and records preserved in archives and views captured in numerous period engravings; but in the case of lesser royal buildings, which follies and pavilions were considered to be, authoritative evidence may simply have vanished: such is the remarkable case of the Hermitage at Compiègne—built and subsequently expanded for Louis XV by his First Architect, Ange-Jacques Gabriel—for which no visual record of the elevations has been found.

C·L·B·   C·P·R·

Pavillon de Saturne

An elevation of the proposed Pavilion of Saturn at Marly, designed by Charles Le Brun and engraved by Chatillon. Such excellent documentation is quite rare for the follies and pavilions of the ancien régime. Authors' collection.

Many lapses in documentation result from the methods employed to build pavilions and follies. The king would commission a building from his Superintendent of Buildings, who oversaw all royal contruction; the First Architect carried out the actual design, employing a staff of architects and draftsmen. Lesser projects were drawn in plan and elevation, with a cursory indication of ornament and detailing, then presented for approval. Construction was swift—harried would be more precise, since every king fancied himself an amateur architect and was mercilessly impatient to see personal projects completed.

Methods were straightforward, often simplistic: as a rule, limestone walls in the city, a stone base and rubble walls coated with stucco in the country. Freshly quarried, limestone is soft and easily carved; blocks were laid like oversize bricks, then sculpted with architectural detail and ornament. Minor inconsistencies are introduced with these procedures; the misalignment of the joint lines of limestone blocks with architectural ornament such as quoins or rustication lines occurs nearly universally. What appears to be a single stone may in fact be composed of three or more separate blocks, and even these decorative quoins may vary by several inches in height as they rise on a facade to ensure that a false joint aligns with a window molding or meets a string course; just such liberties are found on the facade of the Orangerie at Coubert.

Detailing was overseen by the First Architect, who often created an allegorical program that determined the choice of exterior and interior embellishments. For example, the architect's elevation of the Hermitage at Fontainebleau includes a cartouche in the arched pediment; as built, these pediments carry allegorical sculpture of the seasons. A fine drawing survives of the pediment for Summer, depicting a portion of the entablature, the stone balustrade, and the urns that once graced the Hermitage, but precise secondary documentation such as this is an exception proving an unfortunate rule. Moreover, ornamental

André Le Nôtre, Designer of the King's Gardens under Louis XIV, preferred the title of gardener. This unassuming man of genius would create the most ambitious— and influential—gardens of the age. Portrait by Carlo Maratta. Musée de Versailles, Versailles.

sculptors and plasterers were considered artists in their own right, not mere craftsmen, and could be given considerable leeway to interpret thematic directions, and often the only record of their work is the building itself, if it still stands and has not been altered.

The buildings at the Hameau serve as excellent examples of the distorting effects of renovations; the details of the Queen's Mill—built of thatch, timber, and stucco over two centuries ago and therefore in constant need of maintenance—have changed slightly but kaleidescopically in successive photographs. The mill is in fact more a Platonic idea than a structure and has been recreated over the generations with greater and lesser degrees of authenticity, though its most recent restoration is an exemplary one.

For the aristocracy and the financiers—the other great patrons of folly building—architectural recordkeeping was erratic at best. Plans of their garden buildings, assuming such plans existed, are terrific rarities. Creating these follies was blithely uncompli-

*T*he Oyster Party
by Jean-François De Troy, 1734. Musée Condé, Chantilly.

cated, particularly during the reign of Louis XVI, when chinoiserie summerhouses became a rage, and a pagoda may have been built, enjoyed, and destroyed with no record retained for posterity. It has been estimated that several hundred pagodas were built in France in the decades before the Revolution; three remain—the pagodas at Chanteloup and Cassan are illustrated here, and a small kiosk stands in Normandy—and perhaps a few dozen such structures, although destroyed, have any surviving visual documentation.

Engravers and Artists

Scenic engravers and the artists who sketched or painted gardens often reinterpreted their subjects for their own artistic ends; a comparison of the various period representations of the Luxembourg Grotto reveals a spectrum of slightly differing designs. Conscientious, considered draftsmanship did not become at all widespread until the late eighteenth century, casting further doubts upon many period documents. The Grotto of Thétis, an important commission early in the reign of Louis XIV, is unusually well-documented with numerous engravings, some superb in their accuracy and artistry, as well as with canvases, and in several views urns appear atop the parapet. Urns also appear on the grotto in Pierre Patel's 1668 view of Versailles, but Patel, otherwise highly accurate, has painted one more urn than warranted by the number of piers on the grotto's obscured facade. Although urns may have graced the grotto during some of its twenty years of existence, we have opted for conservative course and have not introduced them.

We have dismissed buildings—of which sadly there are far too many—that offer scant evidence for an accurate reconstruction. The results would have been little more than conjecture, akin to those fecund ruins in the Roman Forum that generated staggeringly varied reconstructions by successive generations of students at the École des Beaux-Arts. Nonetheless we also readily admit that in every case

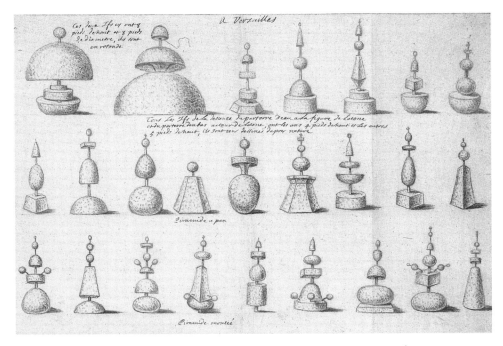

*T*he art
of topiary: designs for the yews bordering
the Latona Fountain, from the album
"Interior Decoration and Gardens
of Versailles." Musée de Versailles,
Versailles.

of reconstruction, including work upon extant buildings, our efforts were repeatedly hampered by the unknowable.

When dealing with these buildings on such a detailed level, the questions that arise are both myriad and mundane. Identifying materials from schematic plans is often a leap of informed faith: was a roof sheathed with lead sheets or slate shingles? If shingles, what shape: rectangles, fishscales, or trapezoids? Did they grade (diminish in size) as they rose? And so on. Apart from stucco and stonework—often, but not always, quarried locally—color is most difficult to document. The color schemes of the pagodas presented here, precious few of which are recorded, are largely based upon chinoiserie representations found in period artwork and interior decoration. Can we trust engravings colored in the period as accurate? We include a contemporary scheme for the Lake Pagoda at the Folly Saint-James, though it is impossible to judge its accuracy.

We have thus realized from the outset that much of our work is of necessity flawed, for the answers to these questions are irretrievably lost or muddled; we present this work as an example, a possibility, and a basis for further investigation, and whatever new light it may shed is welcome. Over and again in our research we were reminded how little can remain— not only of these buildings but of the lives of their architects and those who commissioned them. Time ablates surely and irrevocably, whether it be kings or their monuments, and casts a profound shadow of ignorance. In this sense, a building such as the Orangerie at Coubert, whose facade still stands— windowless, detached, yet intact—is more lost to us because of our ignorance of its history than the Grotto of Thétis, razed over three centuries ago yet remarkably well-documented.

We hope that if we have achieved anything, it is a fuller appreciation of these buildings and the history that permeates them and what they in turn preserve for us all. We hope also to impart the wish to visit those that survive, to know the folly of another age.

LOUIS XIII AND THE REIGN OF THE CARDINALS: A *COUP D'ŒIL* AT ITALY

And to think I will have to leave all this behind.
—Cardinal Mazarin's last words, 9 March 1661

*A*fter decades of civil and religious strife, France achieved a period of relative internal stability during Louis XIII's reign (1610–1643), which fostered resurgent artistic and architectural patronage. The king and Cardinal Richelieu, his supremely able minister, inherited a rich cultural legacy: campaigning French kings and two Medici queens—Catherine and later Marie—had brought skilled Italian artisans to France, and the country was deeply influenced by Italy in all the arts. The architects of the period, dominated by the brilliant François Mansart, firmly established a tradition of French classicism, creating from diverse precedents richly inventive and uniquely French châteaux.

The elements that characterize the baroque French garden— vast axes, geometric precision, and martial rigor—had neither been fully developed nor fully alloyed, and gardens still owed much to the additive, inward-looking designs of the Renaissance. Italianate grottoes typified the garden architecture of the age; their robust facades celebrated the elements of earth and water, and their elaborate shellwork interiors harbored fiercely aggressive water games.

Grottoes and their intricate hydraulics held a singular fascination; Jean Héroard, physician to the future Louis XIII, reported that the young Dauphin's favorite pastime was to spend his afternoons in the workshop of Thomas Francini, who later was appointed the Royal Intendant of Waters and Fountains. Together they built toy fountains, and the Dauphin would awake brimming with excitement for the coming day's adventures, one morning spinning in his bed while imitating the sound and movement of a water jet.

*A*llegory of Wealth
by Simon Vouet.
Musée du Louvre, Paris.

THE MEDICI LEGACY

To My Aunt, the Grand Duchess of Tuscany—
Being of a will to build and furnish a house
to lodge myself in Paris, and wanting something
to guide me of the form and model of
the Pitti Palace, it would be a singular pleasure if you
would have a plan drawn up in its entirety, with
elevations and perspectives of the buildings …

THE NIECE WRITING WAS Marie de Medici, the newly widowed queen, now Regent for ten-year-old Louis XIII. It was little more than a year since the murder of her husband, the extraordinarily loved and extraordinarily capable Henri IV, founder of the Bourbon dynasty. The Medici princess—granddaughter of an emperor, daughter of a grand duke—could not abide living in the degradingly medieval, perpetually unfinished Louvre, and planned a palace of her own, grand and commodious, and most importantly, *not* French.

Rank and wealth were her only allure. Vain, plain, and imperious, she was among the least-loved of French queens. Hers was quite an accomplishment, considering how France loathed its poor foreign princesses, but Marie de Medici seems to have actively encouraged her reputation by behaving as if she

Alexandre Francini, master builder of the royal fountains. Engraving by Bosse, 1631. B.N.F., Paris.

The Luxembourg Grotto in its original state. Built circa 1630 and attributed to Alexandre Francini. Marie de Medici intended a grand, Italianate fountain, but today the grotto is the backdrop for a reflecting basin and sculpture (authors' rendering).

had been sent into cultural and artistic exile. She made her disdain readily apparent by never bothering to master the French language and by preferring to socialize with her Florentine retinue—particularly her confidante Leonara Galigai, who was eventually burned as a witch for her rapacious fidelity.

To a degree, the queen had reason to look upon France as she did: France itself, at times grudgingly, at times with alacrity, had acknowledged Italian cultural superiority for over a century, and its artists, sculptors, and architects were not considered masters until they had studied in Italy. Despite the successive encouragements of François I and Marie's forebear Catherine de Medici, the received weight of tradition and feudalism, Voltaire noted, had kept the country "steeped in ignorance" and mired in "Gothic barbarism."[1]

"That fat bankroll,"[2] as Madame de Verneuil, Henri IV's mistress, dismissed her, had the taste and discernment of the Medici in her blood and instinctively sought the most esteemed artists Europe could offer to enhance her glory: Rubens would paint a remarkable allegorical cycle of the queen's life to hang in the Luxembourg Palace, and she would commission paintings from his rival Van Dyke as well. She also employed the Francini brothers, who had been sent to France by her uncle, the Grand Duke Ferdinand, and

with them came an advanced knowledge of garden architecture and hydraulics that would serve to embellish and animate the greatest of French gardens.[3] Marie de Medici selected Salomon de Brosse to design the Luxembourg Palace, and the combination of his architectural talents and her artistic tastes resulted in a building of singular importance in the development of French architecture, "an island of the most sumptuously modern Italianism in the Gothic Paris of Louis XIII."[4]

Marie de Medici began her regency by liberally bribing the great lords who would—and did—naturally oppose her, and with a modicum of stability thus bought, began purchasing land in 1611 in the Saint-Germain district.[5] The rural Left Bank appealed to her memories of the Pitti Palace, just across the Arno from Florence: a country seat with extensive gardens so near to, yet removed from, the capitol. Suffering from indecision, the queen sought advice from nearly all the prominent architects and courts of Europe before settling upon de Brosse,[6] and in 1614, amid the tumultuous normalcy of whirling court intrigues, the palace's cornerstone was laid. During construction, the queen found novel ways to economize, appropriating a valuable cache of Italian marble intended for the

𝒯he garden
facade of the Luxembourg Palace
with the grotto in the distance.
Engraving by La Belle. B.N.F., Paris.

𝒯he Birth
of Louis XIII by Peter Paul Rubens,
a panel of the allegorical cycle of Marie
de Medici's life commissioned
for the Luxembourg Palace. Musée du
Louvre, Paris.

Valois tomb from the Abbey of Saint-Denis.[7] The palace was not habitable until 1624, and the queen would enjoy her estate for only six years, for she was to provoke her own spectacular exile on the Day of the Dupes in November 1630,[8] and would die impoverished in Cologne in 1642.

The Gardens

From the outset, the queen's simple joy of planning her gardens was unexpectedly thwarted by the neighboring Carthusian order, which refused to cede the land required for the projected main axis. Of necessity a cross axis was substituted, running parallel to the palace's garden facade and culminating to the east with the grotto; the land for today's extended main *allée* was yielded only after the Revolution. Thus from the garden's inception its stunted main axis inspired a plan echoing that of the Boboli Gardens, where a short, steep hillside rising behind the Pitti Palace had forced a similar solution.

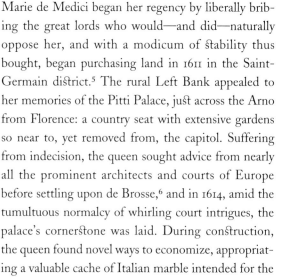

The grotto brought the cross axis to a close and was the garden's main architectural ornament,[9] a grand echo of Medici pride and heritage. The queen's coat of arms surmounts its central niche, flanked by allegorical figures of the Rhône and the Seine,[10] and the facade is richly ornamented with carved coagulations suggesting falling water and known as *mousse*, revived from ancient Roman sources to become a ubiquitous architectural symbol for all things aqueous—as vermiculation came to symbolize earth.

The grotto's design was inspired by triumphal arches common in early seventeenth-century Italy—appropriate for a celebratory garden ornament—and its resemblance to the facade of the Nymphæum at Wideville has led to conjecture concerning the authorship of both grottoes.

De Brosse has been suggested, then ruled out, mainly because he was dismissed in 1624 and died two years later, making it extremely difficult for him to have carried out work at the beginning of the next decade. Jacques Le Mercier, the architect of several outbuildings, has also been proposed, but the Francini brothers are more compelling candidates: Thomas held excellent credentials, having been named Intendant of the Waters and Fountains of the Royal Châteaux and Gardens by Louis XIII in 1623, and is widely believed to have built the Arcueil aqueduct that fed the Luxembourg's fountains.[11] (A descendant still held the post in 1784, illustrating the tenacity of hereditary offices during the *ancien régime*). Thomas' brother Alexandre, who supervised the waterworks at Fontainebleau, published a collection of Italianate facades and gates in 1631;[12] the vigorous baroque spirit of the designs offers convincing proof of his taste and abilities, and almost certainly the brothers' collaboration resulted in the queen's grotto.

Ironically, the grotto which had no *grotte*—thus often called the Medici Fountain—also had no fountain. The queen was exiled before its completion and the need for a water display lost a great deal of its urgency.[13] The grotto has changed dramatically since

The Luxembourg Grotto in a view drawn by an anonymous artist in 1766, before nineteenth-century interventions. B.N.F., Paris.

its construction: originally, walls with false arches extended to either side, blocking views to neighboring properties; these were removed in 1855, and the grotto itself has undergone a series of restorations and transportations.

In 1802, the architect Jean-François-Thérèse Chalgrin supervised a much-needed renovation, and in 1862 Baron Haussmann's public works forced the grotto's displacement. Alphonse de Gisors, architect of the palace's additions, salvaged the Fontaine du Regard from the baron's vast store of razed monuments and employed it as the basis for the decorative pastiche built against the grotto's exposed back.

Gisors raised the grotto upon a high stone base, isolated it with low, stepping cascades, and excavated a sunken reflecting basin before it, distorting the grotto's proportions and destroying the sense of grounding essential to expressing its nature. He also bears responsibility for clogging its main niche with the monstrously overscaled sculpture group of *Acis and Galatea Surprised by the Cyclops Polyphemus;* what originally had been conceived as a rustic void enlivened by the splash of a small water jet is now overwhelmed by marble and bronze. In all, Gisors' interventions created a bosky, secluded setting that never had been intended, yet the grotto, insensitively reset, remains one of the Luxembourg Gardens' great pleasures.

SOURCES OF WEALTH: THE NYMPHÆUM AT WIDEVILLE

Fortitude Subdues the Tempest
—The motto of Claude de Bullion

CLAUDE DE BULLION—Lord of Bullion, Wideville, Bonnelles, Esclimont, Paufou, and Villiers; Baron of Maule; Marquis of Galardon, Montlouet, and Long-Chêne; ambassador under Henri IV; Counselor to the Parlement of Paris; Master of Requests, Ordinary Counselor, Keeper of the Seals, and finally, and most lucratively, Finance Minister to Louis XIII—was among the wealthiest men of his day.

In one way or another, he was related to nearly all the great families of the Nobility of the Robe and relentlessly pursued his own advancement. He was "engaged in some kind of business for the Comtesse de Sault," reported Gédéon Tallemant des Réaux, who added: "the countess was fond of little Monsieur de Bullion, and encouraged him and obtained work for him." The chronicler continued: "M. de Bullion . . . was small, fat, red, and loved expensive things,"[1] and implied that massive wealth more than compensated for his small stature.

The Lord of Wideville, Claude de Bullion. Portrait by Philippe de Champaigne. B.N.F., Paris.

The Nymphæum at Wideville. Built circa 1635 and attributed to the Francinis. The Italianate grotto faces the garden facade of the château (authors' rendering).

In 1632, Bullion—clever, compliant, and capable; a political survivor—was appointed Finance Minister, an office he seemed destined to hold. In influence and remuneration, the post was second only to that of the king's First Minister: Bullion was required to raise the funds necessary for all the king's undertakings, be they waging wars, constructing châteaux, or lavishing gifts upon favorites.[2] Vast sums could be demanded at a moment's notice, and intimacy with the great usurers of Europe was a *quid pro quo,* for a Finance Minister borrowed against his own personal credit, not that of the crown. Bullion relished his position and flaunted his wealth: for a dinner to honor the Maréchal de Gramont, he substituted three bowls of gold coins for the usual dessert of candied fruit.[3]

Bullion served Louis XIII and Cardinal Richelieu with distinction and scrupulously avoided the appearance of excessive profiteering, and he later would be cited as a model of financial discretion by Nicolas Fouquet's accusers.[4] Due to poor oversight and primitive accounting methods, a Finance Minister's opportunities for personal gain were nearly limitless, and no minister—excepting the disgraced, imprisoned Fouquet—died anything but a rich man. Their estates often rivaled those of the king, and Wideville was no exception.

Bullion purchased Wideville in September 1630, two years before he became Finance Minister, indicating he came to office already a wealthy man. He ordered plans most probably from Jacques Le Mercier; the new château retained a decorative moat and was built with a picturesque mixture of materials: limestone quoins and window surrounds contrasted with red brick infill on the walls, and a high slate roof was enlivened by domed corner pavilions and richly figured dormers. Work progressed rapidly, and Louis XIII, the king who lent his name to this architectural style, hunted and slept at Wideville in February 1634.

Antoine Laine was employed to lay out the extensive park, though little else is known about him. A garden designer was then called a *terrassier* or *dessinateur des jardins,* and he traced, or more literally drew, the parterres and *allées* of a garden. Garden design was known as *pourtraiture*—the art of discerning and exploiting the *genius loci.* The intellectual background implicit in these terms, both in mathematics and artistic composition, reveals a great deal about the fundamental conception of French gardens, their geometric clarity and their artistic inspiration.[5]

A Realm of Fantasy

The Nymphæum, the park's architectural centerpiece, stands at the end of the château's main axis. Today freestanding, it was once flanked by brick walls holding statues in niches, much as was the Luxembourg Grotto, and is the last survivor of several structures that Bullion commissioned for the park.[6] The Nymphæum's facade, an interpretation of Italian triumphal arches, is remarkably similar to that of the Luxembourg Grotto. Ironwork of extraordinary artistry fills its arched openings; the tracery of gilded lilies, tulips, and fleurs-de-lys was executed by François Marchant, justly celebrated for this work alone. Warm ochre limestone, Tuscan columns banded with

PLAN ET COUPE DE LA GROTTE

CHÂTEAU DE WIDEVILLE

A river god.
Academic nude by Antoine Coypel.
École nationale supérieure
des Beaux-Arts, Paris.

mousse,[7] and elegant, gilded grilles create a facade at once robust and refined.

Crossing the grotto's threshold brings the visitor into a metaphorical undersea world where the familiar is transformed into a realm of aquatic fantasy. The decor, reminiscent of the polychromed marble rooms of the grandest Italian interiors, has been reduced and interpreted in intricately patterned shellwork. Impish masks composed of rare tropical shells, shards of multicolored glass, and anthropomorphic keystones add notes of whimsy, as did the hidden water jets with which Bullion once sprayed unsuspecting visitors,

Left: section and plan
of the Nymphæum, documenting
its richly sculpted ceiling and elaborate
shellwork interior. Engraved
by C. Sauvageot. B.N.F., Paris.

though the hydraulics for these water games have long since fallen into disrepair.

Grottoes as ambitious as that at Wideville were as much a statement of power and prestige as they were garden embellishments. Such complex and costly buildings, requiring the work of skilled artisans, nearly always had been royal undertakings, but in the early seventeenth century wealthy financiers had begun to rival the patronage of the highest nobility.[8] Bullion sought the greatest talents of his day to enrich Wideville, and the Nymphæum's elaborate, coved ceiling, with river gods and nymphs resting upon the cornice, features frescoes attributed to Simon Vouet; Jacques Sarrazin was commissioned to carve sculpture for the estate and was almost certainly the sculptor of the nymph gracing the grotto's central niche.[9] He also has been proposed as the Nymphæum's architect,[10] but the Francini brothers, who were intimately involved in the creation of Wideville's gardens, are the more likely authors: Thomas Francini engineered the garden's hydraulics, while the Nymphæum's resemblance to the Luxembourg Grotto suggests his brother Alexandre as its architect.

Most work at Wideville was completed by 1636, though a few commissions were not finished until 1640, the year of Bullion's death from a seizure. Louis XIII was surprisingly moved by his passing and wrote to Richelieu: "The more I consider, the more I miss him for his firmness. . . . I do not think we can find another like him."[11] The estate remained in the Bullion family's possession for over two and a half centuries, and though still privately owned, it has changed hands in recent years.

*T*he Grotto at Richelieu.
Built in the mid-1630s by Jacques
Le Mercier. The pair of grotto-pavilions
are nearly all that remain of Cardinal
Richelieu's vast estate (authors' rendering).

"WHAT GOES ON THERE?" THE GROTTOES AT RICHELIEU AND RUEIL

The château is immense . . .
—Voltaire in a letter to Claude Thiériot,
25 October 1721

THE CHÂTEAU DE RICHELIEU is one of a few lost domains, such as Louis XIV's fabled Marly, that can never be described adequately. The château was all-encompassing, built on a scale that impressed with unparalleled grandeur while it repulsed by ostentatious waste: visitors passed nearly half a kilometer of buildings before reaching the entrance, yet the cardinal and his heirs rarely stayed there. The estate was conceived as the physical embodiment of the cardinal's power, for it had no other use, and its sterile purity of vision encapsulated the ambitions of the age.

Cardinal Richelieu was the perfect political being, a man who furthered the interests of the state as he furthered his own and who was guided by cold reason unhindered by compassion. Marie de Medici, on being told that he had wept five times while apologizing for some especially infuriating bit of intrigue, replied bluntly: "That doesn't surprise me at all; he cries at will," and scoffed that at one moment he

A man of many faces: Triple Portrait of Cardinal Richelieu *by Philippe de Champaigne. National Gallery, London.*

could appear cheerful, the next stricken.[1] She had encouraged his rise but later would spend years in poverty and exile ruing her initial support.

The château, begun in 1625, was conceived as an integral part of Richelieu's ministry, a monument to his personal glory that the cardinal hoped would obscure his family's obscurity with "the most handsome and magnificent château that one could ever see."[2] Set on ancestral lands to the southwest of Tours, the estate was a political shrine above all else, and one went there as one did to a place of pilgrimage—in homage. Preserved at the château's heart—as later at Louis XIV's Versailles—was a wing of his father's house, sheltering the room in which he had been born, and though it stood in an awkward spot in Richelieu's enormous park, the church in which he had been baptized likewise was piously retained. These sentimental fragments were embalmed in a setting assembled with characteristic *sang froid.*

The cardinal forced nearby nobles to relinquish their estates for a fraction of their value, then demolished their châteaux in the hope that, by laying waste

The cour d'honneur *of the château with the hemicycle and the flanking grottoes beyond. Engraving by Perelle. B.N.F., Paris.*

Intimations of Versailles: a bird's eye view of the estate of Richelieu. Engraving by Perelle. B.N.F., Paris.

to his neighbors, he would magnify the glory of his own domain. Royal châteaux were not exempted: he persuaded the king to cede him Chinon and colluded with Gaston d'Orléans, La Grande Mademoiselle's father, to exchange the child's estate for another obtained at a forced discount. He then demolished Mademoiselle's Château de Champigny and sought papal permission to raze its Sainte Chapelle, where the princess' mother was buried, citing its imminent collapse. Incredulous, Innocent X despatched a papal legate, who found a magnificent chapel in excellent repair. Tallemant des Réaux mockingly noted that, stymied, Richelieu "didn't dare dig tunnels beneath it, then claim the result was a blow from Above."[3]

The mordant chronicler—anticipating the Duc de Saint-Simon's tirades against Versailles—drew conclusions about Richelieu well worth noting: "Look at the folly of this man, who would make the most obscure corner of France the most illustrious, who thought that joining a huge building to his father's house would greatly increase his glory, without considering . . . that the spot was neither beautiful nor healthy, because despite all the privileges he has showered upon it, no one lives there."

A Vacant Splendor

In 1631, the cardinal founded the town of Richelieu, which he ordered built to exceptional standards, but it was a melancholy marvel that greeted La Grande Mademoiselle: "I passed through a truly beautiful street, where all the houses are well-built and neatly aligned and so quickly constructed that one had to be amazed. . . . In all the windows were paper lanterns of every color that made the most delightful effect in the world."[4] Yet behind these festive stage-sets most buildings were empty. The celebrated poet Jean de La Fontaine wrote that, of all the estate's faults, "the greatest is that there aren't any hosts. . . . Its founder wanted to build a famous town but blundered badly; something he did not do often."[5]

La Fontaine also wrote of the immense forecourts: "If I describe the rest of the château in proportion to the entrance, this will not be a letter but a book: What goes on there?" Even Jacques Le Mercier, the cardinal's personal architect, visited Richelieu only rarely, preferring to oversee commissions in Paris while his brother carried out his orders.

The château was built on a marsh, and though a moat drained the park, guests found the ground floor moldy and dank and the main, second floor little better. The interiors, though, were sumptuous: the château housed one of the world's great art collections, including Michelangelo's *Slaves,* as well as a wealth of Old Master paintings that would later form a substantial fraction of the Louvre's collections, displayed in a gallery seventy meters long.

The Grottoes

The park was conceived on the same enormous scale as the château, though the marshland thwarted lush plantings. The design elements that first appeared at Richelieu—radial avenues leading to the forecourt of the château, an infinite main axis, and a strong cross axis that orders the garden—signaled a transition in the development of the French garden and would shortly achieve their full integration and elaboration in the work of André Le Nôtre, but as yet they remained additive elements lacking a creative synthesis. The garden's main and secondary axes crossed beyond the château at the moated Roman Parterre— so named for the antique sculpture placed there. Beyond the parterre stood a pair of grottoes which framed an amphitheater of trimmed philaria, with

The Château de Richelieu viewed from its forecourts. Engraving by Jean Marot. B.N.F., Paris.

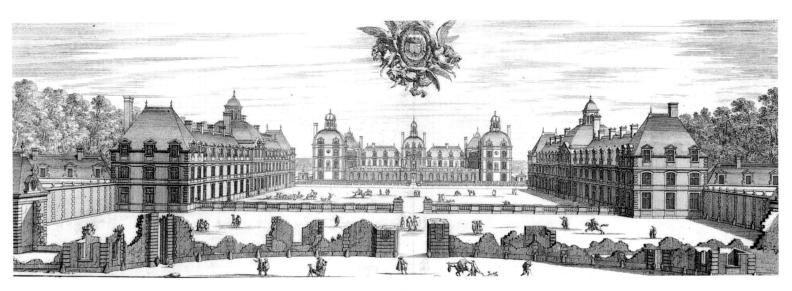

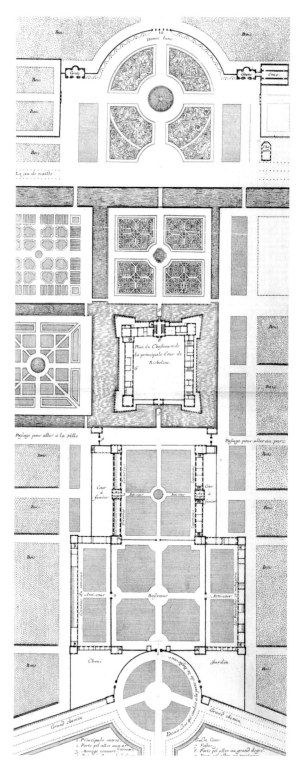

*Additive geometries:
the plan of Richelieu's main axis.
The château was approached from the
bottom, with three avenues converging
at the circular entrance. Lower courts,
forecourts, a moat, and the* cour
d'honneur *led to the château proper, seen
at center. Above was the Roman Parterre
and the hemicycle, bracketed
by the grottoes, seen at top. Engraving
by Jean Marot. B.N.F., Paris.*

sculpture ſtanding within niches clipped in the hedge; the ensemble faced the château and conſtricted the main axis, funneling it into a *grande allée* leading to the hunting park.

Though the pavilions' interiors were never completed, their plan, with a small exedra flanked by shallow niches opposite the entrance, indicates that they were intended to serve as grottoes. They found use as cellars, and one building housed a grape press and a wine vault, but their moſt important function was æſthetic: as a unit with the hemicycle, the grottoes blocked and contained the projected momentum of the château's axis. The same function is performed by the arcing facade of the Nymphæum at the Villa Barbaro in Maser, which muſt have been their inspiration. Their simple, pedimented facades are markedly similar to that of the Italian grotto, and although the Villa Barbaro Nymphæum is curved and niched, it appears Le Mercier deconſtructed and reconfigured Andrea Palladio's design: the paired grottoes retain the Nymphæum's almoſt poſtmodern outline, and its curving, niched facade is reiterated by the semicircular hedge between them.

With a single pavilion of the château, these grottoes are all that remain of the cardinal's undertaking. His great-nephew, the Duc de Richelieu, preferred his own eſtate of Gennevilliers; but Voltaire, visiting the château with the duke nearly eighty years after the cardinal's death, wrote wonderingly: "I truly am in the moſt beautiful château in France. There are no princes who have such beautiful ſtatues or so many of them. Everything reflects the cardinal's grandeur."[6] Excepting that Voltaire was then a young snob on the rise and his sentiments little more than an eighteenth-century poſtcard, it is revealing that he does not mention Versailles. Such was the impact of Richelieu.

RUEIL

Though the house is not of the greatest,
the gardens about it are so magnificent,
I doubt whether Italy has any exceeding
it for all rarities of pleasure.
—John Evelyn in his *Diary*,
27 February 1644[7]

WHAT DO YOU THINK GIVES me the most pleasure?" asked Richelieu. "To improve the well-being of France," answered Jean Desmarets de Saint-Sorlin. "Not at all," Richelieu told the poet: "It's writing vers-

The Rocaille Grotto
at Rueil. Built in the mid-1630s
by Jacques Le Mercier. Destroyed.
This Italianate "Mouth of Hell" was the
centerpiece of Rueil's gardens, ending
a Grande Allée (authors' rendering).

es."[8] There is no doubt that the cardinal wrote most of his verses at Rueil. It was his favored retreat, a simple manor set amid Italianate gardens that was his great joy, and he once remarked wistfully that "the solitude of Rueil is better for me than the demands of Fleury."[9] Midway between Paris and the king at Saint-Germain-en-Laye, Rueil was a place where Richelieu could entertain and be entertained by the writers and actors he so admired. The cardinal lavished far more time and attention upon the estate than upon the vast domain of Richelieu and only months before his death was planning a major reconstruction of the château.

Marie de Medici introduced the cardinal to Rueil, and as a child Louis XIII played among its gardens and fountains and grew to love them passionately, as would his son Louis XIV in his turn. Rueil then was "a place so full of retired walks, so sweetly and delicately contrived, that they would entice a man to melancholy; because in them even melancholy would seem delightful."[10] After seeing the meddlesome Queen Mother off to exile in 1631, Richelieu began his own visits to Rueil, taking possession of the estate in 1633 and finally purchasing it two years later. Jacques Le Mercier was called in to renovate and enlarge the rambling manor, and its decorative program was overseen by Simon Vouet and Philippe de Champaigne.

Rueil was often the backdrop for Richelieu's adventures, for the forbidding cardinal was in private a prankster. A passage of his journal drily records three stories about court dwarfs, including that of Mademoiselle Lavau, fluent in six languages, who was presented to the queen in a cage as if she were a parakeet.[11] Such freakish acquisitiveness thoroughly tickled his connoisseur's soul, for the cardinal collected characters as well as objects. Among the former was the improbably named Zaga Christ, who claimed descent from the late king of Abyssinia. Having failed to recover his kingdom, Christ fled via Egypt and Jerusalem to Rome; the Duc de Créqui brought him to Paris, where he became a society amusement in the years before his short life and doubtful exile ended at Rueil.[12]

The Gardens

Rueil's gardens were the domain's true wonders and delights and the source of its renown. The estate of Richelieu had been a static conception, drafted by a single hand with a singular vision, and had suffered as a result. Rueil was entirely the opposite; chance and serendipity had played an essential part in its creation, prompting an early visitor to observe: "It seemed a grove, an orchard, and a vineyard, so variously interwoven and mixed together, as if it had been the purpose of the artist to make a man fall in love with

*Jacques Le Mercier,
the favored architect of Cardinal
Richelieu. Detail of a portrait by Philippe
de Champaigne, 1644.
Musée de Versailles, Versailles.*

*Rueil's Orangerie
stands at left; the triumphal arch was
painted in trompe-l'œil, hence
its name, the Perspective. Engraving
by Israël Silvestre. B.N.F., Paris.*

confusion."[13] Rueil has been destroyed so thoroughly that we know only the vague outlines of the gardens and only approximately how major ornaments related to one another. Well-intentioned modern attempts to recreate its plan in a sense are misguided, for Rueil's appeal sprang from its almost total lack of plan—the felicity of trial and error, the intuitive juxtapositions of the grand and the bucolic, of open *allées* and cool, shaded waters. Rueil was a piecemeal creation, but that was its essential beauty, and the pleasure of the creative process was clearly as important as the gardens that resulted from it.

Wondrous ornaments were set about the grounds. The cardinal's passion for rare plants prompted the construction of a fine Orangerie housing citrus fruits and tropical specimens, and a trompe-l'œil triumphal arch stood perpendicular to the structure. Richelieu loved tulips, then fabulously expensive, and baptized one crimson-veined variety, the color indicating a cardinal's rank, *la chancelière*.[14] Flowers for Rueil came from the Tuileries gardens, and cypress and almonds were among the unusual trees planted in profusion. Le Mercier imposed order upon the gardens with an *allée* some eight hundred meters long that acted as its spine and afforded views of the most impressive monuments. The latter were modeled on Italian precedents and were seen in France for the first time: the Great Stair, the Cascade, and the

Rocaille Grotto that terminated the northern end of the Grande Allée.[15]

Water is the life of a garden, and an enormous expense, and at Rueil it was everywhere, "a prodigious quantity of water: you see it thrown to incredible heights and then falling precipitously with an imposing thunder," wrote the Jesuit Father Papin. "You see there preciously worked fountains . . . a floodgate of immeasurable grandeur spews forth a roaring deluge of water."[16] The site's gentle hills were cleverly exploited for their picturesque potential: ponds and basins were linked by low waterfalls, fountains, and a grotto that had been built at the beginning of the century.[17] Of the amusements it held, one contemporary noted: "Visitors were obliged to leave their swords at the door because of the disorder that sometimes arose when someone became angry at the soaking they had received."[18]

The Mouth of Hell

Unique in France, the Rocaille Grotto left an indelible impression, reported Father Papin: "here is a frightful chimera that vomits torrents. One is stunned by the sea that seems to come from its vast entrails." The enormous head was made "of fine stone, with a great open mouth three or four times the height of a man, with large ears and a powerful throat, frightening from a distance. The niche was fashioned like a rock, with shells and snails, and contained a fountain," noted another contemporary.[19]

The grotto's prototypes were similar anthropomorphic portals at the Palazzo Zuccaro, Frascati, and Bomarzo, known collectively as "mouths of Hell"; however, the cardinal's grotto, far from being a slavish copy, is a singularly French interpretation of these Italian precedents. Schematically, it echoes the facade of the Nymphæum at Wideville and bears a particular resemblance to the grotto in the Luxembourg Gardens: a large central niche featuring *mousse* detail was flanked by minor niches and paired Tuscan columns and displayed a fountain in its central basin. Both grottoes terminated major garden axes, though at Rueil an imposing mask supplanted the arched

A perspective view of the Rocaille Grotto of Rueil, engraving by Perelle. B.N.F., Paris.

One of the best period accounts of a grotto describes the interior of one of the grottoes at Rueil:

"It is . . . everywhere artistically furnished with fine sculpture and figures, flowers, snails, agates, mirrors, coagulations, and other materials. In four of the angled corners are satyrs, in the other four nymphs, all life-size, prettily formed from sea shells and snails; each character makes a strange gesture with the hand, sometimes placing a finger on the thigh, sometimes on the mouth, while the other hand directs the membrum virile *into the air and water spouts from it; on four of the sides there are fountains with fine oval basins; near each stand three marble figures likewise discharging water from their genitals. On the four other sides are benches, to which one is careful to retire when all the jets are playing. . . . When the whole grotto plays, water spouts from all quarters . . . as if a heavy shower was falling and the wind blowing from all sides. . . . But in particular many jets are directed toward the exit, so that people who try to slip out that way are just the ones who are the most wetted. Near the door are two monkeys who squirt water, and in front of the grotto, on each side, two bronze marksmen . . . hidden behind a fine green hedge aim together at the fugitives and fire their muskets at them." [22]*

panel bearing the Medici coat of arms. In light of these similarities, the suggestion that the Francini brothers were the grotto's architects is convincing.[20]

Richelieu endured a Rueil under near-constant construction or renovation and died less than a decade after taking possession of the estate. He bequeathed Rueil to his niece, the Duchesse d'Aiguillon, who guarded it passionately and continued to augment its gardens. In 1666, Louis XIV, who remembered Rueil as an enchanted refuge from the Fronde, ordered Jean-Baptiste Colbert to negotiate its purchase. The duchess wrote humbly that she would make a "great sacrifice" and part with Rueil, "for the king is the master." However, she and her uncle had made extensive improvements and must be compensated for them; the costs were then enumerated in excruciating detail.[21] The king thought the better of his pursuit; he had just begun work at Versailles and turned his attention there.

Rueil was confiscated during the Revolution and fell into serious decline; Empress Joséphine would eventually incorporate part of its lands into the estate of Malmaison, and today nothing remains of the grand cardinal's pleasure ground.

THE TEMPLE OF TASTE:
THE GROTTO AT MAISONS

The Château de Maisons...
is of such singular beauty that there is not one curious
traveler who would not go to see it, for it is one
of the most beautiful things we have in France.
—Charles Perrault,
Les Hommes illustres

I N DECEMBER 1642, A STORY RECOUNTS, René de Longueil brought François Mansart to his domain of Maisons—a village and woodland bordered to the west by the royal forest of Saint-Germain-en-Laye and to the south by the Seine. They walked from the village in silence, the great architect pausing from time to time, surveying the rise and fall of the land through the bare trees, grunting to himself and moving on, the anxious nobleman following. At the very edge of the property they came upon a rise overlooking the river where the view opened to the south and the village behind them was obscured. "It will be here," Mansart told Longueil, that he would build one of the greatest of French châteaux. The story would be perfect except that the site Mansart chose happened to be occupied by the old Château de

François Mansart, architect of Maisons. Engraving by Gérard Edelinck after Louis de Namur. B.N.F., Paris.

The Grotto at the Château de Maisons. Built circa 1650 by François Mansart; its sculpture is attributed to Jacques Sarrazin. The gate is based upon period precedents (authors' rendering).

Maisons, which would be demolished to make way for his masterpiece.[1]

From the outset, Longueil had intended to build a château of unparalleled magnificence. He chose Mansart, already considered by contemporaries the greatest architect of the age, and gave the tortured genius "A free hand in choice of materials, drawing up plans, on the worksite, no matter if it should cost a fortune," which it would.[2] Longueil specified only that a suite of rooms to lodge the king be a component of the château's program.

François Mansart was notoriously temperamental and suffered from a creative torment that rivaled Leonardo da Vinci's, though his perfectionism involved an infinitely more expensive medium than canvas. He composed in stone, and if a section of building did not please him, it was demolished and rebuilt; he would not, and could not, build otherwise. Work at Maisons did not alter from his established pattern and would carry on—with walls climbing and falling and climbing yet again—for eight years, commencing in 1643.

"La Mansarade"

Three years after construction began, a pamphlet appeared condemning Mansart's incompetence and Longueil's indulgence.[3] The writer, though undoubtedly an envious fellow architect, had reason for his diatribe: a wing of the château had reached the second floor before Mansart noticed a fatal error, and the entire structure was pulled down in Longueil's absence and at his expense. The incensed pamphleteer was delighted to add, "The collapse of the entry vestibule . . . also shows that he does not know how to build solidly and is ignorant of the first rules of the art." Overlooked in this indictment was an even more fundamental error: the ground plan of the dependency intended to house the royal entourage fell across an adjoining property, and Mansart could do nothing to mask his error but propose a stage-set facade.

Neither Longueil nor Mansart paid much attention to such blunders and the sniping that resulted from them, and work proceeded apace in the following years, with Maisons completed in 1651. To many it was a revelation—a country palace built entirely of warm, ochre Chantilly limestone, not the traditional brick and stone mix, and a sophisticated manipulation of the classical orders enriched an equally sophisticated disposition of volumes. The ideas that made Maisons so extraordinary were immediately

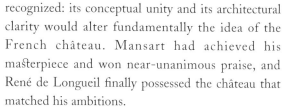

René de Longueil, indulgent architectural patron and lavish host, in an engraving by Michel Lasne. B.N.F., Paris.

The garden facade of Maisons; the second projected grotto has been introduced to the right of the stair. Engraving by Israël Silvestre. B.N.F., Paris.

recognized: its conceptual unity and its architectural clarity would alter fundamentally the idea of the French château. Mansart had achieved his masterpiece and won near-unanimous praise, and René de Longueil finally possessed the château that matched his ambitions.

Longueil did not have many friends but did enjoy the satisfaction of a brilliant career, rising quickly to become President of the Parlement of Paris.[4] Extraordinary political instinct and a talent for intrigue had fueled his ascent, though he distinctly lacked tact and personal charm and never failed to remind fellow *parlementaires*, mostly members of the bourgeoisie who had bought their titles with their positions, of his ancient, though dubious, lineage.[5]

With the death of Richelieu, whose creature he was, Longueil's career appeared to have ended; it was to almost general despair that he soon managed to ingratiate himself with Richelieu's successor, Cardinal Mazarin. Longueil became a major figure in the ensuing Fronde and in 1650, after initiating a spirited cabal, was appointed Finance Minister in reward for his services as a conciliator. A wag noted: "The finances are in good hands . . . the greatest thief gets the purse."[6]

His ministry lasted but a year, yet Longueil found sufficient time to plunder the treasury, erasing the expense of Maisons and all his other debts as well. His gluttony reached its apogee when he hosted a royal feast of Roman proportions at Maisons in 1651. Thirteen-year-old Louis XIV and the Queen Mother made their progress across a carpet of yellow and white flowers, and the amount of food consumed was staggering: whole vats of stews, 1800 pieces of game, 500 loaves of bread, and 154 bottles of wine, which guests drank "like a sponge."[7] Marzipan obelisks towered above it all. A month later Longueil was dismissed in disgrace; unflappable, he explained his newfound fortune with the story that he had discovered a cache of forty thousand gold pieces hidden in his townhouse.[8]

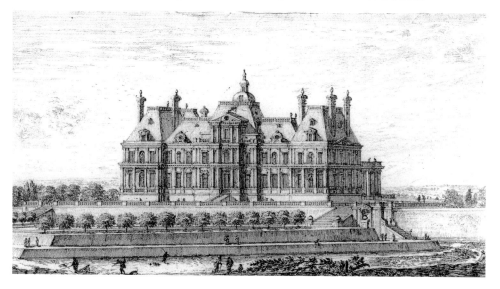

The Grotto

Today the garden facade of Maisons faces a small parterre and a once-magnificent view of the Seine. Its grotto is part of the retaining wall that forms the château's dry moat, a decorative remnant of medieval fortifications that created a plinth elevating and separating the palace from its gardens. A second, mirroring grotto was planned but never completed, which is surprising considering that Longueil supervised improvements at Maisons until his death in 1677, and the rough stone enframement that was to be sculpted can still be seen at the wall's eastern end. The grotto's position and its relative seclusion—a visitor first views it after descending to the parterre and turning back toward the château—heightens the air of surprise and mystery inherent in its discovery.

The vigorously sculpted facade is strikingly Italianate: Jacques Sarrazin is credited with carrying

The unexecuted project for the Baths, the extensive fountain and grotto complex bordering the Seine at Maisons. Designed by Jean Marot, engraving by Jean Mariette. The garden facade of the château is seen in the distance. Musée de l'Île-de-France, Sceaux.

Louis XIV arriving at the Château de Versailles in 1668; the Grotto of Thétis appears at right. Detail of the painting by Pierre Patel. Musée de Versailles, Versailles (overleaf).

out Maisons' sculptural program and would have overseen the carving of this monumental composition. Yet the whole is intimate: a single, arched portal leads to a small, vaulted interior that today is a rough stone cave, bare of embellishments. One of the intriguing questions about Maisons concerns the extensive sub-basements, tunnels, and vaults that underlie the château and its immediate grounds; the small grotto and its unfinished twin may have been planned as entries to this underground complex, used both for purposes of domestic service and for unobserved movements.[9] A grand, bayed grotto known as the Baths had been designed by Jean Marot to overlook the Seine and terminate the parterre, and its arcades and fountains would have transformed the retaining wall into a magnificent terrace. Certainly it would have been linked to this subterranean network; thus the existing grotto should be seen as a true portal to the underworld.

Maisons was revered in the eighteenth century; Voltaire praised its nobility in verse,[10] and Denis Diderot rhapsodized: "Its architecture is simplicity itself . . . everywhere one is moved by elegance, nobility, and lightness. . . . I felt something there which I have never felt anywhere else, that the longer I lived there, the more I would enjoy it; the longer I looked, the more I would find to admire; because I discovered, even in the smallest details—even in the ironwork—that harmony of spirit between the place itself and the rank and character of its owner."[11] Queen Marie Leczinska considered purchasing Maisons, but worried that the necessary renovations would ruin its integrity and regretfully passed it by. The centuries following have been far less considerate, and Maisons has suffered tremendous losses. Today the park is a town, with the estate's old *allées* forming its present-day streets; nearly all the outbuildings have been destroyed, and the grand axis across the garden and the Seine is now defiled by a cruelly sited highway bridge.

LOUIS XIV:
AN AGE OF MAGNIFICENCE

I do not wish to build anymore; everyone gives me too much grief.
—Louis XIV to Jules Hardouin-Mansart,
upon Colbert's death in 1683

*A*n indefatigable builder, Louis XIV (reigned 1643–1715) directed the creation of the château and gardens of Versailles and installed his government there in 1682. The king's patronage inspired buildings of unrivaled richness, intricacy, and splendor that testified to his extraordinary confidence and ambition. The royal demand for constant attendance at court set in motion a movement for aristocratic retreats in the Île-de-France, as courtiers sought to escape the cramped confines of their allotted apartments.

Though the formal French gardens created by André Le Nôtre are understood today as the reflection of an absolutist state and a hierarchically ordered society—with their taut Cartesian geometries the physical embodiment of an age of rational enquiry—such a definition explains these gardens only in theory and with hindsight. Among the most important and least-appreciated reasons for the growth of formal gardens was the dramatic increase in leisure time within the aristocracy during the reign of Louis XIV: as a stage for pageantry and a means to absorb a courtier's measured idleness, a garden such as that of Versailles was an eminently practical solution.

Louis XIV himself composed a detailed itinerary for his gardens, La Manière de Montrer les Jardins de Versailles, *after one prominent visitor became hopelessly lost in the bosquets, saw nothing of Versailles' wonders, and returned to the château parched and annoyed.*

The king's tour requires several hours; leads the visitor from the grand to the intimate, from sun-washed parterres to shaded garden rooms; highlights both single fountains and sweeping vistas; and reveals his implicit understanding of the elemental contrasts that are the life of any garden.

André Le Nôtre, who preferred the simple title of gardener, perfected the formal French garden, but the purity of his conception held little room for such willful, eccentric buildings as grottoes and pavilions. His precedent had enormous impact, and those structures built were mostly hidden away in bosquets carved from the residual green spaces between tree-lined allées. *Nonetheless, even the smallest garden ornaments became part of unified conceptions, their art a celebration of glory.*

*T*he Grotto of Thétis at Versailles.
Built 1664–1668 by Louis Le Vau
and Claude Perrault. Destroyed in 1684
(authors' rendering).

"QUELQUE CHOSE DE PLUS MAGNIFIQUE": THE GROTTO OF THÉTIS AND THE BOSQUET OF FAME AT VERSAILLES

Almost nothing is more innocent than hunting and the taste for a country house, provided that you do not spend too much on it.
—Point thirteen of Louis XIV's *Instructions to the Duc d'Anjou*, 1700

PERHAPS NOT TOO PARADOXICALLY for anyone who has ever attempted to restore an old property, the greatest destruction at Versailles was not caused by time or natural catastrophies, but by its owners. The losses are painful to recount, and certainly high on that list are two nearly forgotten garden structures, the Grotto of Thétis and the Bosquet of Fame, that stand parenthetically at the beginning and end of the Sun King's *jeunesse dorée*. They are virtually unknown simply because they no longer exist, but each in its day was celebrated as one of the foremost ornaments of the château's gardens.

For much of his reign, Louis XIV was as fond of tearing down Versailles as he was of building it. He entrusted Louis Le Vau, Charles Le Brun, and André Le Nôtre with the major renovations in the early 1660s, and a small cubic loggia was begun just to the north of

Pastel portrait of Louis XIV by Charles Le Brun. Musée du Louvre, Paris.

the château in 1664. The most curious element of what was to become the Grotto of Thétis was its roof, which served as a reservoir, and in Pierre Patel's painting of 1668 its still waters reflect the pale sky of the Île-de-France. Le Nôtre's gardens required enormous amounts of water—the fountains at Versailles would in time consume more than Paris—and Pierre and François Francine[1] devised the hydraulics to raise water from the pond at nearby Clagny to the roof of the grotto, which then fed the Latona and Dragon fountains as well as the château's lesser water displays.

In his memoirs, Charles Perrault claims to have invented the iconography of the grotto, inspired by Ovid's *Metamorphoses*.[2] If this is true, he elaborated one of the great modern mythological allegories—that of the Sun King, with the young Louis XIV representing Apollo, charioteer of the sun, whose selfless labors enlighten the world. The king, whose love of flattery knew no excess, provided it was done well, delighted in the comparison and adopted the myth of Apollo as a metaphor for his reign. The execution of the allegorical program was nearly flawless, save that at Versailles the sun god arose from the sea at the

Bassin d'Apollon and traversed the skies eastward to set at the Grotto of Thétis.

The Palace of Thétis

Le Vau, the king's First Architect, designed the grotto's exterior.[3] The arches of the earlier loggia scheme conveniently echoed a triumphal arch, and the grotto's piers were embellished with panels of *mousse*. Bas-relief rondels depicting putti astride dolphins were sculpted at the spring of the arches—an allusion to the Dauphin, heir to the throne, then only four years old. Above the cornice was a frieze of three plaques, depicting Apollo in his chariot riding across the sea at the end of his day's labors, flanked by a court of tritons and nereids heralding his arrival at Thétis' undersea palace.

Faced with limestone and modeled in low relief, the grotto's facade would have been rather unremarkable but for the extraordinary trio of gilded, sunburst grilles fitted into its arches. Charles Perrault magnanimously credited his brother Claude with their design, knowing that they were among the finest pieces of ironwork ever created. The six rondels centered on each gate depicted the four known continents and the polar regions, and the king's motto, *Nec Pluribus Impar*, Not Unequal to All, was inscribed on ribbons in the side arches. The effect of seeing the grotto for the first time is reported to have been breathtaking, and to the chronicler André Félibien it appeared as though the sun, setting within the walls of the palace of Thétis, still blazed forth from within.[4]

The Interior

Stepping inside the grotto, the royal guest entered a subaqueous world. The interior walls were richly encrusted with shells, coral, colored stones, and shards of glass, and the floor was geometrically patterned with marble. Birds and animals depicted in shellwork were modeled "after those that the king kept in the Menagerie, which are very rare and little-known," noted Félibien. Shellwork grotesques peered from corners and mirrors caught and distorted candlelight

*T*he youthful court before the Grotto of Thétis; the King rides a white horse, Madame de Montespan descends steps at right. French school, seventeenth century. Musée de Versailles, Versailles.

from chandeliers, some of which also harbored jets to shower water upon the unsuspecting.

The dry warmth of the daylit world fell away as visitors approached the scene of Apollo's repose, and the massive piers that supported the reservoir created an ambiguous, complex space that was neither one room nor many, but evoked a labyrinthine, vaulted cave. The unearthly atmosphere was enhanced by the sound of trickling water and "music of the countryside" echoing from a hidden hydraulic organ, "making one indeed believe that one was standing in the middle of a grove where thousands of birds were singing to one another," reported Mademoiselle de Scudéry.[5]

On reaching the central niche the encounter of Apollo and Thétis was not to be seen; rather, the sun god was portrayed at rest, attended by nymphs. In the side niches, tritons groomed Apollo's horses and fed them ambrosia; the Marsy brothers, Gaspard and Balthazar, sculpted the far superior group to Apollo's left, which gained wide esteem for its movement and vigor. Jean Le Pautre's engraving of 1676 provides an excellent visual record of the grotto's interior, but is somewhat misleading: the paired abstract shapes on the floor indicate the positions of piers, and it was impossible to see the ensemble as depicted; visitors discovered the unearthly tableau scene by scene and could never encompass the whole.

The interior shellwork was begun in the summer of 1665, and when the king visited the following spring the work had been essentially concluded. Plaster models of the statuary were set in place in 1672, but the marble figures would not be installed until four years later. The completed grotto received great acclaim, of which

Above: section through the grotto illustrating the placement of the Baths of Apollo *sculpture group; structural piers have been eliminated for clarity. Engraving by Jean Le Pautre, 1676. Left:* Masks of Shells and of Rocailles. *Engraving by François Chaveau illustrating André Felibien's* Description de Versailles, 1676. *B.N.F., Paris.*

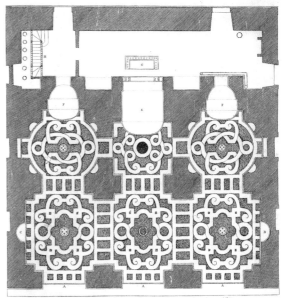

Right: floorplan of the grotto; the water organ was concealed in the long service room at top. B.N.F., Paris.

Félibien's accolade was typical: "there is no other place in all this Royal House where Art has succeded so happily as in the Grotto of Thétis."[6]

Time and again the grotto served as the setting for the fetes and banquets of the young court; among these was an outing to honor the Prince of Tuscany, "where there was a reception with excellent music, with a beautiful display of fruits and desserts in great bowls set upon pedestals in every corner, lit by an infinity of lights around the cornice."[7] With the grotto as their backdrop, the composer Jean-Baptiste Lully and the poet and scenarist Philippe Quinault staged splendid ballets, lasting endless hours, yet undoubtedly the most imposing celebration marked the conquest of Franche-Comté in 1674; the pageantry spanned a week, and the third day of festivities came to a close with a performance of Molière's *Le Malade Imaginaire,* staged before the illuminated grotto.

Exactly a decade later the grotto was destroyed to make way for the château's northern wing. Only twenty years had passed since its construction, at a time when Versailles was still a small pleasure ground enlivened by the young king's conquests and a succession of amusements. Versailles' vast additions were designed by Jules Hardouin-Mansart, a distant nephew of François Mansart, who, Saint-Simon avowed, had ursurped the great man's name as soon as he had died and could no longer defend it. An anecdote relates how the architect came to the king's attention: the Abbé Lambert recounts how Louis XIV, visiting the construction site of the Place Vendôme, spied a young man of noble bearing. The king approached, discovered that he was an architect and a great-nephew of Mansart, and immediately challenged him with a commission at Versailles. Flattering to both himself and the king, this story may well have been Hardouin-Mansart's own invention; in truth, Le Nôtre recommended the young man after working with him at Chantilly,[8] a favor he would have ample opportunity to regret.

*J**ules Hardouin-Mansart,
First Architect to Louis XIV and
indisputably the most successful architect
of the* ancien régime. *Detail of a portrait
by Jean-François De Troy.
Musée de Versailles, Versailles.*

*T**he floorplan
of one of the pavilions in the Bosquet
des Dômes. The color scheme of the marble
floor is based upon similar work
at the Château de Versailles
(authors' rendering).*

*F**acing page: a pavilion
at the Bosquet des Dômes at Versailles.
Built 1675–1679 by Jules Hardouin-
Mansart. Destroyed. Perhaps
the ultimate party tents, the paired
pavilions were a stage for elaborate
fetes early in the reign of Louis XIV
(authors' rendering).*

Saint-Simon despised Hardouin-Mansart for his false bonhomie and recounts how he would lay traps for the king, humbly applauding as his insinuations returned to him as his patron's own ideas.[9] In this fashion, Hardouin-Mansart revamped the Envelope constructed by Le Vau and rebuilt his Orangerie, reworked Le Brun's interiors, and continually meddled in Le Nôtre's bosquets.

The Bosquet of Fame

Hardouin-Mansart's first undertaking at Versailles was the Bosquet des Dômes, originally named the Bosquet of Fame. In 1675, the king commissioned Le Nôtre to lay out a bosquet just to the north of the Tapis Vert, to be dedicated to his own renown. Le Nôtre, also a supremely able architect who designed many of the structures required in his gardens, appears to have modeled the bosquet after a fountain at the Villa Montalto in Rome, with a hexagonal basin surrounded by two rings of gilded bronze balustrades.[10] The inner balustrade supported eighteen small fountains hidden in the piers, and Gaspard Marsy, under the supervision of Le Brun, was commissioned to cast a statue of *Fame* for its center.[11] Eight marble statues were set before the encircling palisades, among them *Acis* and *Galatea* from the destroyed Grotto of Thétis.

materials, the pavilions were built of white French marble enlivened by columns of colored marble from quarries at Givet and Rance. The structures were perfect squares in plan, fifteen feet to a side, and stood twenty feet tall. All sides were open to the elements, and only the pediments facing the fountains disturbed their symmetry. The military trophies placed between the pilasters were an innovation in France; the inspiration was Roman, and later Palladio had adopted them, but Hardouin-Mansart, in a characteristic flourish, thought to cast them in gilded bronze, creating a decorative sensation that would endure for centuries.[13]

The bosquet's completion in 1679 followed the signing of the Treaty of Nijmegen in the previous year, which confirmed France as the undisputed power of Europe. Elaborate nocturnal celebrations inaugurated the Bosquet des Dômes; the music of Lully and Marais played as courtiers danced and mingled among the gilded fountains and the illuminated pavilions. The Marquis de Dangeau described an entertainment held after a grand supper in the Dauphin's apartments in 1685: ". . . the king came with the ladies to the gardens, and we found the [bosquet] ablaze with light, and in the pavilions were oboists, and so we danced, and Mademoiselle de Nantes finished the ball by dancing the most wonderful *dame gigonne* in the world."[14]

With the destruction of the Grotto of Thétis in 1684, the king ordered the *Baths of Apollo* statuary moved to the bosquet to create *"quelque chose de plus magnifique."*[15] The central statue of *Fame* was replaced by a high fountain jet, and the bosquet became known as the Baths of Apollo. Jean Cotelle's painting recorded the new arrangement; it was a rich ensemble, but with much of Versailles' gardens, it fell into disrepair after the spectacular reversals that overshadowed the end of Louis XIV's reign.

The *Apollo* statuary was transferred again in 1704 to the Bosquet Le Marais. The gilded balustrades with their clever fountains, so troublesome to maintain,

The gilding on the balusters had hardly mellowed when Hardouin-Mansart presented his scheme for two domed pavilions to frame Le Nôtre's fountain. He requested a review by the Royal Academy of Architecture, and its members, flattered, spent their mandate dissecting the minutiæ of socles, stereobates, and scotias while the architect's caravan pressed on and work began.[12] Respecting Colbert's decree that the crown's architects employ indigenous

The Bosquet
of the Baths of Apollo, peopled
by a mythological court.
Painting attributed to Jean Cotelle.
Musée de Versailles, Versailles.

Above: Elevation of the Project for the New Baths of Apollo, circa *1704, the last of Louis XIV's projects for his beloved statues. Left: Hubert Robert's watercolor of the* Baths of Apollo *grotto commissioned by Louis XVI. Both Musée de Versailles, Versailles.*

were replaced by marble ones the following year. The Bosquet of Fame, stripped of its statuary and neglected for decades, was razed during the reign of Louis XVIII, but the basin and balustrades remain, and the eight statues that ringed the original bosquet were remounted in 1897.

The Bosquet Le Marais once held a strange fountain in the form of a gilded metal tree, reputed to have been Madame de Montespan's invention. Equally hopeless to maintain and reminding Louis XIV uncomfortably of his former favorite, the bosquet was replaced by the *Baths of Apollo* statuary on the king's order. The statues were ringed with low cascades and protected by three cheerful, gilded baldachinos, but again the bosquet fell into disrepair, and when Louis XVI ordered Versailles' gardens replanted in the 1770s, he commissioned Hubert Robert to design a rockwork grotto for the peripatetic statues on the site.

The *Baths of Apollo* statuary remains in the damp caves of the grotto, and the figures stand admirably cool and white against the dark voids, so distant from the well-trodden *allées* of today's Versailles. Even on the sunniest afternoon the bosquet is tinged with melancholy, partly an intended effect of Robert's dark, romantic caves, but also a result of the inevitable losses these sculptures embody.

A KING'S INDULGENCE: THE PAVILIONS
AT THE VERSAILLES MENAGERIE

*The Menagerie at Versailles
is the most magnificent palace for
animals in the world.*
—Nicolas de Fer, engraver, 1705

*The Duc and Duchesse
de Bourgogne being served refreshments,
from an anonymous late seventeenth-
century French engraving.
Musée de Versailles, Versailles.*

*A pavilion projected
for the Menagerie at Versailles. Designed
in 1698 by Lassurance the Elder for
the Menagerie's kitchen garden,
but unrealized (authors' rendering).*

ELEVEN YEARS OLD WHEN she arrived in France to marry Louis XIV's eldest grandson, the Duc de Bourgogne, Marie-Adélaïde de Savoie took the heart of the aging king by storm. He found her "exactly to my wish" and described her enthusiastically in a letter to Madame de Maintenon: "She has the most perfect grace and figure I have ever seen, dressed fit to be painted . . . eyes bright and beautiful, eyelashes black and admirable, complexion as smooth, white, and red as could be desired. . . . The more I see of the princess, the more satisfied I am."[1]

Marie-Adélaïde, a granddaughter of the king's brother, the Duc d'Orléans, known as Monsieur, appeared at a court desperate for diversion. A decade earlier, Madame, Monsieur's wife, had complained that Versailles was "growing so dull that people were getting to loathe it, for the king imagined that he was pious if he made life a bore."[2] Operas, ballets, and midnight fetes had long since given way to three rather dreary nights of *trictrac* a week,[3] and no one yearned more for distraction than the king himself. Even Madame de Maintenon admitted, "I cannot bear it any longer; I wish I were dead!"[4] With the child's arrival, prayers seemed to have been answered. "Light as a nymph, she was everywhere, a whirling breeze, bringing life and gaiety," wrote Saint-Simon.[5]

The high-spirited princess could not have been more different from her earnest, devout husband,

whom Madame described with Germanic bluntness: "The Duc de Bourgogne is quite awry. One of his legs is much shorter than the other, so much so that, when he wishes to stand, the heel of one of his feet is in the air, and he only touches the ground with his toes."[6] Marie-Adélaïde never loved him, though he adored her, and once took to imitating his hideous limp in Madame de Maintenon's apartment; the laughter and applause still rang in the air as a courtier ran to inform the duke, who, needless to say, was not at all pleased with her, reported Madame de Noyer.[7]

Louis XIV could deny the little duchess nothing: the crown jewels were hers soon after he first laid eyes upon her, and when she declared in the spring of 1698

Marie-Adélaïde, the Duchesse de Bourgogne, at fifteen years of age. Painting by Pierre Gobert. Musée de Versailles, Versailles.

that she would like a menagerie, "the king offered various buildings in the park . . . from which to choose the one she liked most."[8] She listlessly visited a few buildings, and the king soon understood that she wanted not any menagerie, but his own. He offered it happily, and within two days Dangeau reported that the princess had "already planned all the lodgings at the Menagerie, and the king ordered work begun immediately." Rarely was a royal present more enjoyed, and in a letter home to Turin, Marie-Adélaïde recounted her whirlwind campaign: "They are working on my Menagerie. The king has ordered Mansart to spare nothing. Imagine, dear grandmamma, how it will be!"[9]

Begun by Le Vau in 1662, the Menagerie had been one of the king's earliest projects at Versailles,[10] an exotic diversion in the days before the Grand Canal had been completed, and once the vast, cross-shaped lake had been excavated, the king's zoo became a destination for fashionable boating parties. Guests viewed such wonders of the seventeenth century as pelicans, peacocks, ostriches, porcupines, a crocodile, and an elephant from the salon in the central pavilion,[11] where the animals' portraits were hung "as if in preparation for what one was about to see," wrote Mademoiselle de Scudéry.[12] In time, the Menagerie had fallen from favor, with only expenses to remind the king of its existence, but the willful child's wish would restore it to the center of court life.

Almost a century before Marie Antoinette would escape to the Hameau, the barely teenaged princess delighted in the same bucolic fantasy at her Menagerie, surprising the king with the fresh butter she churned there. Courtiers swooned over its taste, and duchesses plotted to spend afternoons with the child baking cakes. The Menagerie became Marie-Adélaïde's miniature palace, and its interior was transformed by Hardouin-Mansart into a royal dollhouse. The princess maintained both summer and winter apartments; each contained a suite of rooms on the tiniest scale—one barely seven feet square—and their delicate paneling was enriched with carvings of shells, birds, and arabesques that offered a hint of the coming age of *rocaille*.[13] Louis XIV threw himself into the project's minutest details and specified the entire decorative program, writing to Hardouin-Mansart, "Childhood must infuse everything."[14]

The Court of the Storks

The Menagerie's exterior changed little during renovations, but the courtyard nearest the canal was transformed completely.[15] A small kitchen garden seemed appropriate to complete the diminutive château, and the walled Court of the Storks, its plan regularized and its garden replanted, became a secluded retreat. Two cubic pavilions were built into its northernmost

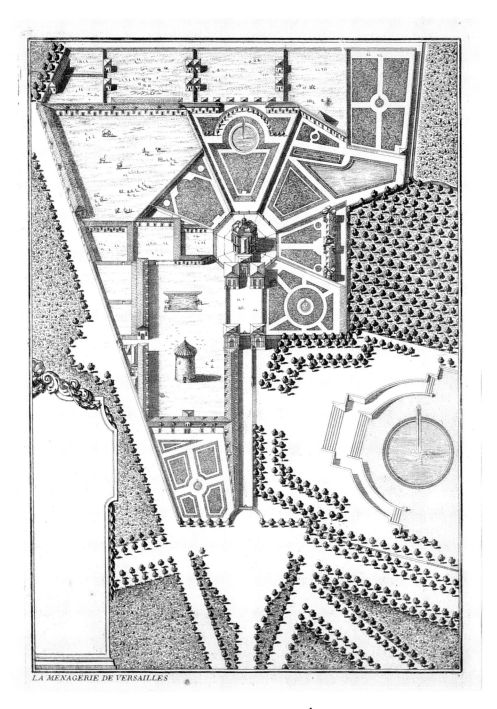

LA MENAGERIE DE VERSAILLES

*T*he Versailles Menagerie.
Engraving by Nicolas de Fer, 1705.
Authors' collection.

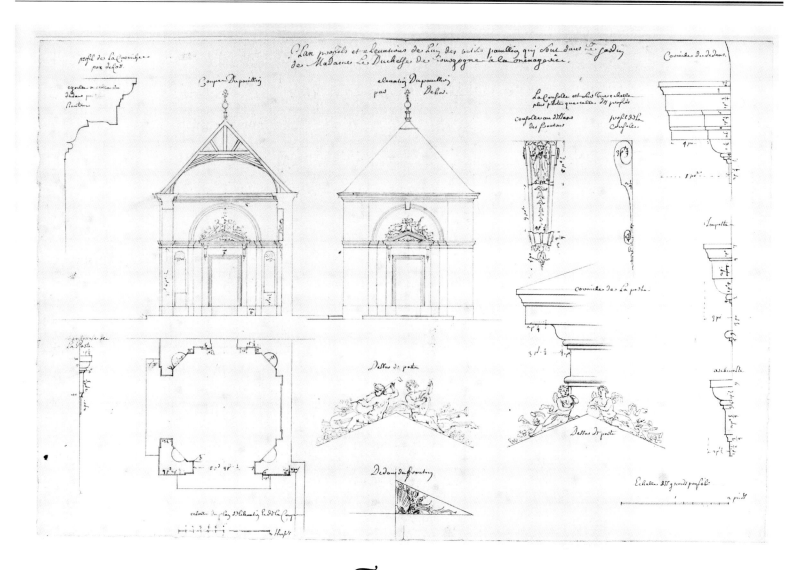

corners, and their shaded stone benches offered the perfect vantage-points from which to contemplate a small fountain and the beauty of well-tended vegetable beds. Lassurance the Elder, Draftsman of Royal Buildings, provided the unexecuted design depicted in the watercolor. The graceful dome echoes that of the Menagerie's octagonal salon, though the simple, pitched roofs of the pavilions that were built possess the more tangible grace of economy. As constructed, the pavilions' facades were more severe, having lost their Ionic pilasters and pediments, though the interiors received an enriched decorative program that fea-

*T*he plan, profiles,
and elevations of the pavilions finally
constructed for the Versailles Menagerie
in an anonymous French drawing
of the seventeenth century.
Musée de Versailles, Versailles.

*R*ight:
A ballet typical of those held at Versailles.
B.N.F., Paris.

tured sculptures of putti playing musical instruments and reclining atop the pedimented overdoors.

During the first decade of the new century, overshadowed by the disastrous War of the Spanish Succession, members of the court, desperate for diversion, visited the Menagerie time and again. A typical evening in 1705 began during the endless summer twilight so characteristic of France; Louis XIV bid adieu to a boating party from the balustrade at Trianon, overlooking the Grand Canal. In the gilded gondolas were the Old Pretender, recognized in France as James III, Marie-Adélaïde, the Duc de

Berry, "and many young English and French ladies." Over two dozen guests set sail for the Menagerie, "to promenade and to dine; where they were accommodated magnificently by the duchess' household. . . . After dinner they danced to songs and played games in the salon."[16] The party returned by lantern-light near midnight, only to learn that the king had retired.

These carefree excursions ended tragically in February 1712, when nearly the whole of the king's family succumbed to smallpox. The first was his beloved Marie-Adélaïde, a week later her husband, then their eldest son. Only the king's great-grandson, the future Louis XV, survived; his governess refused to allow the infamous royal surgeons to touch the infant, thereby saving his life. "Darkness fell over the court and all happiness vanished," wrote Saint-Simon.[17]

After that year the Menagerie, too much the princess' domain, fell from favor forever: the Duc de Luynes would write in 1750 that "Curiosity to see the Menagerie is totally outdated."[18] Louis XVI considered transferring its animals to the Jardin des Plantes and allowing nature to follow its course, but the Revolution overtook him and carried out his will. All that survive today, among ramshackle cottages, are the Menagerie's pavilions, in terrible disrepair and all but forgotten.

MARLY

*You cannot know how agreeable it is to be
at Marly; I find that the court is altogether different
there than at Versailles. The king is
quite relaxed and very playful. They say that at
Versailles he is consumed by affairs, and that Marly
is all his and all for his pleasure.*
—Jean Racine in a letter to Boileau,
24 August 1687

W HEN LOUIS XIV DECIDED that Versailles
would be the seat of his government, he began
to look for "someplace small and solitary"[1] to serve as a
royal retreat. "Behind Louveciennes he found a deep,
narrow valley, completely shut in, swampy and inacces-
sible and without a view, but with a wretched village
called Marly upon one hillside . . . a haunt of snakes,
frogs, and toads." The king was overjoyed, continued
Saint-Simon incredulously, and "the hermitage was
made. At first it was for sleeping from Wednesday to
Saturday, two or three times a year, with a dozen
courtiers. But slowly it grew. Hills were leveled to
make room for buildings, and at the end [of the valley]
they were paired to create the resemblance of a view."

*T he Jupiter
Pavilion at Marly. Built 1679–1685
by Jules Hardouin-Mansart
and frescoed by Charles Le Brun.
Destroyed during the French Revolution
(authors' rendering).*

*F ollowing pages:
Hawking Party at Marly by
Jean-Baptiste Martin. The company
stands upon a nonexistent hill.
The Royal Collection, London.*

Marly became the aging king's obsession; he tinkered endlessly with its gardens, and a dizzying succession of bosquets and basins, fountains and *allées*
appeared and disappeared like so many stage sets.
Hundreds of men worked through the night by
torchlight to carry out extraordinary transformations
between visits, and one Swedish visitor commented
that there half a year's work was compressed into a
week.[2] These extravagances led Saint-Simon to
claim, "It is a modest estimate to say that Versailles
did not cost as much as Marly," but the result of all
these labors was to him "A fairies' palace, unique in
Europe."[3] The otherworldly metaphor was invoked
repeatedly to describe Marly: "Everything there
seemed to have been created by the magic of a fairy's
wand," wrote Madame Campan;[4] "Fauns and sylphs
people its shadows," wrote Abbé Jacques Delille;[5] for
Madame, fairies worked in its gardens; for Diderot, it
seemed a monument to a great, departed race.

Origins
Construction began in 1679 under the supervision of
Jules Hardouin-Mansart. Marly's inspiration

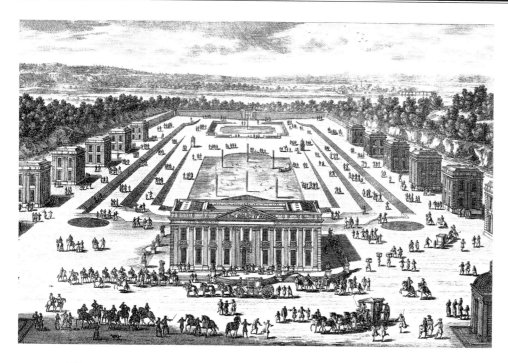

derived in part from the architecture of Palladian villas and in part from imaginatively conceived Italianate gardens such as Rueil,[6] which the king remembered from his youth; the pavilioned complex of the Trianon de Porcelaine, the king's first hermitage and likewise richly polychromed, was a crucial precedent. Louis XIV, in selecting a site that inverted all the usual requirements for a château, challenged his architect with a new conception of a royal residence and Hardouin-Mansart succeeded brilliantly, retaining the sense of isolation that characterizes villas such as Palladio's Rotunda while fully exploiting the strong cross axes their plans imply. The King's Pavilion, square in plan with identical facades, was the indispensable center dominating the compound, particularly the Courtiers' Pavilions, which stood six to a row to either side of the Pièce d'Eau—the central reflecting basin—creating the

Marly viewed from the future site of the Cascade. The King's Pavilion stands in the foreground, Madame Campan's theatrical perspective of Courtiers' Pavilions flanks the central basin. Beyond lies the fantasy landscape of the engraver, Jean Mariette. Authors' collection.

Above: plan, and right: section and elevation of a Courtiers' Pavilion, with one small apartment on each floor. The last pavilion of either row held bathing facilities. Archives nationales and B.N.F., Paris.

COUPE DU PREMIER PAVILLON A DROITE.

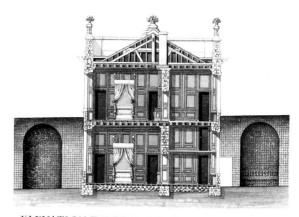

ELEVATION DU PREMIER PAVILLON A DROITE.

*O*ne of the Courtiers'
Pavilions representing the seasons.
Destroyed during the French Revolution.
The watercolor reconstructions
present two pavilions as we believe they
originally would have been frescoed.
The Apollo Pavilion (right), one of four
facades representing the seasons,
is a revision of Le Brun's initial scheme
for the Pavilion of Saturn. The Jupiter
Pavilion (page 52) is also part of this
revised scheme and can only be considered
restrained in the light of its predecessor. It
is impossible to recreate definitive color
schemes for these facades, for the period
documentation is simply too sparse.
A series of grisaille gouaches[7] records
Le Brun's initial designs, dedicated to
ancient deities—not, as is often claimed,
to the Zodiac. A pair of paintings
by Pierre-Denis Martin[8] record Marly
during the Regency, and though the
buildings are too small to read details,
close study reveals the colors used for
the principal decorative elements. A series
of elevations document the facades of
Marly's main buildings[9] but, being tinted
quite freely, offer only vague hints
as to their color schemes. However,
the polychrome marblework created for
interiors at Versailles during the same
period affords numerous examples
of the vocabulary of materials depicted on
the pavilions' facades, and has been an
invaluable aid.[10]

illusion of a theatrical perspective, noted Madame Campan.

The pavilions sat amid trellised bowers trained with honeysuckle and clematis, small guest cottages with one upstairs and one downstairs apartment, notorious for their smoking fireplaces, for the king did not wish chimneys disfiguring their silhouettes. Caught midway between the intimate bosquets and arbors and the open vista of the Pièce d'Eau, the Courtiers' Pavilions were a metaphor for Marly itself, suspended between worlds: "These pavilions, isolated and almost embowered in a forest, seem to be the dwellings of subaltern spirits," wrote Diderot.[11]

Charles Le Brun's extensive and innovative use of fresco made Marly unique: the facades of all main buildings were richly decorated with trompe-l'œil architecture. Exterior frescoes were rare in France, but appeared most prominently at the Gondis' country house at Saint-Cloud and at Cardinal Richelieu's Rueil. At Marly, for the first time on such an unprecedented scale, illusionistic skill replaced architectural elements and paint mimicked lavish materials. Fresco was in part chosen for its economy: Le Brun had designed a flamboyant decorative cycle, yet when the first pavilions were completed, Louis XIV, for once of the opinion that less was more, ordered subsequent facades limited to variants upon alternating schemes, one featuring pilasters, the other a central medallion, busts, and terms.[12]

"Sire, Marly!"

The words echoed a hundred times as Louis XIV passed through Versailles. An invitation to Marly was the most coveted honor at court and yet another instrument with which the king controlled the aristocracy. Bontemps, the royal valet, announced the chosen few a day before each journey, and the voyages, during which the king paid all expenses, were so exclusive that Madame remarked: "Not even ambassadors or envoys are allowed there." Obsessed by rank, she fretted that "there was nothing resembling a

The King's playground. Above: the Escarpolette, drawn by Aveline, and below: La Ramasse, the royal rollercoaster, from an anonymous garden plan (detail). Musée Promenade de Marly-Le-Roi-Louveciennes and Archives nationales, Paris.

court" at Marly:[13] men were permitted to wear their hats during the royal promenade and almost everyone was allowed to sit in the king's presence. For her, confusion reigned. Madame exaggerated, but Marly's relaxed atmosphere gave rise to many of the court's lightest moments. It was there that the king actually sang, accompanied by one of his daughters, and where little Marie-Adélaïde surreptitiously sewed a seventy-year-old duchess to her *tabouret*, then had firecrackers lit beneath her.

The gardens offered more profound pleasures, described by Diderot: "Countless yews clipped in a hundred-thousand ways border a parterre of the grandest simplicity, leading to bowers of indescribable lightness and elegance. They rise up the hillsides, leading the eye into the depths of the forest; only the closest trees are clipped, the rest are left rustic and wild . . . this progression from nature to art, and from art to nature, creates a veritable enchantment. Leave the parterre, where the hand and mind of man are used so exquisitely, and go to the hillside above—it is isolation, silence, wilderness, the horror of Solitude. It is simply sublime. What a mind conceived these gardens!"[14]

To counter the sublime there was also the ridiculous. *La Ramasse*, a rollercoaster on wooden rails, ran

for nearly a half-kilometer; dukes and duchesses sat in the blue-and-gold wagon while the king stood at the back, a royal trolley conductor. Another bosquet held a large communal swing, and there were the quieter diversions of admiring the flowerbeds—replanted daily, which absorbed eighteen million bulbs in four years—or enjoying twilight concerts as members of an orchestra played to one another from hiding places throughout the gardens. Madame de Maintenon wrote: "We act at Marly like idlers. All day long the king of France plants and the king of Spain hunts, and all night long they play games in my room."[15] Madame found only praise for Marly, where she thought fairies worked: "Where I left a lake, I find a grove and a bosquet; where I left a forest, I find a large reservoir, into which some thirty admirably beautiful carp will be thrown this evening."[16]

The Royal Carp

"I have built Versailles for the court, Marly for my friends, and Trianon for myself," Louis XIV once declared;[17] but this was not quite true, unless one understands that when he spoke of his friends, he was referring to his carp, kept in porcelain-tiled basins near the château. His mania began at the turn of the century,[18] and as word spread of the old king's new passion, barrels of carp arrived from across France. The Dauphin sent blue carp from Meudon, the Duc de La Rochefoucauld pink carp from the moats of Liancourt, and green-and-gold carp arrived from Fontainebleau. The king was so obsessed by their beauty that Saint-Simon quipped that he would soon order the royal painters to freshen their scales. The fish were constantly shifted from basin to basin as their master carried on an obsessive quest for the perfect carp pond, while a baker spent his days baking biscuits, their only food, thereby increasing their staggering mortality rate, despite the fact that carp are the hardiest of fish.

The king often described himself as the shepherd of his aquatic herd, and his favorite was a golden carp named *La Dorée*. He always stopped to talk to it dur-

ing his daily promenade, but one day he could not see the fish and ordered the basin emptied, only to find *La Dorée* dead. When the queen died, he had been merely inconvenienced; Madame de Montespan's death passed almost unnoticed, and Louise de La Vallière died for him the day she took the veil; but *La Dorée's* demise was a terrible blow. He would not speak for the remainder of the day and even refused to see the diplomatic courier.

After Louis XIV's death, his nephew, the Regent Philippe d'Orléans, planned to demolish Marly to recoup the expense of its maintenance, but Saint-Simon, a member of the Regency Council, learned of his decision and dissuaded him. Louis XV and Louis XVI were indifferent to the domain; the former preferred his own retreat of Choisy, the latter visited mainly to hunt. The Revolution devastated Marly; it was first pillaged, then sold to an entrepreneur and converted to a textile mill. Napoleon attempted to save the estate, but the Courtiers' Pavilions had already been destroyed and the King's Pavilion was razed soon after. The loss was irreplaceable, for had Marly survived in any recognizable state, it would rival Versailles as one of the wonders of France.[20]

*T*hat the king was mourning the death of a fish did not escape Parisian wags, and a verse soon appeared:

A courier arrived at Marly
That one had better see,
But the Hussar who guards the door
Told him, "Take yourself away!
The favorite carp is no more
And no one will be received today!"[19]

Above: a carp basin at Marly, from a plan of 1709. Archives nationales, Paris.

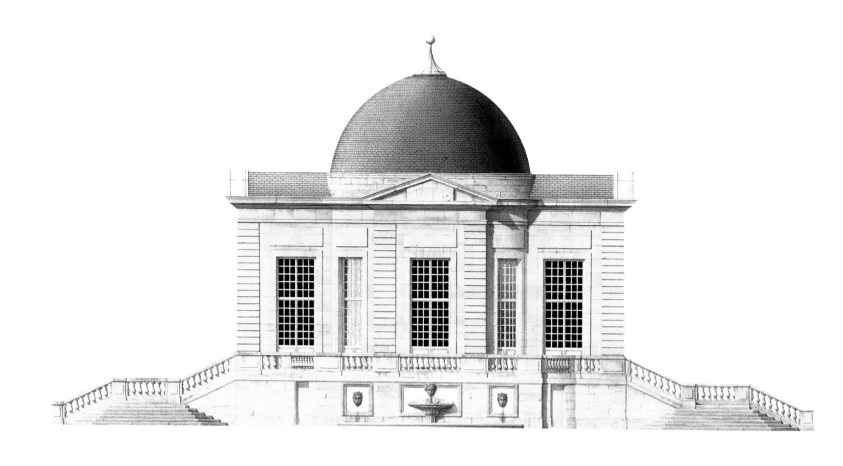

*T*he Aurora Pavilion
at Sceaux. Built circa 1672 and
attributed to Claude Perrault. The
clarity of its volumes and sober details
reflect the taste of the pavilion's
commissioner, Jean-Baptiste Colbert
(authors' rendering).

FIDELITY AND INTRIGUE:
THE AURORA AND MENAGERIE
PAVILIONS AT SCEAUX

The love that this great minister had for
the fine arts, architecture, painting, and sculpture,
and his good taste in recognizing all their beauties,
brought them to their last perfection
during the time of his ministry.
—Charles Perrault, *Les Hommes illustres*

JEAN-BAPTISTE COLBERT WAS an extraordinary man, not so much because he typified his age—he surely did not—but because, through immense strength of will, he sought to impose a "grand design" of rational order upon France. He was unlike any other figure of the *ancien régime;* a man of diligence, of probity and fidelity, and above all of modesty. Amid a riot of colored silks and velvets, of gold-and-silver embroidery spangled with pearls and diamonds, he wore the somber black of the Dutch burghers he so envied and worked at an ebony desk covered with a worn black cloth.[1] His study was lined with busts of Roman emperors and senators, and he kept an ebony chiming clock that rang each precious quarter hour. His carriages were lacquered black, with black linings, and were drawn by black horses.

Jean-Baptiste Colbert, Louis XIV's supremely able minister. Pastel by Robert Nanteuil, 1676. Musée Condé, Chantilly.

He could not bear disorder or slovenliness or abuses of power and personally administered the royal botanical gardens when he saw that they had fallen prey to cronyism. Later, while touring the gardens, he came upon a vineyard for the administrators hidden in a plot intended for specimens; livid, he grabbed a pickax and uprooted the vines himself. And when the court arrived from "urine-soaked" Versailles for the reception he hosted to display his newly completed estate,[2] courtiers took as much note of the château's "marvelous cleanliness" as they did of its furnishings,[3] described as "more in good taste than richness, or rather with a modest magnificence, if one may be permitted to say."[4]

Colbert rose to power as the protégé of Cardinal Mazarin and was the cardinal's greatest legacy; he would prove indispensable in imposing order upon a disordered kingdom, affording Louis XIV the luxury of his building and his conquests. Colbert worked tirelessly and allowed the king to believe it was an order when the latter wrote, over and again in the amazing laundry-list letters from the glorious battlefronts of his youth, "Do what you think is best."[5] Remarkably,

Above:
Jean-Baptiste Colbert in a
contemporary engraving.
Authors' collection.

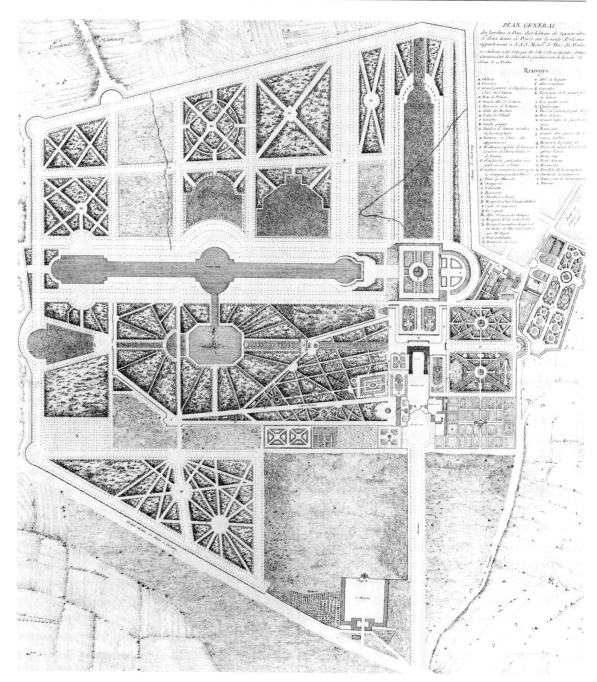

The plan of the estate of
Sceaux, circa *1727. The château is seen*
at center right, the Aurora Pavilion
stands amid the rectangular beds of the
kitchen garden at lower right,
the Menagerie Pavilion in the angled
parterre at far right. Engraving
by Jean Mariette. Musée de l'Île-de-
France, Sceaux.

Colbert always did. He was always deferential to the king, for he understood his vanity too well, but increasingly Louis XIV would thwart his carefully considered—and often vital—plans for bettering the nation. Colbert sensed a looming financial disaster in the swampy "toad hole" of Versailles[6] and sought to divert the king's energies toward the languishing Louvre, to no avail. A letter arrived from the siege of Besançon, demanding: "Let me know how the orange trees look at Versailles when they are properly arranged"; another appeared, exhorting: "Think above all of the water pumps!"[7] Colbert loved the idea of France more than any person or thing, but staggered under the weight of the king's appetites, and eventually Louis XIV would force him to witness the reversal of much of his life's work. It is no wonder he wore black.

Colbert purchased Sceaux in 1670, nearly a decade after coming to power. The château dated from the time of Henri IV, and thinking both of Fouquet's great fall (which he had masterminded) after building the overly impressive Vaux-le-Vicomte and of the king's example in retaining the original château of Versailles amidst new additions,[8] Colbert decided to remodel and enlarge the manor rather than demolish it and start anew. He employed the artists inherited from Fouquet and passed down through the king: Le Nôtre designed the gardens, Le Brun carried out the decorative work, but there is no evidence to indicate an architect, although Claude Perrault is most often suggested. Gilded balconies and antique busts on consoles in the manner of the Marble Court of Versailles were added to the château's garden facades, and a handsome courtyard flanked by a chapel and an orangerie gave the entrance court a quiet air of grandeur.

The garden at Sceaux is one of Le Nôtre's greatest works, taking full advantage of the site's gentle slopes and hollows to create a landscape whose extraordinary beauty unfolds as a series of surprises, or more aptly, revelations. Its centerpiece was the Cascade, which so entranced Louis XIV when he first saw it during the fete of 1677 that he stopped his promenade and sat down to study it carefully.[9] Ladies of the court, dressed in a rainbow of silks, floated by on gilded gondolas poled by white-uniformed gondoliers, wooing him to join them, but the king paid them no attention and climbed instead to the top of the great stair of water, where he discovered singing and the music of oboes emanating from the hedges. (Colbert rejected Le Nôtre's proposal for a grand canal to complete the garden's cross axis, stating that it was too extravagant a work. Following his death, his son, the Marquis de Seignelay, who had no such scruples, ordered it dug

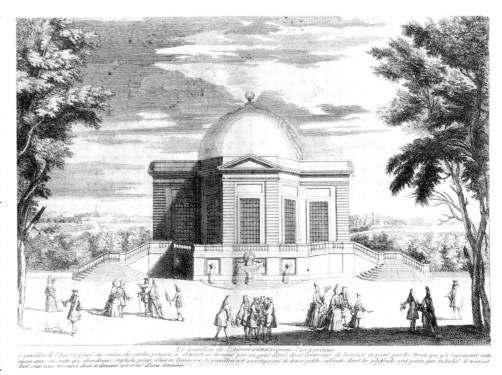

Le pavillon de l'Aurore à Sceaux comme il est présent

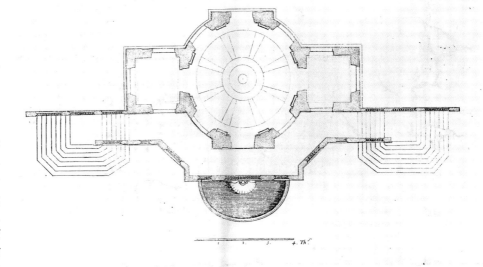

Plan du Pavillon de l'aurore ou Salle des festins au milieu des jardins potagers de Sceaux.

The Aurora Pavilion (top) and its plan (bottom) seen in two anonymous seventeenth-century French engravings. Both Musée de l'Île-de-France, Sceaux.

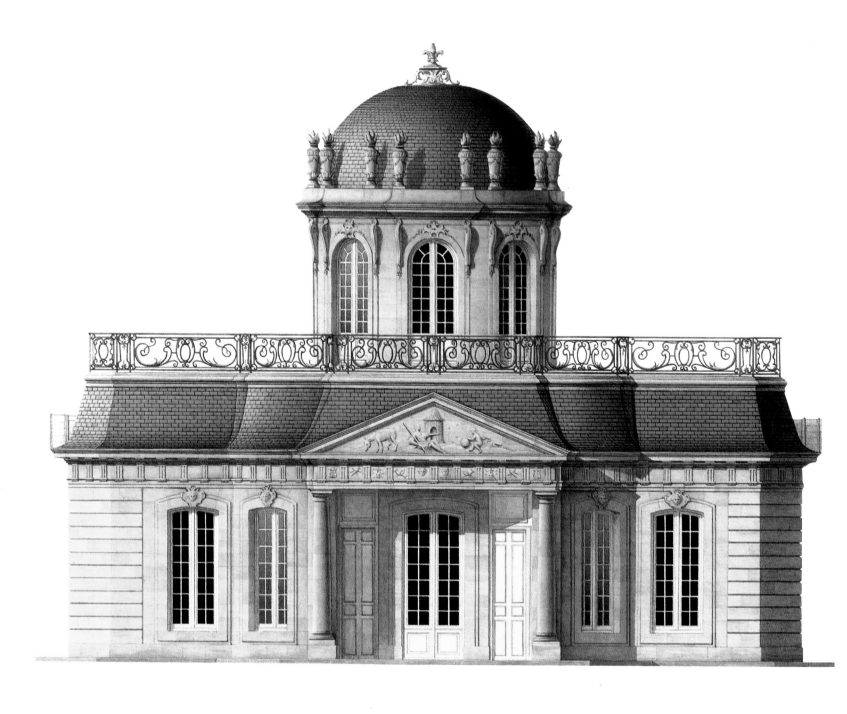

forthwith.)[10] The evening ended with a festival of fireworks that included synchronized rocket displays from neighboring villages lighting the horizon. After a performance of Racine's *Phædra* in the orangerie, the company discovered the villagers—whom Colbert had relieved of paying half a year's taxes that morning—celebrating under lantern-lit trees. The king was thoroughly enchanted.

The Aurora Pavilion was most probably built in 1672 to the designs of Claude Perrault[11] and is an essay in refined geometries. The pavilion is raised upon a high plinth featuring three wall fountains that play into a semicircular basin, in turn bracketed by generously spilling flights of steps. This graceful plan permits an elevated prospect of the gardens from the interior rooms and the balustraded terrace and creates a richly modulated pyramidal composition. The cylindrical main salon is flanked by two small cubic wings, and the entire interior is filled with light, for the walls are little more than piers holding enormous window frames. The salon's circular ceiling features Le Brun's painting of Aurora, goddess of Dawn, banishing Night and harnessing Apollo's chariot in preparation for his glorious transit across the skies—an allegory so befitting the minister's relationship to the Sun King that it requires no elaboration.

Colbert genuinely enjoyed the pavilion and used it personally whenever he could. He would have his desk brought there in summer, to work and write amid the neat rows of his kitchen garden in peace and solitude. He once held a meeting of the Académie Française there as well, an occasion remembered primarily for the cruel length of Philippe Quinault's poem in praise of Sceaux—some six hundred lines read after a large dinner. With the exception of the gatehouses supporting Antoine Coysevox's allegorical statue groups of *Fidelity* and *Purity*, little survives of Colbert's Sceaux but this remarkable remnant, today beautifully restored, having escaped the domain's destruction after the Revolution and the ravages of three wartime occupations.

Cleopatra of the French court: the Duchesse du Maine in a portrait attributed to Pierre Gobert. Musée de Versailles, Versailles.

The Menagerie Pavilion at Sceaux. Built circa 1710 by François de La Guepière. Fortunately Jean Mariette documented the Menagerie Pavilion with a set of engravings in the early eighteenth century;[12] the elevation presented here is faithful to his work, and not only depicts all architectural details but carefully renders schematized building materials—stone, slate, lead, wood, and wrought iron—thus lifting the veil formed by an antiquated mode of representation that has hindered proper appreciation of the building (left, authors' rendering).

"The Royal Ragdoll"[13]

"People are talking about Sceaux being sold," wrote Madame de Sévigné soon after the Marquis de Seignelay's death in 1690,[14] but the Colbert family did not sell the estate until 1699. Its purchaser, the Duc du Maine, was one of Louis XIV's illegitimate sons, whom the king inexplicably adored. Saint-Simon loathed him: "He had the mind of a devil," he wrote, "whom he matched in viciousness, moral corruption, and devious ways . . . but he also had the devil's talent to entertain and distract when he wished to please. Morally and intellectually, he was an enormous coward, and an especially dangerous one. . . ."[15] Du Maine found a soulmate when he married the Grand Condé's granddaughter; they quarreled incessantly and were avoided at court, and though Sceaux was an enormous estate, the duke found refuge only in his study and was not at all missed by his overbearing wife, who eventually became known as "the queen of Sceaux."

The Duchesse du Maine, "No taller than a ten-year-old, had rotten, crooked teeth," wrote Madame.

A longitudinal section through the Menagerie Pavilion, revealing the domed salon and its roof terrace. Engraving by Jean Mariette. B.N.F., Paris.

"She was not too fat, but she was painted with rouge. She had pretty eyes and was pale and blonde. When she shut her mouth she wasn't that ugly."[16] Saint-Simon was no more fond of her than of her husband. "The duke was egged on by his wife in all his schemes. Her spirit—and she had lots of it—was totally corrupted by bad novels and plays. . . . She branded her husband a craven coward; his pathetic maneuverings filled her with outrage, and she drummed it into him that his greatest honor was to have married her. She railed and mocked him, and he never said a word for fear that she would finally go mad."

Nonetheless, the duchess knew how to entertain and soon created a small, frivolous, and mutinous court. Near Paris, Sceaux was far enough from Versailles to escape the oppressive atmosphere of rectitude and the constant pall of mourning for dying heirs and lost battles that hung over Louis XIV's interminable twilight. Sceaux became known as "the abode of delights,"[17] where the great wits and spirits of the day, whom the duchess called "my beasts" and "my galley slaves"—among them the young rake, the Duc de Richelieu, and the ever-present Voltaire—vied to create the wickedest and wittiest of wordplays.[18]

The duchess concocted the Order of the Beehive, and membership in the secretive little cell became a coveted honor: initiates received from the Queen Bee a commemorative medal struck with her portrait, and meetings were held in the salon of her Menagerie Pavilion. Initiations were followed by ostentatious banquets which in time became the Grand Nights of Sceaux, elaborately staged revels that ended at dawn. The fifth and last was the most notorious of all, employing the solar eclipse of 1715 as "a pretext for a debauchery in verse."[19]

The Menagerie Pavilion

The Menagerie Pavilion doubtlessly was inspired by Le Vau's Menagerie at Versailles, though it housed no animals and sat instead in a flower garden at the edge of the estate. Its dome echoed that of the Menagerie's octagonal salon, as did its ironwork balconies, which permitted the flat roof to be used as a terrace. Set on a low plinth and surrounded by parterres and orange trees in tubs, the pavilion was entered through vestibules framed by Doric columns supporting an entablature embellished with alternating metopes of the sun and a female mask. The pediment carried the symbols of the duchess' order: the hive with bees, suggesting industry; a shepherd, representing moral guidance; and a putto holding a globe, symbolizing a passion for knowledge. The interior was paneled and mirrored and richly furnished throughout, and the drum beneath the dome held a circular salon featuring eight glazed arches. Reached by a small spiral stair, the magnificent belvedere was "of complete beauty, as much for its sumptuous furnishings as for its tapestries, its daybeds and armchairs, but no one is lodged there," reported a contemporary guidebook.[20]

The pavilion straddles the transition in architectural styles at the end of Louis XIV's reign, retaining a baroque spirit while anticipating the geometric concerns of French neoclassicism. François de La Guepière's overly ambitious plan is an elaboration of the circle, the cross, and the octagon, and a maze of vestibules and passages perfectly expressed the building's role as a hive of intrigue. Sceaux was confiscated during the Revolution; the pavilion shared the château's fate and was demolished in 1798, but its plinth and entrance columns remain and have been incorporated into a public park.

The Home of Intrigues

In 1714, the aged Louis XIV, hoping to avoid a possible crisis of succession, proclaimed the right of the Duc du Maine and his brother to inherit the throne. After the king's death, Philippe d'Orléans, Regent for the five-year-old Louis XV, annulled the proclamations and stripped the duke of his remaining military commands. Du Maine acquiesced impotently, but the Queen Bee was furious. The thwarted duchess, allied to a clique of intriguing ambassadors and nosy *abbés*, would respond by launching one of France's most embarrassingly amateurish cabals, the Cellamare conspiracy.

The Prince of Cellamare, the Spanish ambassador, plotted to install a Regent controlled from Madrid; Philippe d'Orléans knew of the intrigue from its inception, and waited for the *frondeurs* to act. With the meetings of the Beehive Order in the Menagerie Pavilion providing their cover, the conspirators made their plans and the duchess urged her husband forward as a malleable candidate, but the Regent intercepted their correspondence and banished most of them to the hinterlands or to the Bastille. The duke, who said an insane asylum would have been the better choice, was sent to the Citadel of Doullens, while the duchess, wailing, was removed to the Château of Dijon.

She returned to Sceaux a year later, somewhat humbler; the duke avoided her for years, but gradually they reestablished a smaller, less audacious court. Voltaire should offer the final words about them: "Her court was charming; one was as amused there as one was bored at Versailles. She loved all pleasures on account of her high spirits, her imagination, and her fantasy. One couldn't have ruined one's husband more gaily."[21]

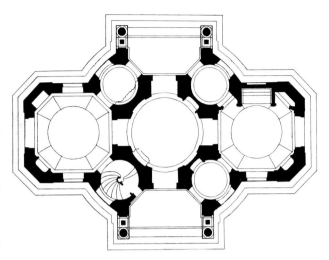

The plan of the Menagerie Pavilion, a celebration of geometries. Engraving by Jean Mariette. B.N.F.

The Pause in the Hunt by Carle Van Loo, favored artist of Louis XV. Musée du Louvre, Paris (overleaf).

LOUIS XV
AND MADAME DE POMPADOUR:
THE AGE OF INTIMACY

What a terrible emptiness in the grandeur and the pleasures of Courts,
that the ignorant desire unknowingly!
—Madame de Pompadour in a letter to the Comtesse de Brézé, 1750

*M*adame de Maintenon's old fear (or hope) that Versailles would not outlive its builder eventually came to nothing when the Regent brought twelve-year-old Louis XV back to his great-grandfather's palace in 1722. The boy was delighted to return, but for some time after remained paralyzed by its physical grandeur and the lingering ghost of Louis Le Grand. He grew to become an intelligent man, given to melancholy and boredom, and his life was a constant struggle to escape both. To Cyril Connolly he was "the gracefully bored,"[1] a man with an enormous capacity for fatalism and bemused indifference. Trapped in the amber of Louis XIV's autocratic state, he would not consider major changes in Versailles and its gardens until well into the second decade of his reign (1715–1774), and resigned himself to the Sun King's daily rituals, both rising from and preparing for a bed in the Grand Apartments where he no longer slept. He endured the balletic charade only to slip behind a hidden door once it was over and take the little lift to Madame de Pompadour's rooms, there to dine with a few select friends late into the night.

The perpetual, unstated bankruptcy of the state, thrown to a crisis pitch after the disaster of the Seven Years' War, would mean that bills simply were not paid—not that expenses were seriously curtailed. Indeed, much of the history of building during Louis XV's reign is one of empty coffers bringing about the delay, reassessment, and often abandonment of entire projects. Royal architects, clerks, and draftsmen worked years without pay; gardeners starved and finally deserted; maintenance was deferred and broken windows were replaced by oiled paper. The king would say most famously: "All this, as it is, will endure as long as I do."[2] But it was glorious while it did last. All things moved toward refinement, enveloped in a spirit of intimacy and vivacity. Architecture achieved unparalleled grace and clarity, complemented by interiors designed according to increasingly sophisticated rules of accomodation. Public rooms diverged irrevocably from private ones, with the latter evolving into retreats of splendid comfort. The effusive sensibility that characterized the style known as Louis XV was truly never that of the king, though more the taste of his mistress; however, both patrons encouraged restraint as they matured—in part due to a lack of funds and in part in response to a resurgent interest in the architecture of antiquity. This austerity eventually evolved into the neoclassicism credited to Louis XVI, though it can be detected in the French Pavilion at mid-century and reached its first maturity in the Petit Trianon.

L'ART DE VIVRE:
THE PAVILION FOR THE DAUPHIN,
THE FRENCH PAVILION, AND THE
PETIT TRIANON AT VERSAILLES

IN SEPTEMBER 1729, nine months after she had prayed for an heir on the day of the Immaculate Conception, Queen Marie Leczinska gave birth to a male child and France erupted in celebration. The Dauphin's birth was witnessed by the entire court—or by those who managed to squeeze into the queen's State Bedroom—and the infant was baptized by the Grand Almoner and bestowed with the Order of the Cordon bleu, then carried to his governess, the Duchesse de Ventadour. Spoiled by the court, the Dauphin grew to be a likeable, though strong-willed, child. His mother, in whose ear he whispered a thousand secrets a day, found him handsome and headstrong, with a precocious wit. When she once scolded him, "Naughty child, you're causing me chagrin," he retorted: "You would be even more

Louis de France, the Dauphin, son of Louis XV. Detail of a portrait after Louis Tocqué. Musée de Versailles, Versailles.

The Pavilion for the Dauphin at Versailles. Built 1736 and attributed to Ange-Jacques Gabriel. The Dauphin's playhouse, set in a small bosquet in the château's park, stood for little more than a decade (authors' rendering).

chagrined, Madame, if you did not have me!"[1]

Following custom, the Dauphin was entrusted to a male tutor at age seven. His well-rehearsed speech for *Maman* Ventadour was deluged by tears, which ended only with the appearance of a new marionette theater. Officially the prince could now appear at court, receive ambassadors, and maintain his own household. "If nature continues to favor [the Dauphin] with her gifts, he will be the most handsome and perfect prince in the universe!" one writer proclaimed,[2] but his bigoted governor, the Duc de Chatillon, molded the spirited boy into a moralizing prude who would later bore the court and make life uncomfortable for Madame de Pompadour and his father.

The Pavilion for the Dauphin

In 1736 he was still "an angel, a child of bliss, whose name birds and fountains praise,"[3] and Louis XV, with painful memories of an orphaned youth, was determined to give his son the pleasures of a childhood largely denied him. To that end, he instructed the Gabriels to construct a playhouse in the small park of Versailles. The site, near the Bosquet Le Marais, had been earmarked by Louis XIV for the Bosquet of Diana, but that work had never been carried out. At this time, both Jacques V Gabriel and his son Ange-Jacques were employed as royal architects, the former as First Architect. No records clarify which of the Gabriels designed the pavilion, though opinion tends to favor Ange-Jacques, who immediately acceded to his father's office after Jacques V died at Fountainebleau in 1742.

The pavilion's design was founded upon the precepts of architectural appropriateness: classical proportions lent it dignity while spare details and a stuccoed exterior expressed its rank as a minor garden structure. Similar detailing was echoed in a group of garden pavilions built at Dampierre several years later and subsequently was reprised by Ange-Jacques Gabriel for the French Pavilion at Trianon.

The Dauphin's Pavilion, but one octagonal salon and two small cabinets, sat at one end of the bosquet, on a horseshoe-shaped terrace defined by three steps. The salon housed a marble fireplace, a rock crystal

Detail of Red Macaw and other Birds *by Willem Frederik Van Royan. The Wallace Collection, London.*

Below:

The Dauphin's Pavilion, flanked by its birdcages. Engraving by J.B. Scotin. B.N.F., Paris.

chandelier, and a Delft-tiled floor, and the angled walls between its arched French doors were painted with cartouches of children at play.[4]

The building was completed within a few months and readied for the Dauphin in the summer of 1736. The salon was reserved for refreshments, but the bosquet outside was the boy's great joy: two large, intricately worked birdcages, "of the latest taste and of the last magnificence,"[5] flanked the pavilion, and at the garden's center was a fountain with an infant riding a dolphin—symbolizing the Dauphin—watched over by statues of the king and queen depicted as Jupiter and Juno. Turtles swam in the fountain's basin, exotic ducks gathered at the Rocaille Cascade in a far corner, and the Dauphin grew vegetables in the flowerbeds to feed the tortoises that roamed about his oasis.

The enchantment lasted no longer than the Dauphin's childhood; when Jacques-François Blondel wrote of the bosquet fifteen years after its construction,[6] a lawn had replaced the pavilion; in 1778 the remains of

*T*he French Pavilion.
Built 1750 by Ange-Jacques Gabriel amid
Louis XV's gardens and menageries
at Trianon (authors' rendering).

the bosquet were razed to accomodate Hubert Robert's rockwork grotto for the *Baths of Apollo* statuary.

The French Pavilion at Trianon

Louis XV was a passionate builder, as Louis XIV had been before him; Madame de Pompadour said he was never happy unless he had plans waiting on his desk, and we know from the Duc de Croÿ that he had collaborated closely with his First Architect Ange-Jacques Gabriel in the spring of 1749 in designing the small cross-shaped French Pavilion at Trianon—so much so that he considered himself its architect. Thus we also know that when the king bid the duke to remark, "This is the style in which one should build,"[7] he was fully aware not only of the nature of what he had just created but also of what was to come.

The king was a dedicated amateur botanist and spent a great deal of time at Trianon; the future site of Marie Antoinette's English-style garden was then his botanical garden, with greenhouses for acclimatizing exotic plants and large trial fields, all under his direct supervision. A menagerie housing exotic waterfowl stood nearby, as did informal gardens composed solely of evergreens; both were novelties at the time. The pavilion was roofed in August 1749 and its interior completed a year later. In 1751, the Duc de Croÿ wrote in his journal: "Today, the king brought us to the Trianon to see the greenhouses for rare plants, those for flowers, and the menagerie for poultry that he loves—the marquise has given him a taste for all these little pleasures—the pretty pavilion, the flower gardens, the herb and vegetable gardens; it was all laid out with great taste and expensively executed."[8]

The pavilion still stands at the center of a small formal garden—hence its common name, the French Pavilion—and was conceived by the king primarily as a place where he could "dally and chatter in peace with Madame de Pompadour" amid scented flowers.[9] It contains a small kitchen in one cabinet and a central salon where the couple could dine or entertain informally. The building was known at court both as

*L*ouis XV
by François Hubert Drouais. Detail of a portrait painted in August 1773, when the king was aged 63, exhibited in that year's Salon. Musée de Versailles, Versailles.

*A*nge-Jacques
Gabriel's elegant study in interlocking geometries: the floorplan of the French Pavilion at Trianon. Musée de Versailles, Versailles.

the Pavilion of Company and Games and the Menagerie Pavilion.

The building is stuccoed, reflecting its status as a garden structure, and softening its geometric severity are details freely mixing rococo ornaments. The four keystones above the arched doors feature masks of the seasons, and flower vases and sculpture groups of children at play—favorite decorative motifs of Madame de Pompadour—animate the balustrade. The salon is dominated by an inlaid marble floor, and its white-and-gold decor suggests a metaphorical rotunda of engaged Corinthian columns with scenes of wildlife depicted in the encircling frieze.

The pavilion's plan—a cross inscribed in a circle of steps, containing a circular salon—exhibits the fascination with perfect geometric figures that would increasingly dominate French architecture, culminating with the immense utopian schemes of Étienne-Louis Boullée and Claude Nicolas Ledoux late in the century. The complex, overlapping architectural elements that characterized the influential work of François Mansart—particularly at Maisons—were deconstructed and simplified over the course of the eighteenth century, permitting each constituent geometric figure to stand in purity and clarity, thus freeing it to

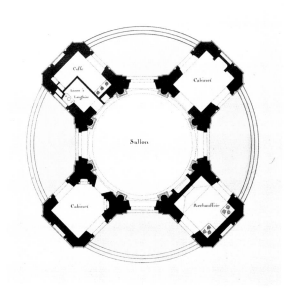

Louis XV viewing the gardens of Trianon, the Menagerie and its dependencies, the French Pavilion, and the Treillage Portal. Gouache attributed to André-Jacques Portail. Musée de Versailles, Versailles.

contribute its own characteristic beauty to a scheme.[10] François de La Guepière's awkward Menagerie Pavilion at Sceaux struggles at the beginning of this process, but with the French Pavilion these ideas crystallize—ideas that would fundamentally alter architectural æsthetics as the century progressed.

The Aurora Pavilion at Sceaux has been cited as an important precedent, due to its elegant, centralized plan;[11] however, the Aurora Pavilion was not conceived to stand free and originally its primary facade brought an axis to a close. A group of five pavilions at Dampierre, of which only the central one survives, are more intriguing precedents, for the group—a central salon and four satellite cabinets—shared a similar architectural vocabulary and formed a conceptual cross in plan. Another striking precedent is Bernini's overlooked plan for the royal chapel at Saint-Denis, which, despite its scale, is nearly identical to Gabriel's plan.[12] The Comte de Fels, writing at the turn of the twentieth century, dismissed the

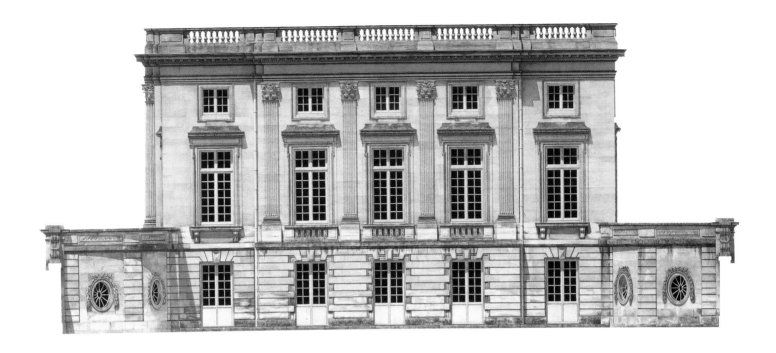

French Pavilion for "its bizarre design, the heaviness of its decorative details, and the groups of infants atop the balustrade."[13] He attributed these lapses to "a certain breakdown of French taste with which Louis XV's reign began" and would only be appeased by the austerity of the Petit Trianon.

Though his designs could affront conservative taste, Gabriel has been denigrated as a reactionary or has received the ambiguous praise of being named the last great architect of the Renaissance tradition.[14] He is neither, and must be the least-understood of France's great architects. To those with progressive opinions, he is seen as fighting a rearguard action, impeding architecture's inevitable progress toward the visionary schemes of the Revolutionary era. There is an element of truth in this view when assessing his

Above left and right: the Petit Trianon, entry and garden elevations. Built 1761–1768 by Ange-Jacques Gabriel, and universally acknowledged as his masterpiece (authors' renderings).

great public projects—which Louis XV wished to reflect royal grandeur as defined by Hardouin-Mansart and the Sun King—and we can be thankful that his sterile project to obliterate the entrance facade of Versailles proceeded no further than it did. However, even Gabriel's defenders consistently

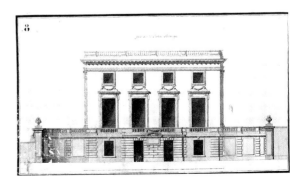

underestimate the importance of his minor works: these seemingly inconsequential garden pavilions, hermitages, and hunting boxes, with so little in the way of programmatic needs to constrain them, were in fact the perfect laboratories for exploring ideas that could never be carried out elsewhere.

Below left and right: the entry and garden elevations of the Petit Trianon in Ange-Jacques Gabriel's project of 1761, before expansion to a five-bayed structure. Note the entrance facade's lack of pilasters and poorly resolved ground floor, and the coupled columns of the garden facade. Archives nationales, Paris.

The Petit Trianon

The Petit Trianon has been a lightning rod for an amusing and enduring debate concerning the two foremost architectural movements of eighteenth-century Europe: English Neo-Palladianism and French neoclassicism. Unsurprisingly, views on the merits of each school split cleanly along national boundaries. English critics proclaim that their Palladian country houses are characterized by bold-ness, clarity, and vigor and dismiss the French châteaux and hôtels of the period as effete, pedantic rehashes of an outdated Kentian style, with the Petit Trianon as the greatest offender of all. In turn, the French find the English style bombastic and clumsy and consider their beloved Petit Trianon to be the epitome of sophistication, elegance, and architectural

refinement, the apex of the French classical tradition. The Petit Trianon is beautifully planned, its symmetries elegantly adapted to the requirements of its site and its program. Its three-story entrance and service elevations and two-story garden elevations masterfully employ the classical orders to express function and purpose, with a richly modeled Corinthian colonnade *in antis* facing the formal garden of the French Pavilion, pilasters at the entrance and secondary garden facades, and a nearly bare facade facing what at the time were Louis XV's botanical gardens.

Terracing and retaining walls cleverly knit what is essentially a cubic structure seamlessly into the surrounding landscape, shaping and defining the character of the land and harmonizing it with the building's facades. The pavilion is an essay in grace, with an air of effortless inevitability that belies the extraordinary talent and diligence of its architect.

The Petit Trianon was the last and grandest of Madame de Pompadour's hermitages, and Gabriel's original elevations depict a three-bayed pavilion, a direct descendant of the Hermitage at Fontainebleau. However, the king's increasing seclusion—two mechanical tables would be designed by the engineer Antoine-Joseph Loriot to permit dining without

servants[15]—and an acute shortage of space in the Hermitage at Fontainebleau combined to expand Trianon's program to one approaching that of a small château; in plans dated May 1762, Gabriel had lengthened the facades to five bays and departed from a design based on the perfect square in response to the proportions required to accomodate a colonnade and pilasters on adjoining facades, a necessity which subtly enriched the building.

Construction began in 1762, but was halted that same August due to lack of funds; the foundations lay bare that winter, and work was resumed anemically during the following two years. In 1764, the king announced that he wished construction to be completed swiftly, and the shell of the building was roofed that fall, though a second hiatus of over two years would impede the outfitting of the interiors. Pierre de Nolhac gallantly dissimulates that "The house, which was to become so famous, was built without haste, as it was desired to make it perfect."[16] Gabriel presented the keys for the unfinished pavilion in 1768, though the king would not spend his first night in the Petit Trianon until 9 September 1770, in the company of Madame Du Barry, and it was there, in late April 1774, that he fell mortally ill with smallpox and was told by his surgeon that it was at Versailles that one should be ill.

Upon his accession to the throne, Louis XVI gave this haunt of mistresses to Marie Antoinette in a pointed gesture of fidelity, and the Petit Trianon became the queen's private domain. Admittance to its grounds was by invitation only, an order which included the king; the queen composed rules of conduct, commissioned special liveries for the servants, and succeeded in recreating the atmosphere of carefree informality that had characterized her youth in Vienna. None of this seclusion would in any way endear her to a hostile court or to the people of France, but for posterity the Petit Trianon is imbued with her spirit.

LA CHASSE: THE HERMITAGES OF MADAME DE POMPADOUR

THE STORY OF MADAME DE POMPADOUR, that most perfect mistress, is too familiar and too rich to be encapsulated here. With Louis XIV, she is the most fascinating figure of the *ancien régime* and has been the subject of numerous biographies, yet none has managed to penetrate the essential mystery of her character. Though "few human beings since the world began can have owned so many beautiful things"[1]—the auction of her belongings required two years—she could write earnestly: "I have never wanted material things."[2] She loved houses and precious objects and her daughter Alexandrine, but most of all she loved Louis XV, even more than her own life. She was a faultless courtesan; she lived to serve him, spent her considerable capacities inventing every kind of

*The Hermitage
at Fontainebleau. Built 1749
by Ange-Jacques Gabriel. The watercolor
depicts the pavilion in its first state,
before flanking one-story wings were
added (authors' rendering).*

La Belle Jardinière: *Madame de Pompadour*
by Carle Van Loo. Musée de Versailles, Versailles.

entertainment to banish his ennui, and surrendered her delicate health to a brutally demanding regimen that ensured she would never fail to please him.

In return, she achieved enormous influence over the king and the affairs of France; out of his depth and knowing it, Louis XV surrendered his prerogatives gratefully. "My heart and mind are forever upon the king's business,"[3] she would write, and she became a great power behind the throne, airily dismissing ministers by claiming that they turned the king a bilious yellow. As with Louis XIV, Madame de Pompadour's sense of mission forced her to modulate her personality to achieve her ends, thus making her true self essentially unknowable and creating a mythic persona that became the embodiment of her age.

She possessed seventeen residences in her lifetime—a shocking number until one considers that both she and Louis XV were restless nomads who could not remain in one place for more than a few days at a time. She planned many of her houses with and for the king; royal outings were organized to oversee their construction and the laying out of gardens, and a further wave of interest and enthusiasm was generated with their decoration. Once finished, they would be inaugurated with ingenious entertainments, then visited periodically and tinkered with endlessly. Houses were an infallible antidote to the king's boredom, absorbing countless hours (and *livres*) and a brilliant means for the marquise to consolidate her position and retain her influence once she no longer slept with the king. Louis XV was by nature a recluse, and the more she enticed him to her intimate refuges, the greater her power became, and so it is not surprising that she wrote, "the cost of my houses makes me very upset. But it is all for my Master's pleasure, and there is nothing more to say about it."[4]

The Hermitage at Fontainebleau

Madame de Pompadour's first hermitage was a small house she ordered built at Versailles, "a certain hermitage near the Dragon Gate where I spend half my life. It is sixteen yards by ten, nothing above, so you see how grand it must be; but I can be alone there, or with the king and a few others, so I am happy."[5] Rustically decorated with painted furniture and *toile de Jouy*, with a garden of scented flowers and an enormous marble basin that was once the Sun King's bathtub, the house so amused Louis XV that she planned similar hermitages for the other major royal châteaux. The Duc de Croÿ soon bemoaned that the couple were building these precious little hermitages "at just about every one of the king's and the marquise's houses, [and that] their terrible predilection for small buildings and their little details proves immensely costly, without leaving anything of beauty to posterity."[6]

Fontainebleau, ancient seat of French kings, was by tradition the setting for an annual fall hunting voyage of several weeks. The château was vast, and each monarch felt compelled to make it a bit vaster, and thus it was the sort of palace Louis XV would have wished to avoid. Madame de Pompadour's hermitage stood across the road from the château's main gates, and the king, dressed for the hunt, would gallop off in the mornings to double back to the pavilion, whiling away the autumn days among the curios in her "simple but extremely pretty rooms,"[7] the flower and botanical gardens, and the small farmstead and dairy stocked with goats, cows, and exotic poultry.

The project began in 1748 with designs by Lassurance the Younger, architect of the marquise's houses at Bellevue, Crécy, and Versailles. Documentation is too sparse to be definitive, but Gabriel, then First Architect, seems to have made major revisions at the king's urging, changing the pavilion's plan from a rectangle to a perfect square and substantially redesigning the facades.[8] Construction began in January 1749, and the building shell of rubble walls finished with stucco was completed by mid-May. The king did not formally present the hermitage to Madame de Pompadour until 1753; she owned it for the rest of her life, but her brother the Marquis de Marigny sold it

A garden party in a bosquet at Versailles in 1678; the table's headboard prefigures the facade of the Hermitage. Engraving by Perelle. B.N.F., Paris.

to the man who had built and paid for it soon after her death. In 1754, Gabriel was called on to design a pair of one-story wings: that to the left of the entrance was a dining pavilion faced with trelliswork; the other, built to retain symmetry, was a treillage garden room constructed of iron and lath.[9]

The courtyard facing the château was arranged symmetrically with walls that hid the stables and outbuildings from view; the garden facade faced a formal parterre, with the kitchen garden and specimen plants in rectangular beds arranged to one side. Almost all of this has long since been lost, as the Duc de Croÿ feared it would be, but the hermitage itself has remained remarkably intact and for the past decades has been privately owned.

The elevational watercolor depicts the pavilion in its original state, before the treillage wings were added. The balustrade has been rebuilt poorly; it was originally of stone, with the roofline enlivened by vases holding flowers, as at the French Pavilion at Trianon. The four arched pediments contain sculpture groups of children playing amid attributes of the seasons; otherwise, the pavilion is enormously

*T*he Butard Hunting
Pavilion. Built 1750 by Ange-Jacques
Gabriel. The watercolor presents
Gabriel's idealized vision for Butard;
the sculpted stags' heads have
vanished, and, as built, the domed roof
above the salon was greatly
reduced (authors' rendering).

restrained, with only the slightest ornament of garlanded keystones appearing above the French doors on the rusticated ground floor. The squat attic story is lightened by pilasters capped by foliage evoking Corinthian capitals; the interplay of the rusticated piers and the pilasters they support with the volume of the protruding central bay creates a facade of great visual wealth on so small a scale. Poised between court and garden, the hermitage presented the same facade to four different prospects; thus it had much in common with the King's Pavilion at Marly and was in some measure the couple's own interpretation of Louis XIV's retreat, rescaled for their love of intimacy and recast for their own interests.

The Butard Hunting Pavilion

Despite his charades at Fontainebleau, Louis XV loved to hunt. Four or five afternoons each week he rode into his forests in search of wild boar one day, roebucks, wolves, or stags the next. He maintained more than 350 horses solely dedicated to deer hunting and regularly exhausted two or three packs of seventy

Ange-Jacques Gabriel's original plan for Butard, with its corresponding elevations. Archives nationales, Paris.

hounds; when he did not ride, courtiers liked to say: "The king does nothing today."[10] His obsession verged on the perverse; Madame Campan avowed that "The king thinks of nothing but the hunt," and after killing over eight hundred pieces of game at Gennevilliers, the Duc de Richelieu reported that he ate "like a real hunter—nothing but freshly killed meat, bloody and quivering, if you will."[11]

Inevitably, it was Louis XIV who had regularized the uniform and etiquette for the hunt, which remained substantially unchanged until the Revolution.[12] To be admitted to the royal hunt, a nobleman was first presented by the king with a turquoise jerkin trimmed with gold and silver braid; he also wore a red vest and riding breeches, a braid-trimmed hat, and deerskin gloves that reached to his elbows. Ladies also followed the hunt and outfitted themselves in stunning costumes; Madame de Pompadour first caught the king's eye when riding in a small carriage in the forest of Sénart, and Madame Du Barry was reported to have worn a white silk robe, a pearl-grey, man-tailored jacket trimmed with silver,

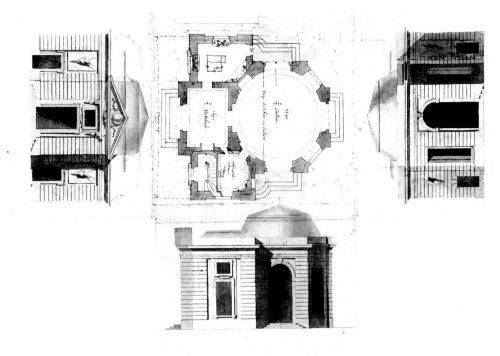

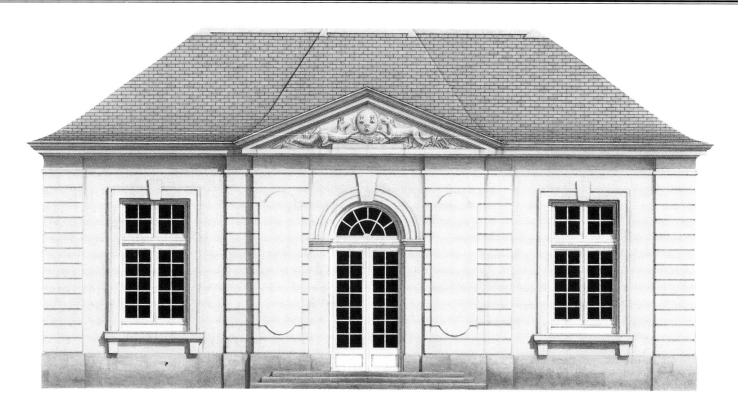

"and a rakishly angled tricorn atop her beautiful blonde hair."[13]

In 1750, at a time of numerous royal commissions after the Treaty of Aix-la-Chapelle ended the War of the Austrian Succession, the king directed Gabriel to design a hunting pavilion for a site equidistant between Versailles and Marly overlooking a small ravine—a butte, hence the name Butard. This was the first and grandest of a series of hunting boxes built in the royal forests, an unsurprisingly short distance from Madame de Pompadour's retreat at La Celle-Saint-Cloud. The pavilion sat in a forest clearing at the end of a hunting *allée*, with dependencies before it and a grille with stone piers forming a *cour d'honneur*. Gabriel designed an extraordinarily handsome building, a rectangular block conjoined with an octagonal salon overlooking the forest. The entrance vestibule protrudes slightly from the facade and is topped by a pediment carved

A project for the Hermitage at Compiègne. Designed in 1753 by Ange-Jacques Gabriel. The watercolor is based upon the only known elevational drawing of the Compiègne hermitages, and is nearly identical to hunting lodges Gabriel had designed at Fausses Reposes and Pont-Colbert, and later was used as the model for a house built in the town of Versailles[14] (authors' rendering).

with a boar being felled by hounds. The pavilion is built of tawny limestone; its crisp rustication and severe detailing was originally enlivened by sculptures of stags' heads mounted on panels above the doors and windows; these have disappeared, and there is some question as to whether they were oval medallions or busts. The watercolor elevation presents sculpted stone busts, as depicted in Gabriel's original sketches and corroborated by scars on the facade.

The pavilion's interior has been altered significantly:[15] the magnificent circular salon featured carved paneling and French doors which opened onto a terrace with an expansive view of the surrounding forest. A high, deeply vaulted ceiling was planned for the room but in fact a shallower vault was executed, and the watercolor elevation presents Gabriel's original roof profile.

After the Revolution, Empress Joséphine owned Butard; Pasteur later considered it for a laboratory, but the pavilion was instead allowed to molder. After being restored privately, Butard was reclaimed by the government and is today kept under lock and key.

Compiègne

Compiègne was a musty, forgotten palace until Louis XV discovered the wealth of game in its forests; in 1747 he initiated an enormous building program that would span three decades and create a château rivaling Fontainebleau in size. It soon became a fixed destination on the royal itinerary, offering an excellent hunting park and a fine site for military maneuvers.[16]

During the first years of construction, the king and Madame de Pompadour planned and built a new hermitage at Compiègne nearly every year; as the château was barely habitable, they created a series of camps in clearings in the park.[17] The first hermitage, built before 1749 and known as the King's Cabin, had the rustic air of a military encampment: a wooden lodge in the shape of a tent was surrounded by a small garden and enclosed by a canvas fence. In 1749, Gabriel designed a second hermitage: two small pavilions were erected in one corner of a square plot, and nearby stood a pair of wooden tents "of Asiatic magnificence," gifts from the Turkish Sultan.[18] The compound included a fountain and a parterre, a large birdcage, and a curious garden; its plan, lacking hierarchy but with numerous local symmetries, recalls the Labyrinth at Versailles, though its winding paths and artificial streams were unique for the time and anticipated the Anglo-Chinese gardens that were to appear in France decades later. This second hermitage may in turn have been supplanted by a third complex designed in 1751.

Finally, a permanent pavilion was commissioned to complement the vast neoclassical château rising nearby, a reiteration of the Hermitage at Fontainebleau. Initial plans were sketched by Lassurance, then revised by Gabriel; unfortunately only floorplans have survived, and the building's appearance is unknown. Its conception, though, is clear: as at Fontainebleau, the cubic pavilion was poised between a walled *cour d'honneur* and a formal garden, with its

salon facing the château's Grand Parterre. A notable innovation was Madame de Pompadour's dairy—a pavilion within a pavilion, with its own forecourt and garden—which anticipated the dairies of Marie Antoinette.[19]

Construction began in late 1753, but lack of funds delayed the pavilion's completion for two years. In 1756, after the Duc de Richelieu's astounding feat in conquering Port Mahon—his cook would invent "Mahonaise" during the siege—the king and the marquise jointly hosted a celebration for foreign ministers at the hermitage; the euphoria marked the pinnacle of France's fortunes in a war that would soon turn toward disaster; shortly thereafter the king authorized additions to the pavilion, but even this minor work was delayed again by the precarious state of the royal finances. Louis XVI later gave the hermitage to the Vicomte de Laval, but its subsequent history is obscure and no trace of it remains.

*La Sultane:
Madame de Pompadour relaxing in Turkish garb, perhaps in her wooden tent at Compiègne, a gift of the Turkish Sultan. Painting by Carle Van Loo. Musée des Arts décoratifs, Paris.*

*T*he project for
a Triumphal Arch at Crécy. Designed in
1749 by Lassurance the Younger
but unexecuted. The arch's monumental
scale reflects the ambitions
Madame de Pompadour held for the
estate of Crécy (authors' rendering).

CRÉCY

*We leave tomorrow for Crécy . . . I know
that you do not doubt the extreme pleasure
these voyages give me, my only regret
is that they are so short; I would like to
spend my whole life there.*
—Madame de Pompadour in a letter
to her father written in 1750

CRÉCY WAS THE FIRST, THE LARGEST and the most expensive of Madame de Pompadour's estates,[1] a gift from the king shortly after she became his titled mistress in 1746, and the marquise immediately began renovations with a view to receiving him there. The Duc de Luynes, who accompanied her on her first journey, found Crécy already "well-furnished and very beautiful,"[2] but for the marquise it was not beautiful enough, and she shuttled constantly between Crécy and Choisy—a favorite royal residence—to oversee construction.

The marquise faced criticism of her growing passion for architecture and cleverly explained: "Everywhere one criticizes the folly of building; personally I approve of that madness, which feeds so many of the poor."[3] She commissioned Lassurance the Younger,[4] who would become her preferred architect, to modernize the château and transform Crécy into a royal residence. Lassurance's major contribution was a vast *cour d'honneur*: the château's existing side wings were demolished and replaced by curvilinear additions which, though hardly unknown in French architecture, were considered Italianate by contemporaries, an impression reinforced by the use of flat roofs surmounted by balustrades punctuated by trophies. Despite the precedent of the garden facade of Versailles, such roofs were rare for country

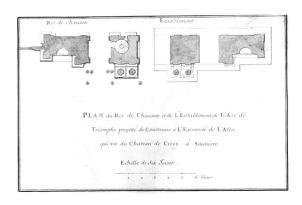

*The plan
of the Triumphal Arch. Drawing
by Lassurance the Younger.
Archives nationales, Paris.*

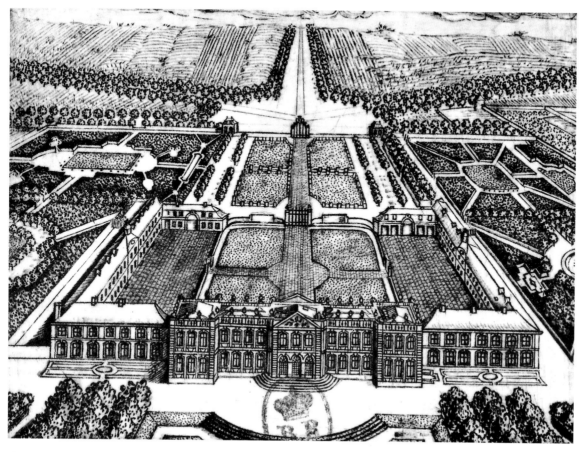

châteaux of the period, and approving them was an early indication of Madame de Pompadour's intention to seek out the vanguard of artistic and architectural movements.

The most beautiful room in the château was the octagonal library, which featured François Boucher's cycle of infants at play with the attributes of the arts and sciences, today in The Frick Collection in Manhattan. Life at Crécy, unfolding like a country-house outing, centered on the grand salon facing the garden: afternoon suppers were held there and courtiers lingered to chat, play cards, and gamble. Louis XV worked in an adjoining room until dinner, after which play resumed. The king loved gaming and was quite adept, playing until the small hours while the marquise entertained.

The gardens at Crécy were designed by Garnier de l'Isle. The Duc de Luynes found them "not very large, consisting of a parterre facing the château which leads to a terrace and two wooded areas flanking the house and garden, newly planted by Monsieur de l'Isle in compartments and bosquets."[5] The duke also noted the incomparable site, a plain one hundred and fifty feet above the river Blaise, from which a hydraulic machine brought water to the gardens. The château faced a terrace fifteen hundred feet long and overlooked the river; the valley floor once held a long reflecting basin, and the forests on the far hills were cut by hunting *allées*, thus incorporating the entire landscape into the estate's design.

The Triumphal Arch

Madame de Pompadour's most ambitious project for Crécy was never realized—an enormous triumphal arch that would have commenced a grand axis leading to the château. The roof of the arch was to have held

a reservoir—as at the Grotto of Thétis—to replenish the garden's fountains and provide water for the village. Modeled upon the arch of Septimus Severus in Rome, it was one of several projects for triumphal arches inspired by the Prix de Rome competition of 1747, and was contemporary with the architect Emmanuel Héré's triumphal arch at Nancy. The central arch was to have been flanked by coupled Ionic columns; secondary gateways to either side would have been surmounted by niches containing bas-relief sculpture of the elements, and a small spiral staircase embedded in one of the piers would have led to the reservoir and its small pavilion.

A pair of short wings rusticated with *mousse* flank the central composition; these unusual additions are reminiscent of Italianate grottoes built in the preceding century, and in particular recall Cardinal Richelieu's trompe-l'œil arch at Rueil. The wings underscore the arch's intended function as a reservoir, but also reflect its architect's brash eclecticism. As at the Château de Crécy, Lassurance juxtaposed architectural elements in unexpected contexts, creating surprising and innovative buildings by freely mixing French classicism with the Italian precedents he had studied in Rome.

The grand arch never did greet Louis XV: Crécy was simply too far from Versailles and too expensive for the chronically insolvent king to justify. The annual sojourns the couple so enjoyed ended in 1755, and two years later Madame de Pompadour sold her "small and poor Crécy"[6] to the king's cousin, the Duc de Penthièvre. Crécy shared a fate common to many châteaux of the *ancien régime,* first confiscated during the Revolution, then sold and resold before finally being demolished in the nineteenth century.

The Maréchal de Richelieu has built a rotunda
that he has named the Temple of Love; it sits
atop an ice cellar and so is known as love on ice.
—The Marquis d'Argenson,
Journal et mémoires

F EW FIGURES IN HISTORY have ever enjoyed themselves more, for a longer period of time and at so
many others' expense, than the Duc de Richelieu. He
was "the living incarnation of the eighteenth century for
his contemporaries and for posterity,"[1] a man with a
fecund imagination who concocted whatever he found
lacking in life, from the minutiæ of court protocol to a
celebrated sleeping coach with bed and pantry. He held
no allegiance but to his own interests and reveled in
scandal; he was mockingly irreligious and dabbled in
the black arts, and carried on his infamous affairs with
ingenuity and witty élan. Two of his first twenty-one
years were spent within the Bastille, and though high
political office eluded him, he was an animated figure at
court from Louis XIV's last decade until the eve of the
Revolution—a "moth-eaten mummy,"[2] older in the
end than much of Versailles and its furniture.

T he Aurora Pavilion
at Gennevilliers. Built circa *1755*
by Giovanni Servandoni.
This first folly-rotunda in France was
destroyed early in this century
(authors' rendering).

B elow: the Maréchal Duc de
Richelieu. Pastel by Jean Valade, circa
1750. Authors' collection.

Presented at court in 1710, he scored an immediate
triumph by rescuing the Duchesse de Bourgogne
from a gaffe during a ball at Marly, but his pursuit of
Marie-Adélaïde—he was dragged from under her
bed, then caught with his hand up her skirts—would
result in the first of three confinements in the Bastille
at the tender age of fifteen.

The duke carried on his affairs as a kind of public
theater; to enhance his reputation, he ordered his carriage to stand all night before the houses of beautiful
women. The novel *Les Liaisons Dangereuses* by
Choderlos de Laclos is but one of many thinly veiled
accounts of a mere handful of his exploits; Jean-
François Hénault, President of the Parlement of Paris,
dubbed him "the greatest lady-killer of the century; he
tamed all women, to such an extent that one remarks
those who managed to resist him."[3] Most notoriously,
the duke rented rooms abutting Madame de La
Popelinière's townhouse and connected their bedrooms
with a revolving fireplace—silver fireplace charms soon
became a Parisian fad—and cruelly humiliated two
mistresses who were friends by separately inviting them
to the same rendezvous; he then sat between them on a

himself in the bloody hides of freshly slaughtered cattle. He wore higher heels as he shrank, stretched his wrinkles flat and hid the tape under his wig, earning a thousand cruel nicknames, yet he was always the courtier; he ignored Louis XVI's suggestion that he retire to Guyenne, and in the end the Creaking Machine of Gallantries prevailed,[4] presenting the king his warmed bedshirt with all the good humor he had shown his grandfather. In 1778, he danced at a masked ball with the wizened Maréchale de Mirepoix, Madame de Pompadour's great friend, and the court was touched and chastened by the sight of the two octogenarians "dancing a minuet with as much grace and lightness as youths of twenty."[5] At the end of his life, Richelieu achieved a certain dignity by upholding the courtiers' unique *joie de vivre* that was fast being consumed by rising discontent—a living relic who once remarked to Louis XVI: "I have seen three reigns: during the first, one remained silent; during the second, one whispered; but today, one shouts."[6]

The Aurora Pavilion

"My fleeting affairs, academic intrigues, and the circus of the court did not at all suffice to fill my leisure in 1749, without my little house at Gennevilliers, which soon became, thanks to Servandoni and myself, a beautiful château, a rendezvous for hunting and for love, a theater for gastronomic prowess and bacchanals where Louis XV did not disdain to play his role, but this time without the marquise, and showed himself, fork in hand, a most distinguished actor."[7]

So wrote *Son Excellence* about Gennevilliers, where he fancied himself a country squire and host to kings. His architect, Giovanni Servandoni, was a Florentine known throughout Europe for his theater and festival designs and is best remembered for the facade of Saint-Sulpice in Paris. He rebuilt Gennevilliers' park and château along the simple, rustic lines of a hunting estate and included a large rectangular garden, "one of the first to be designed in the English style, rebelling against the majestic and monotonous tradition of Le Nôtre's masterpieces."

couch and cajoled them into drawing lots for the privilege of being the first to visit his bedroom.

The duke was an extraordinary dandy and embalmed himself in musks and ambers. One day the queen commented on a bishop's strong perfume, but the prelate had merely sat in a chair used by Richelieu some hours before. The duke was no less extravagant in dress. As ambassador, he rode through Vienna preceded by seventy-five servants in silver-trimmed velvet; he himself wore a gold-embroidered suit and rode in a gilded carriage, and his horses were shod with silver shoes held by a few nails, so that they flew off, creating clamoring mobs in his wake. This embassy earned him Louis XV's favorite nickname, *Son Excellence*, and as First Gentleman of the King's Bedchamber, he became one of those few the king allowed every indulgence.

Richelieu sought bizarre enhancements in old age, bathing in almond milk and alcohols and wrapping

Unfortunately, the claim is questionable; portions of the duke's memoirs appear to be apocryphal, and Labrière's redrawing of the park along "English" lines in 1785 reveals traces of an earlier, rectilinear design.[8] However, the garden included a folly-rotunda dedicated to Aurora, goddess of Dawn, that anticipated the rage for Anglo-Chinese garden follies by nearly two decades—the ancestor of countless temples of love that would appear in French gardens for generations to come.

Richelieu was extremely proud of this rotunda and recalled it in detail:

"I want only to speak of my icehouse, an elegant rotunda . . . imitating the Temple of the Sybil at Tivoli that harbored in its womb cellars where wine was perfumed in the chill air. Above that precious cavern . . . was a round dining room with twelve doors of Venetian glass, unique in clarity and quality. Boucher had decorated the paneling with his voluptuous inspirations and a swarm of putti, painted in the proper style of Madame de Pompadour, with a portrait of the king strewn with roses.[9] We dined amid baskets of rare flowers and cages filled with tropical birds, on my Saxony porcelain . . . and as one ate, with a mosaic floor at one's feet, one's eyes were everywhere refreshed by the mellow mixture of greenery and statues, one's brow was caressed by nocturnal breezes wafting gently through opened windows, with the most refined gustatory pleasures joined to the most free and easy conversation."

Constructed of stuccoed rubble walls and wood painted to imitate marble, the rotunda was surmounted by a balustrade supporting statues of classical deities, and a gilded Mercury stood atop its dome. The cellars formed a pyramidal, rusticated base, and the salon above was reached by exterior stair ramps, its elevated position creating a secluded setting: the pavilion overlooked a basin at one end of the garden and a large artificial lake lay behind. The picturesque ensemble, combining two disparate garden elements—an ice cellar-*cum*-grotto and an Italianate rotunda—anticipated an essential characteristic of

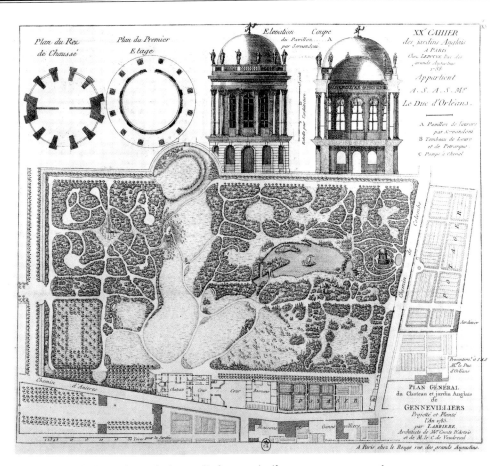

later garden follies, whose designs relied upon similar additive pastiche. The pavilion also reflects Servandoni's immersion in mid-century festival architecture, in which unusual designs such as domed rotundas served as short-lived centerpieces for public celebrations. Though ignored or slighted, undoubtedly because of the impossibility of judging anything pertaining to the Duc de Richelieu impartially, the Aurora Pavilion deserves wider recognition for its unique place in French garden history.

Son Excellence grew tired of the country in his old age and sold the estate to the Duc de Choiseul in 1764; seven years later Richelieu's son bought Gennevilliers, and in 1783 the premiere of Pierre Caron de Beaumarchais' *Marriage of Figaro* was held in his father's orangerie. The dilapidated pavilion was photographed at the turn of this century but was destroyed not long after.

The garden plan of Gennevilliers in 1788 with the plans and section of the Aurora Pavilion. The pavilion is seen to the right of the lake. Engraved by Georges-Louis Le Rouge. B.N.F., Paris.

THE ORANGERIE AT COUBERT

THE FRENCH PASSION for orange trees began with military campaigns in Italy in the fifteenth century. In the wake of marauding kings and two Medici queens, Italian gardeners enticed across the Alps had introduced new horticultural practices, and naturally it was an Italian, Dom Pacello di Mercogliano, who built France's first orangeries for Louis XII at Blois and Amboise.[1] François I brought orange trees to Fontainebleau; later Diane de Poitiers, mistress of Henri II, commissioned hothouses at Anet; and another glasshouse was recorded at the Louvre; but the word *orangerie* would not appear until the early 1600s, first employed to describe Henri IV's Orangerie at the Tuileries Palace.

Built following Roman principles, these early orangeries were little more than wooden frames fitted

*The Orangerie
at Coubert. Built* circa *1740
and attributed to Germain Boffrand.
Tragically destroyed in the 1960s, though
its stone facade survives
(authors' rendering).*

*The most beautiful
orange tree in the world: a detail
of* The Progress of Love: The Lover
Crowned, *by Jean-Honoré Fragonard.
The Frick Collection, New York.*

with glass and heated by braziers in winter. Some were designed to be dismantled each spring, much like the *logis des orangers* at Heidelberg described by Salomon de Caus.[2] By the mid-seventeenth century collecting these precious, expensive trees and building shelters for them had become a craze, comparable only to the tulip mania that seized Europe at the same time, and an orangerie became as much of a status symbol as an Italianate grotto had been only shortly before. Cardinal Richelieu's Orangerie at Rueil, a stone building with large, arched French doors, set a new standard of opulence in the 1630s, but Louis XIV's vast Orangerie at Versailles remains the most imposing monument to man's unreasoning love for these trees.

The king began his collection with trees confiscated from Vaux-le-Vicomte. His arboreal *La Dorée* was a tree named *Le Grand Bourbon*, allegedly sown at the beginning of the fifteenth century by a princess of Navarre, which had graced the grounds of Chantilly before François I removed it to Fontainebleau. Louis XIV ordered the tree to be transferred to Versailles, where it remained until its death in 1894.

The modest Jean de La Quintinie tended the trees, and when he died the king declared that he had not lost a servant but a friend. La Quintinie had written a practical essay on the planning and care of kitchen gardens, a bestseller in France and England;[3] every detail of cultivating orange trees was discussed, and the forthright gardener advised against using decorative (and Italianate) terra-cotta pots, for they offered very little stability, though others recommended terra cotta because it trapped the sun's warmth, promoting growth.

At Versailles, trees were displayed in bronze vases or in wooden tubs painted in a variety of colors or, as in the Hall of Mirrors, in solid silver urns. Though not easily portable—the combined weight of the silver and soil must have strained the back of many a footman—the king thought nothing of ordering the trees moved constantly about the château, perfuming

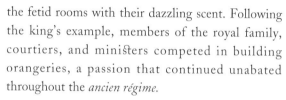

Details of engravings illustrating Jean de La Quintinie's book, L'Instruction pour les jardins Fruitiers et Potagers. *B.N.F., Paris.*

the fetid rooms with their dazzling scent. Following the king's example, members of the royal family, courtiers, and ministers competed in building orangeries, a passion that continued unabated throughout the *ancien régime.*

One of the finest examples of a mid-eighteenth-century orangerie was built at Coubert. The estate was purchased in 1719 by the wealthy financier Samuel Bernard, whose unprecedented invitation to Marly a decade earlier had scandalized the court.[4] The acquisition of Coubert coincided with Bernard's marriage to a noblewoman almost fifty years his junior,[5] and though a septagenarian, he would spend a further twenty years enlarging his estate and hosting parties for his young wife, who was sorely tried by his unforeseen longevity. The château was remodeled, parterres laid out, and a canal excavated to embellish the gardens, which, excepting financial affairs, were the old man's passion.

Bernard died in 1739 and his son, the Comte de Coubert, a President of the Parlement of Paris, inherited the estate and shortly afterward commissioned the Orangerie. Though no records exist, the facade's refined proportions and exuberantly carved pediment indicate a talented architect, and Germain Boffrand is generally credited with the design.

Three arches decorated with delicate, garlanded keystones led into a structure which housed as many as five hundred orange trees, representing a considerable fortune. The pediment features a bas-relief of infants at play amid garden tools and suggests a temple dedicated to the glory of the orange trees and grape vines that were sheltered within.

An ancient *allée* still leads to the site of the demolished château, now occupied by a nineteenth-century building. The Orangerie, still intact at the beginning of this century as photographs attest, was near collapse after the Second World War, and as an unclassified building was razed in 1966. Its facade alone now stands free, a monument to thoughtless vandalism.

MADAME DU BARRY
AND LOUVECIENNES

It's not that bad. In fact it looks rather good.
—Louis XV, upon first seeing the portico
of Ledoux's Music Pavilion

T HE HILLSIDE ABOVE THE SEINE at Louveciennes
was once the site of a vast, infernal contraption
named the Machine of Marly, built by the Flemish

*The Music Pavilion
at Louveciennes. Built 1770–1771
by Claude Nicolas Ledoux.
Destroyed, then rebuilt in the 1930s
(authors' rendering).*

engineer Arnold de Ville to feed Louis XIV's fountains at Versailles and Marly. With large wooden
paddlewheels and countless pumps, chains, and elon-
gated buckets, it somehow managed to raise the
river's water nearly five hundred feet, a marvel of seventeenth-century engineering that became a pilgrimage site for curious, mechanically inclined visitors

from Peter the Great to Thomas Jefferson, though the Duc d'Harcourt sniffed that de Ville could have simplified its workings, "but made it complicated to enhance his reputation."[1]

Atop the hill beside this wheezing monster sat the overseer's house; the consolation for its vibrating walls was a magnificent view of the Seine winding through a pastoral landscape. The Duc de Luynes admired Louveciennes' views and found the house delightful, tactfully neglecting to mention the unbearable noise and the pungent stench of silt and mud stirred up from the river. After de Ville's death, the estate was given to one of Louis XIV's granddaughters, and in 1766 it passed to the Duc de Penthièvre, another of the king's grandchildren. After his only son, the Prince de Lamballe, died at Louveciennes, the disconsolate duke offered the estate to Louis XV.

The king soon found use for the property, bestowing it upon his new mistress, Madame Du Barry, during the summer voyage to Compiègne in 1769. Why he did so is a mystery, but the king's action can best be explained as an act of expediency—the estate was available and his newly ennobled countess, thirty-four years his junior, would be grateful for whatever gifts came her way. Even Ange-Jacques Gabriel could not rid Louveciennes of its neighbor and could propose only extensive interior renovations, begun the same year as Madame Du Barry's presentation at court.

The countess' grip over the aging king swifty became dominion, and any disrespectful talk, at least in his presence, ceased. In truth, the new mistress gained many surprised admirers; typical among them was the Comte d'Espinchal, who avowed: "She is good and generous, and her company is sweet. An excellent friend, kind and obliging; at home and in public she acts with the greatest decency."[2] Her simplicity and warmth were so alien to Versailles that many courtiers were confounded: "She was the first to laugh at all the verses aimed at her," reported another ally.[3]

By 1770, her position was indisputable—announced, as always at Versailles, by a move to a

The icehouse in the park of Louveciennes. Built in the mid-1770s and, because of its monumentality, attributed to Claude Nicolas Ledoux (authors' rendering).

finer set of apartments. Madame Du Barry had successfully established her own party, which included such social pillars as the Duc de Richelieu and the Maréchale de Mirepoix, who specialized in befriending royal mistresses. The Duc de Tresmes was honored to consider himself her monkey since his hunched back amused her, and the future King of Sweden, Gustav III, knowing her passion for jewels, presented a diamond collar to her dog. She enchanted the king with an easy familiarity, most famously by calling from bed: "Look out, France, your coffee's

The Machine of Marly, Louveciennes' rude neighbor, which fed the royal fountains at Versailles and Marly, by Pierre-Denis Martin, 1724. Musée de Versailles, Versailles.

about to bolt!" Though contested by the Marquis de Ségur, the remark illuminates Louis XV's private life as few others could.[4]

The Music Pavilion

That same year Madame Du Barry commissioned Claude Nicolas Ledoux to design a music and dining pavilion at Louveciennes. The existing house was simply too small to accomodate the king's frequent visits and was outdated and architecturally undistinguished as well. The countess intended to build in the latest style and selected one of the most fashionable and controversial architects of the day. Ledoux came to her attention through the acclaim surrounding his Hôtel de Montmorency; the Duchesse de Montmorency was an avid amateur architect and gardener and had allied herself with the countess' rising star. Ledoux's bold volumetric designs—with their spare, almost brutal, classical detailing and provocative proportions—placed him at the vanguard of a coming revolution in French architecture, though at the time of his introduction to the royal mistress, reported an English contemporary, he was very much the picture of a young architect on the rise, "a singularly high-flown personage" styled like a peacock and eager to fill the ears of prospective clients with "courtly blandishments."[5]

The Music Pavilion had a direct precedent in Ledoux's own Hôtel Guimard, built for a well-known actress on the same fashionable avenue as the Hôtel de Montmorency. Its entrance facade, with an enormous coffered niche screened by an Ionic portico, was nearly identical to that of Louveciennes, except that the portion of the niche that rose above the entablature was absent. The Music Pavilion was used only to mount entertainments and dinner parties, and so Ledoux took pleasure in designing a series of geometrically perfect rooms, creating a plan that Cyril Connolly likened to frozen music.

Work began in December 1770, and nine months later the countess hosted a lavish inaugural dinner in the grand Dining Room, evocatively captured in Moreau le Jeune's watercolor. The king, with Madame Du Barry at his side, is clearly recognizable; one can also find the governor of Louveciennes—Zamore, her eight-year-old Bengal blackamoor.[6] Reaction to the pavilion was mixed: to many it was an exquisite, classically inspired jewel set with simple grace in a green park; to others, its preciously worked details—the extraordinary door hinges have been cited—sapped the building of life and suggested a gilded cage for a kept woman.

The inaugural dinner of Louveciennes given by Madame Du Barry in the king's honor, 27 September 1771, captured in watercolor by Moreau le Jeune. Musée du Louvre, Paris.

The Frick Collection's magnificent wall canvases of *The Progress of Love* by Jean-Honoré Fragonard were commissioned but never accepted for the King's Salon; it is not known why they were refused, though some speculate that Madame Du Barry found them outdated or that the king was not amused by his resemblance to Fragonard's ardent young lover. Nevertheless, the king approved of Louveciennes; Ledoux was engaged to build an inexplicably immense palace incorporating the Music Pavilion, and work progressed on the foundations before the king's death sent his favorite into exile.

After a series of unfortunate nineteenth-century alterations, the Music Pavilion was razed in the 1930s by the couturier René Coty, who built a swimming pool in its basement and fractionally enlarged the entire building to accomodate an air-conditioning system. The present pavilion, to which an attic story has been added, is a modern replica.

*M*istress of Louveciennes:
*Madame Du Barry drawn
by François Hubert Drouais.
Location unknown.*

A fanciful view of the garden
*facade of Louveciennes.
Engraved by Bellet after Testard.
B.N.F., Paris.*

LOUIS XVI
AND MARIE ANTOINETTE:
THE RAGE FOR EXOTICISM

I am afraid of being bored.
—Marie Antoinette to Comte de Mercy-Argenteau

*T*he reign of Louis XVI (1774–1792) roughly coincided with the onset of the French mania for Anglo-Chinese gardens. Though neo-classicism continued to evolve—becoming increasingly mannered and deeply influenced by ancient precedents, culminating in what is today termed Revolutionary architecture—in the gardens of the period the rage for exoticism swept up all in its path.

No anecdote so clearly illuminates the confluence of the craving for the exotic with the aristocracy's willful naïveté as the Comtesse de Boigne's story of the exiled Prince of Chios and his son Justiniani, who lived off Louis XVI's bounty at Versailles for several years. Their "accent and a somewhat pronounced foreign bearing assured their success . . . mystifying, to their own advantage, the King of France, his government, and his court, [until] it was discovered that the heirs to the Empire of the East were in fact simply two peasants from Berry," unmasked by a servant of the Comte de Maurepas.[1]

By the time of Louis XVI's accession, formal gardens had fallen from favor, and nobles took as their model the English landscape garden, but crowded all manner of picturesque constructions upon their grounds. These follies offered a boundless repertoire of imagery: pagodas evoked the Orient, innumerable thatched huts hearkened to Edenic idylls, farm villages presented a supremely false vision of peasant life, temples and rotundas echoed the Ancients. All the world and all its cultures were plundered to provide adornments for a nobleman's garden, leading the Prince de Ligne to bemoan in 1781 that "Chinese buildings reek of the boulevards and sideshow fairs," and that "Gothic houses, too, are becoming too common."[2] He proposed instead the hitherto untapped ornamental possibilities of Moldavian huts and allowed that Arab and Turkish styles had not yet been exhausted.

These late follies—brash, colorful, fantastic, and above all impermanent—depict an aristocracy unrestrained in its pursuit of pleasure and blithely unaware of the fragility of the old order.

*T*he royal family inspecting the replanting of the
Tapis Vert at Versailles during the winter of 1774–1775.
Detail of the painting by Hubert Robert. Musée de Versailles, Versailles.

A ROYAL REFUGE:
THE HAMEAU AT TRIANON

If what the queen desires is possible,
it has already been done;
if it is impossible, it will be done.
—The Comte de Calonne, Finance Minister
of Louis XVI

IN 1774, TWO MONTHS after becoming queen, Marie Antoinette was "entirely occupied by a garden in the English manner that she wishes to establish at the Trianon," wrote the Austrian ambassador, Comte de Mercy-Argenteau.[1] She had first requested a plan from the Comte de Caraman, a respected amateur gardener; her visit to his Paris townhouse produced a whirlwind of activity as the garden was readied to receive her, and that same day the count's plan for the Trianon was approved and he was named Director of the Queen's Gardens. In her enthusiasm, Marie Antoinette pursued her project much as a private individual would have done, following the advice of friends in choosing a designer and then commissioning him after inspecting his work. As queen, however, a bureaucracy of craftsmen lay at her disposal and ignoring them generated nothing but hostility. She also alienated the royal

The Marlborough Tower at Trianon. Built 1783–1785 by Richard Mique. The building long ago lost its picturesque, winding stair (authors' rendering).

Marie Antoinette walking in the gardens, drawn by Madame Élisabeth Vigée-Lebrun. Private collection, New York.

architectural establishment by creating a post for her own architect, Richard Mique, and such self-absorbed and ill-advised actions, repeated heedlessly, would in time undermine her reputation at court and color public opinion.

Antoine Richard, who had supervised Louis XV's botanical gardens at Trianon for over three decades, earlier had submitted a plan for an Anglo-Chinese garden that preserved much of his own work, but its every square foot was traced with an impossibly dense network of paths and watercourses meandering between nearly two dozen garden features. The queen dismissed the plan, and Caraman's design was in turn modified by Richard Mique; Hubert Robert is also said to have played a part in the garden's design, and in due course the Prince de Ligne, a confidant of Marie Antoinette and a celebrated garden enthusiast, offered his advice; yet despite its many authors the gardens at Trianon would become a rare, though immensely costly, collaborative success.

The Queen's Gardens

"One thinks one is a hundred leagues from court," wrote the Prince de Ligne of Trianon's gardens, where construction began coincident with Anne-Robert Turgot's dismissal as Finance Minister in 1776;[2] the first structure appeared that same year, the festive, chinoiserie Carousel built immediately to the west of the Petit Trianon.[3] Within two years, Louis XV's botanical fields had been transformed into a landscape park planned about a sinuous watercourse; Mique's acclaimed rotunda, the Temple of Love, was built upon an artificial island planted with scented shrubs and white roses and was inaugurated in 1778 with a reception in the king's honor.

Construction of the Music Pavilion, or Belvedere, began that same year and its interior was completed in 1781. Set on an artificial rise and backed by evergreens, it brought the vista beyond the Carousel to a close and screened greenhouses and flower nursuries from view. The pavilion overlooks a reflecting pond

The queen's garden at Trianon: The Petit Trianon is at left, the Carousel to its immediate right; the Belvedere is seen in the far distance, to the left of the Temple of Love. Watercolor by Louis-Nicolas de Lespinasse. Musée de Versailles, Versailles.

and is approached through a rockwork of extraordinary modeling; the queen took great interest in this work and demanded fourteen models before approving its construction. The Belvedere's design employs a refined classical vocabulary that defers to Gabriel's Petit Trianon, though its precisely faceted octagonal facade and brittle details display the aridity that eventually would sap French neoclassicism of its life and spirit. Polychromed frescoes inspired by those at Pompeii adorn the circular salon, and though the pavilion's furniture has not survived, the correspondence between its architect and the overseer of the royal furnishings is noteworthy: "my dear friend, see whether you can give me a moment for us to decide what to do, for you know our mistress, and that she likes to enjoy her pleasures without delay."[4]

Though costs rose to nearly three times the original budget, the expense of the Music Pavilion was soon forgotten, and it became the centerpiece for the queen's nocturnal receptions, celebrated for their

The Belvedere illuminated during a fete in honor of the queen's brother, Emperor Joseph II, in August 1781. Painting by Claude-Louis Châtelet. Musée de Versailles, Versailles.

*T*he Belvedere
at Trianon. Built 1778–1779 by Richard
Mique for Queen Marie Antoinette
(authors' rendering).

*T*he Hameau:
the Marlborough Tower is at left and
the Queen's House at right. Gouache
by Claude-Louis Châtelet.
Biblioteca Estense, Modena.

*I*ntricately patterned
marblework distinguishes the floorplan
of the Belvedere (authors' rendering).

remarkable lighting effects. One of the first honored the Comte de Provence and was so well-received that it was repeated the next four evenings, though the reception held in June 1782 for the Russian Grand Duke Paul and his wife, traveling incognito as the Count and Countess of the North, was to be the most memorable fete of Louis XVI's reign. After an opera and a ballet, orchestras played as guests strolled the gardens "which were lit—*not* illuminated—producing a charming effect: earthenware lamps, concealed by green-painted boards, threw light upon the shrubs and flowerbeds and brought out their many tints in the most varied and pleasing manner," reminisced Madame Campan.[5]

This decorative approach to nature inevitably influenced the towering, thematic hairdos that were then the rage; for this evening, the Baronne d'Oberkirch hid a vase in her hair, confessing, "The springtime atop my head amid powdered snow produced an unequalled effect." She noted that the grand duchess' wig held a small, jeweled bird that fluttered on a spring at the slightest movement and that "The queen found it so adorable that she wanted one of her own."[6]

The Hameau

Inspired by the farmers' hamlet that the Prince de Condé had commissioned at Chantilly, Marie Antoinette began the planning of the Hameau in 1782. Its twelve buildings were located to the north of the English garden and were grouped about a large, artificial pond. In part an actual working farm and in part stage-set illusion, the Hameau would be the queen's most beloved undertaking and the last royal construction at Versailles before the Revolution.

The Marlborough Tower was the first building to be completed and took its name from an old song that had been revived by Beaumarchais. It dominates the buildings grouped about the lake and was modeled upon the Tower of Gabrielle at Ermenonville, which the queen had admired when visiting the estate in 1780. The stone base, hexagonal in plan, served as a

fishery, above which rises a two-story tower of faux limestone surmounted by a lookout. An elaborate wooden stair, today destroyed, once allowed direct access to the tower, and its picturesque curves and switchbacks added an element of richness and complexity the building now lacks. White-glazed flower-pots with the queen's monogram in blue were placed along the railings, creating what the Comte d'Hezecques called "an aerial flowerbed."[7] Attached to the tower was the Queen's Dairy; its roughly stuccoed walls belie an elegant white faux-marble interior where Marie Antoinette and her guests

The Queen's Mill at Trianon. Built 1783–1785 by Richard Mique. The mill was restored in 1994 to its original state (authors' rendering).

enjoyed fruit and fresh milk brought from the nearby working dairy.[8]

Standing across the lake from the Marlborough Tower, the Queen's Mill is an essay in picturesque scenography; iris plants held the clay of its roof ridges in place, its waterwheel was driven by a small sluice, and the cracks in its stuccoed walls were carefully executed by craftsmen. As the tower once did, the mill derives much of its æsthetic appeal from its rustic exterior stairs, as well as from its seemingly haphazard massing. Destroyed for centuries, the small shed-like room raised upon stilts was rebuilt, along with the waterwheel, when

*Portrait of Richard Mique,
Director of the Queen's Gardens, by Heinsius.
As the major proponent of the gardens
at Trianon, he shared Marie Antoinette's
fate and was guillotined in 1794.
Musée Historique Lorrain, Nancy.*

the building was restored in 1994, and the surrounding vegetable plots were refurbished and replanted.

Daily life at Trianon was enveloped in bucolic peace, as described by the Baron de Besenval: "The king came to breakfast with the queen every morning, without a captain of the guards, and he returned to Versailles to hold his *levée,* came back at two, then went into the garden to read in an arbor, sometimes spending the whole day there, sometimes going back to Versailles for his work and councils, and returning for supper at nine. Afterwards he played games and

*Plan of the French
and landscape gardens of the Petit
Trianon, circa 1785, attributed to
Richard Mique. The French Pavilion
and the Petit Trianon are seen at bottom
left, the Hameau at center right.
Château de Versailles, Versailles.*

left at midnight to go to bed. As there were hardly any bedrooms at Trianon, all the company went to Versailles to sleep and returned in the morning to dine and spend the day."9

It was in the gardens of Trianon that Marie Antoinette first learned of the mob's march from Paris, precipitating the Revolution, and at her trial the Hameau would be invoked repeatedly as evidence of her decadence, a symbol of wanton extravagance. Its cost was indefensible and the myopic insularity it represented inexcusable, yet it evokes the spirit of a most remarkable time.

A ROYAL WAGER:
BAGATELLE AND ITS GARDENS

It was obvious from the start that it was eminently
absurd to attempt to achieve such
an undertaking in six or seven weeks.
—Comte de Mercy-Argenteau, in a letter to
Empress Maria Theresa, 19 November 1777

WITH THE COMMISSION OF BAGATELLE, "The
Comte d'Artois made his entry upon that
fatal destiny which was to ruin his family and his
country. His tastes and his caprices were merely those
of the young men of his time, but he displayed them
upon a stage sufficiently high to make them visible to
the mob,"[1] wrote the Comtesse de Boigne. Twenty
years old in 1777, Artois was tall, dashing, handsome,
and vacuous, with an appetite for all the Bourbon
princes' obsessions: building, gambling, horses, hunting, and women. His partner in his adventures was the
Duc de Chartres, and, bitten by the same all-encompassing Anglomania, Artois affected the appearance
and habits of an English rake, and together the
cousins organized the first horse races in France near
the site of the count's great bauble, Bagatelle.

The Comte d'Artois in hunting dress,
with Bagatelle visible beyond.
Gouache by Alexandre Moitte.
Musée de Picardie, Amiens.

The Philosopher's Pavilion at Bagatelle.
Built in the late 1770s by Bélanger;
today destroyed (authors' rendering).

"In the Bois de Boulogne stands a little pleasure
house named Bagatelle, which as the result of various
arrangements is now owned by the Comte d'Artois.
This prince shows a decided taste for the trowel, and
in addition to the four or five buildings he has already
undertaken, he now wishes to enlarge and renovate
this one, or rather rebuild it completely to make it
worthy of him. He has found a very clever way to
defray its costs: he has bet the queen one hundred
thousand *livres* that the château will be completed
during the voyage to Fontainebleau and that he will
host a party there in her honor when she returns.
There are eight hundred workers, and His Highness'
architect is determined to win."[2]

Artois won his wager, largely by employing
François-Joseph Bélanger, an architect of rare talent
and even rarer organizational ability. Within days of
the royal wager, the old, dilapidated Bagatelle, built
during the Regency as a secluded pleasure ground for
the Maréchal d'Estrées, was demolished, plans for the
new pavilion drawn and approved, and construction
begun. Artois exploited his position as Colonel-
General of the Swiss and Grey Guards, and diverted

building materials entering the gates of Paris to the worksite—to great public outcry—where nine hundred laborers, not the reported eight hundred, worked by torchlight through the autumn nights. After sixty-four days, on 25 November 1777, the new Bagatelle was completed, though the queen would not inaugurate it until the following spring and her payment would do almost nothing to defray its three-million-*livre* cost.

Bagatelle's name and its motto, *Parva Sed Apta*, Small but Fitting, could not have been more appropriate, though the size of the count's "casino" was immediately remarked upon; its critics protested that a great deal of money had purchased very little (due to the premium paid for haste and the high level of artistry with which the interiors were subsequently finished), and questioned why a prince should want to build such a small château when actresses now lived in palaces. The complaints bluntly ignored the count's intentions, though they do underscore how far the aristocracy had recoiled from the grandiose splendors of the Age of

𝓟lan of the ground floor of Bagatelle. Engraving by Krafft. B.N.F., Paris.

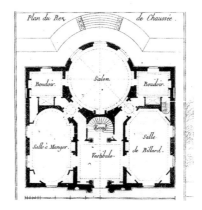

Louis XIV, and in this sense Bagatelle is the perfect illustration of that craving for sophisticated intimacy that today falls under Talleyrand's worn rubric of *la douceur de vivre*.

The Interiors

Bélanger's decorative program carried out inventive variations on the theme of sensuality; the finest artists and tradesmen created an interior of extraordinary quality and luxury, though delicate furnishings suffered from Bagatelle's damp location. Hubert Robert supplied a set of six landscapes for a small mirrored boudoir[3]—a virtual catalogue of the eighteenth century's repertoire of amorous allegory—and ornamental painters and sculptors created numerous variations upon the Amorous Turk, Venus, Cupid, and Mars, all melded into a decor of delicate, sumptuous surfaces. Most notable was the bedroom, conceived as a military tent, with a mantlepiece supported by upturned cannon and bedposts in the shape of fasces—a witty play

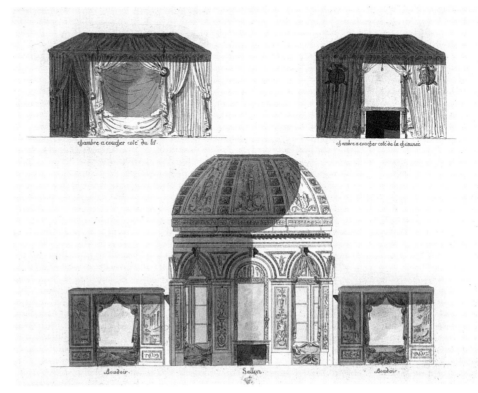

*A*bove left and right:
The entry and garden facades of Bagatelle. Built 1777
by François-Joseph Bélanger and today greatly altered
(authors' renderings).

chambre a coucher coté du lit.

chambre a coucher coté de la cheminée

Boudoir.

Sallon.

Boudoir.

*S*ection through the bedroom
and the salon at Bagatelle, 1777. Watercolors
by François-Joseph Bélanger. B.N.F., Paris.

upon the count's honorary offices and a blunt metaphor for the bedchamber as battleground. Bélanger took great pride in Bagatelle's decor, which presaged a renewed interest in antique Roman and Pompeiian details, then known as Roman grotesques, though credit for the work must be shared with the sculptor Nicolas-François-Daniel Lhuiller, who had traveled to Italy and promoted the style that Bélanger knew only at one remove, having seen the Neo-Palladian work of the Adam brothers and their circle in the course of an English tour he is believed to have undertaken in 1766.[4]

Bagatelle in its original state was infused with this antique spirit, newly fashionable at the time of Bélanger's breathless design. The pavilion's simple cubic mass was accentuated by its approach through a portal at the center of the long-destroyed Commons, whose curved wings figurally embraced Bagatelle across a sunken court. Running before the pavilion,

the courtyard's retaining wall became a rustic plinth inset with arched grotto-basins, and Bagatelle's lightly rusticated, tawny ochre walls and carefully positioned ornaments effectively evoked the novelty of Roman antiquity on the floodplain of the Seine.

The Gardens

As originally conceived by Bélanger, Bagatelle's gardens were rigidly formal and tightly restricted to the area immediately surrounding the compound; this plan was elaborated into a more complex, though still rigorously formal, garden featuring hundreds of rare and exotic trees. During the initial rush of construction, laborers worked through the nights to complete the massive groundwork; the pace would continue, only slightly abated, into the following spring, when the gardens were hastily readied for the inaugural festivities. Terracing and planting continued into fall 1778, when Thomas Blaikie, a Scotsman hired as an "English gardener" for the count's estate of Maisons, was approached by Bélanger to design a picturesque, English-style garden; Bagatelle's grounds were to grow enormously in the next year, when Louis XVI ceded his brother an adjoining plot of land.

The stage was now set for an amusing clash of cultures between Bélanger, the polished courtier-architect, and Blaikie, the contrary, intuitive Scottish gardener, and their diametrically opposed views as to what constituted an English-style garden. Bélanger, the foremost practitioner of the French school of picturesque gardens, designed a dense, folly-cluttered pleasure ground with an intricate web of watercourses and footpaths; Blaikie presented a miniature English park with large pastures bordered by sinuous paths and a few poetic landmarks and lacking—thrifty soul that he was—any horribly expensive watercourses. Bélanger's plan was adopted, but much of the work was carried out under Blaikie's supervision, affording him the opportunity to modify and simplify his rival's plans.

Blaikie strove to integrate the compound with its landscape, in one instance urging Artois to remove a wall dividing the courtyard from the gardens, but the

The plan of the estate of Bagatelle and four chinoiserie follies in its gardens. Clockwise from upper left: the Chinese Bridge, the Grand Wooden Bridge, the Philosopher's Pavilion, and the Chinese Tent. Engraving by Krafft. B.N.F., Paris.

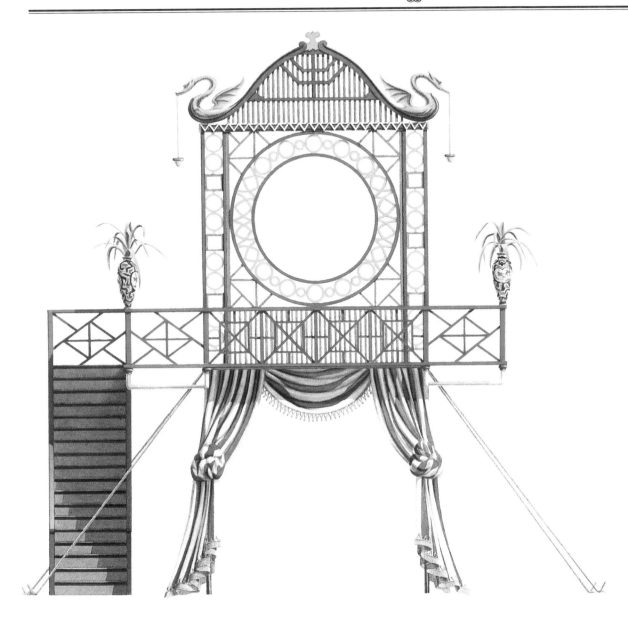

count's retinue, fearing burglaries, would agree only to an iron fence. Blaikie's attempts to impart an English conception of a house in harmony with its gardens proved an exasperating experience, as his diary attests: "Although [French] architects have great taste in their buildings, they are extremely defective in arranging their gardens, all due to the vanity of Le Nôtre, of which every Frenchman brags; certainly his plans were noble, though the reverse of Nature, always with those stiff terraces and extravagant stairs, as if they imagined nothing would be noble without stairs, statues, terraces, and so on."[5]

Bagatelle's garden was indeed a place of pleasure, not nobility, and amusement demanded variety in all

The Chinese Tent at Bagatelle. Built in the late 1770s by François-Joseph Bélanger. Destroyed. The fretwork pavilion sat upon stilts and the curtains below could be drawn to create an outdoor room (authors' rendering).

things: in the plantings, which featured rarities from Asia and America; in the layout, a circuit that led around lakes and across plains, through groves and past waterfalls, over Chinese bridges and under arching rockworks; and most importantly in the numerous follies. These buildings, largely constructed of wood, were conceived on the same intimate scale as Bagatelle itself and were skillfully woven into landscape scenes: "all the objects that one encounters awaken the gentlest sensations in the soul, which their variety redoubles," noted one contemporary guidebook.[6] Among the garden's follies were two thatched hermitages known as Druids' Cabins, a Chinese and a Palladian Bridge, an island with an irreverent Tomb of the King of Hearts, an Egyptian Obelisk, "engraved with mysterious hieroglyphics," a black marble Tomb—"What illustrious cinders does it hold?"—and the "agreeable surprise" of the Philosopher's Pavilion, a small octagonal kiosk perched atop a rockwork.

The pavilion was a composite of Gothic, rustic, and chinoiserie elements that somehow rose above its inherent absurdity to a confectionary brilliance. Its interior was adorned with medallions of Greek philosophers, and "its windows were composed of multicolored glass, through which one views Nature with diverse tints, the emblems of human passions, which make men see different colors in the same object."[7] The grotto beneath offered seats from which to contemplate a ceiling composed as a "tapestry of seemingly all the most agreeable minerals: without a doubt the natural history cabinet of a philosopher, just as the pavilion above is his observatory." The Chinese Tent was its complement, an open fretwork pavilion built on a rectangular platform raised upon stilts, where guests could enjoy an elevated view as well as refreshments. Its theatricality and insubstantiality are emblematic of the garden structures of the period, which were often no more than passing fancies made visible: thrown together in a day, they were intended to survive no longer than the smiles they imparted.

Royal Amusements

A garden party in May 1782 was given in the queen's honor, which Blaikie found to be "conducted with great order and decorum with mirth."[8] Actors had been placed in booths made of greenery, the gardener noted, and musicians played on scaffolds built in the groves "as the company walked round to see the gardens . . . which, with the echo of the trees, made enchanting effects." A pyramid had been erected near the wall that separated the garden from a newly acquired plot; beside it stood "an actor who played the part of a magician, who asked their Majesties how they liked the gardens and what a beautiful view there was toward the plain if only that wall did not obstruct it, but that their Majesties need only give the word and he with his enchanting wand would make the wall disappear. The queen told him with a laugh, 'Very well, I should wish to see it disappear,' and at that instant the signal was given and above two hundred yards [of wall] opposite fell flat to the ground, which surprised them all." The day's festivities ended "with a ball in the pavilion at which everyone danced but the king, who amused himself playing billiards for half a crown a game; at that rate he could never ruin his fortune."

The count hosted other celebrations in the gardens at Bagatelle, but soon the Baronne d'Oberkirch noted: "Parisians and foreigners profited more by it than its illustrious proprietor, who rarely walked there."[9] Blaikie once escorted Marie Antoinette through the gardens, and she inquired innocently if he enjoyed working for Artois; the flinty Scot replied bluntly: "I never saw a lazier man of less taste; he [has] not once come to see the gardens since he [has] lodged there."[10] The queen was thoroughly amused and chided Artois for neglecting both garden and gardener.

Bagatelle survived the Revolution relatively unscathed and under the Empire enjoyed a vogue as a society restaurant. Upon his return from emigration in 1814, Artois reclaimed the property, but untoward events during his reign as Charles X forced his exile in 1830. Lord Hertford purchased Bagatelle in 1835 and

installed his renowned collection; his estate was inherited in 1870 by his natural son, Sir Richard Wallace, who, in an enormous lapse of judgment, destroyed the Commons and raised the pavilion's roof to gain space for his treasures, which today form

A view of the Chinese Bridge; Bagatelle appears through the trees at right. Engraved by Élise Saugrain after Louis Gabriel Moreau l'Aîné. Musée des arts décoratifs, Paris.

The Wallace Collection in London. Bagatelle is now owned by the city of Paris; the pavilion has been restored recently and its grounds, denuded of follies and greatly altered since the eighteenth century, feature a celebrated rose garden.

THE FOLLY OF SAINT-JAMES

Near Neuilly is a garden that would be more beautiful if
there were less of it, and if it actually were a garden.
If M. de Saint-James had spent four
hundred thousand francs less, he would have
been much more successful.
—The Prince de Ligne, *Coup d'œil sur Belœil*

L OUIS XVI, A STORY THAT MAY well be true
relates, was hunting one day in the forest of
Fontainebleau when he came upon a team of forty
draft horses straining to move an enormous boulder
toward Paris. Flabbergasted by the Sisyphean scene,
the king was told that the rock was destined for the
property of the Baron Saint-James and would be
incorporated into the Grand Grotto being built in his
gardens, and forever after the king referred to the
baron as "the Man with the Rock."[1] The story,
consisting in equal part of vainglory and excess, illuminates the singularity of the Baron Saint-James' folly garden at Neuilly; a place of superlatives and
extremes where the rage for the picturesque most
nearly approached parody and madness.

The Baron Saint-James
in an anonymous portrait. B.N.F., Paris.

The Lake Pagoda at the Folly
Saint-James. Built circa *1784*
by François-Joseph Bélanger. As its name
implies, the now-destroyed pagoda stood
in a lake and was reached by a chinoiserie
skiff (authors' rendering).

Claude Baudard de Sainte-Gemmes-sur-Loire
was the son of a wealthy tax farmer, who by various
maneuverings became General Treasurer of the
American Colonies and shared the post of Treasurer
of the Navy with Charles-Robert Boutin, who built
the wildly successful Tivoli amusement park near
Paris. Saint-James, as he anglicized his name, was
commonly perceived as a *nouveau riche* boor;
Madame Vigée-Lebrun (who nevertheless attended)
judged the gatherings in his townhouse on the place
Vendôme more boisterous than elegant. The baron
fueled his social ambitions with an enormous, dubious fortune. The portraitist described Saint-James as
"stout and fat, of medium height, with a very red face
and a fresh complexion, which one can still have at
fifty if happy and healthy."[2] His financial machinations left the baron unperturbed, and he seems to
have found true joy in his schemes and the wealth and
influence they brought.

In 1772, Saint-James had purchased land near
Bagatelle, and in the years that followed he observed
Bélanger rebuild the estate for the Comte d'Artois
and the celebrity that resulted from the undertaking.

Grande Roche d'Après Vernet

Autres, IDÉES *d'Après Nature*

The financier then conceived a scheme to eclipse Bagatelle and its owner with his own pleasure ground, and in 1781, a year after work upon several outbuildings had begun,[3] he offered François-Joseph Bélanger free rein to "Build whatever you like, provided that it is expensive."[4] Artois was not amused by this brazen upstart and is said to have remarked to his brother, "Sire, I wish you would give me the position of General Treasurer of the Navy, for without it I cannot compete in magnificence with my neighbor," and quietly ordered Bélanger, who remained in his employ, to "ruin Saint-James,"[5] a mission which the architect accepted with relish.

House and Gardens

The great surprise when visiting the estate of Saint-James is, as at Bagatelle, the modesty of the residence. The stuccoed house, with an Ionic entrance portico and a vaguely Venetian garden loggia, offers restrained, well-proportioned rooms and an Italianate, trompe-l'œil stair hall, but the facades suffer from

Right:
Section and elevation of the Chinese Skiff which brought visitors to the Lake Pagoda (top), elevation of the Grotto and the Chinese Pavilion (middle), plan of the Grotto and the Icehouse (bottom). Engraving by Krafft. B.N.F., Paris.

Bélanger's tendency toward pastiche and the building sits awkwardly in a cramped and ungainly courtyard. The house, however, was little more than an excuse for its garden, and it was this extensive folly park, bisected by the road to Bagatelle and extending to the Seine, that would absorb much of Saint-James' fortune and tax the limits of Bélanger's creative energies.

The baron's grotto alone absorbed 1.6 million *livres* and was dubbed the Eighth Wonder of the World; the Doric portico set into an artificial mountainside, replete with bathing salon and gallery, inspires far less awe today, and the greater part of its wonder in fact may have resided in its phenomenal cost. Blaikie scorned the folly as simply "ridiculous, as there is neither an elevation nor mountain to form this huge pile of rocks,"[6] a remark that echoes Horace Walpole's damning description of Boutin's Tivoli: "There are three or four very high hills, almost as high as, and exactly the shape of, a tansy pudding."[7] The garden was variously described as English, picturesque, and Anglo-Chinese,[8] but the confused nomenclature aside, Saint-James' seventeen cluttered acres can be seen as the summation of the French folly garden in all its absurd splendor.

Jean-Charles Krafft's description of the park is particularly revealing:

"This grand garden is divided into meadows, groves, orchards, vineyards, vegetable gardens, beds for exotic plants, arbors, flowerbeds, bosquets, lawns, fields, etc. . . . their variety provides alternating views of mountains and valleys, hills and plains. The entire park is also crisscrossed in various directions by roads and winding paths, which sometimes cross or pass over one another, and sometimes continue or surround each other, so that the walks are so myriad that one easily loses oneself and is unable to find one's way out of the compound."[9]

The author was equally unimpressed by the crude effects of the watercourses:

"First there is a large lake fed by a cascade, and then a winding creek, here widening and there narrowing. . . . These streams then vanish below ground and appear again atop a rock, from which they crash down in violent cascades and are collected in a pond. Finally their enchantment wanes and they instead serve the far-different needs of the household, departing without their former noise and arrogance to return to their source."

The Follies

The garden was furnished with amusement foremost in mind, and neither the eye nor the body were allowed a respite. Strolling south from the greenhouse complex, a visitor would have encountered, within a few minutes' time, the Chinese Vases, the Ashlar Bridge, and the Tightrope Walk, then a view of the lake and its Pagoda as one approached the Bridge of Love, which led to the Isle of Love with its statuary and Antique Column. Bélanger exhausted the picturesque possibilities of bridges, producing between ten and twelve by one tally, and by another, fourteen: "bridges of stone or rock, bridges of tiles

Elévation du Bac chinois.

Coupe du Bac chinois.

Elévation de la Grotte et du Pavillon chinois N.º 19.

Plan général du Souterrain, de la Grotte, et de la Glacière et Salle X.

Krafft.

Gravé par Bouley.

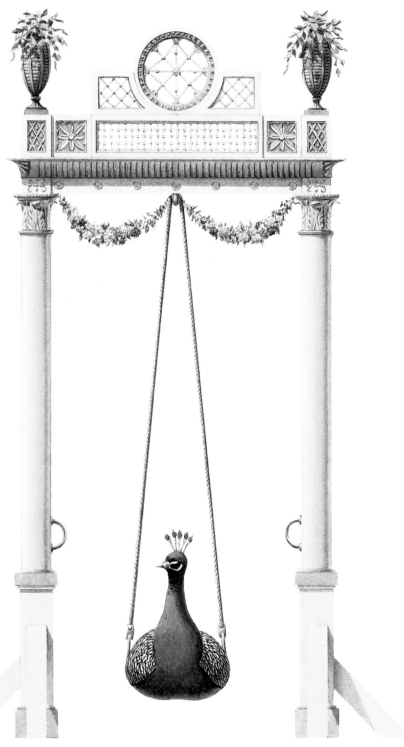

*T he Peacock Swing.
Built circa 1784 by François-Joseph
Bélanger; destroyed. A true folly,
built of wood, lattice, and fantasy
(authors' rendering).*

and wood, swing bridges, Chinese bridges, English bridges, Turkish bridges";[10] the architect likewise depleted the repertoire of folly forms in a desperate search for novelty.

Among the garden's most picturesque follies was the foursquare latticework Pagoda which stood upon pylons in the lake and was reached by a small chinoiserie skiff. It has long since disappeared, as have all the other follies in the gardens, save the Grand Grotto. The Pagoda's watercolor elevation presents a color scheme recorded in a contemporary plan;[11] however, this may be one colorist's fanciful interpretation, though it is consistent with chinoiserie color schemes of the period. Likewise, the Peacock Swing, the hollow bird in which ladies and gentlemen would sit and propel themselves with the aid of handgrips, is also presented in a conjectural color scheme, as is the Gothic Monument. This latter folly, triangular in plan, is a playful admixture of Moorish, Gothic, and Renaissance elements, and served as a shaded bench and yet another eye-catcher.

These three structures typify the visual wealth and stylistic confusion that prevailed in the last gardens built during the *ancien régime.* Eclectically furnished, the garden at Saint-James contained follies created as elements of a rich, colorful, and fantastic ensemble, and their intended effects owed more to the mannered theatricality of the *Comédie italienne*—of Pierrot, Arlequin, and Scaramouche—than to the

*The Gothic Monument.
Built* circa *1784 by François-Joseph
Bélanger; destroyed.
An extraordinary amalgam of the
most diverse architectural elements
(authors' rendering).*

French architectural tradition. The latter, its building methods and the values it represented, had been abandoned in favor of an architecture of illusion, and the pursuit of individual whim gave rise to ephemeral stick-and-lath structures that mirrored a frivolous society heedless of its own fragility.

The Baron Saint-James enjoyed his pleasure ground and the notoriety it brought him—for it did indeed eclipse Bagatelle as a park of ingenious novelty—for only the shortest time: he was declared a bankrupt in 1787 after suffering huge reversals in his speculations and having been drawn unwittingly into the infamous diamond necklace scandal.[12] A shattered man, bereft of animating wealth, he retired of his own volition to the Bastille, where he died some weeks later. When this news reached the king, he exclaimed: "Ah! That was the Man with the Rocks!"[13]

The estate of Saint-James was sold at auction to the Duc de Choiseul-Praslin, a good friend of the Comte d'Artois, for a fraction of its true value;[14] however, the Revolution soon negated any of the count's satisfaction, and by 1812 Krafft would uncharacteristically soliloquize: "Oh vanity of vanities! All this is nothing but vanity; all these monuments to luxury and wealth have been ravaged by time and have disappeared like their owner. . . . A Bélanger is rare, a Saint-James rarer still!"[15] Today the Folly of Saint-James, its park greatly reduced and its follies destroyed, houses a school.

*T*he Music Pavilion
at Montreuil. Built 1783–1784
by Jean-François-Thérèse Chalgrin.
The pavilion has been altered
by the addition of side wings,
a balustrade, and an enlarged attic story
(authors' rendering).

FOR WIFE AND MISTRESS: THE PAVILIONS OF THE COMTE DE PROVENCE AT MONTREUIL AND BALBI

On poor terms with the queen, as well as with her sister the Comtesse d'Artois, she lived alone, spending nearly all her time in her delicious garden at Montreuil.
—The Comte d'Hezecques, recalling Madame

Ground-floor plan of the Music Pavilion. Engraving by Krafft. B.N.F., Paris.

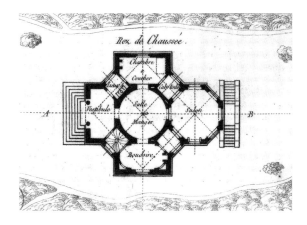

DIPLOMATIC DISPATCHES and state portraits had provided ample warning, but when Marie-Joséphine-Louise de Savoie stepped from her carriage, titters ran through the assembled court. The future Comtesse de Provence was, at seventeen years of age, as small as a child, the result of centuries of inbreeding. "Not tall, but beautiful eyes," wrote the king,[1] employing the last resort of royal praise. Others were less kind. Comte de Mercy-Argenteau, ever eager to cast Marie Antoinette in the best light, wrote to Vienna: "Her bearing is hardly agreeable; she rarely speaks, and if so then without grace; and she offers nothing that is necessary to please this nation."[2] Marie Antoinette mocked her moustache, and Madame Du Barry, whose own toilette could last until the early afternoon, desperately tried to persuade

the stubborn girl to wash or use perfume and mounted a fruitless campaign to convince her to pluck her single, dense eyebrow.[3]

Monsieur, the Comte de Provence, tactfully found her "better than expected"[4] but abandoned his wife after an unsuccessful wedding night. Hopelessly vain, yet obese and balding, he compensated for his physical deficits with an acid wit and a taste for intrigue. Monsieur was far more intellectually accomplished than his brothers, Louis XVI and the Comte d'Artois, yet a subversive element in his character transformed

him into a jealous prince who used his considerable capacities to undermine his elder brother's authority.

Neglected and apathetic, Madame became a brooding recluse, seldom missed and rarely invited to leave her quarters. The arrival of her younger sister, who would marry the Comte d'Artois, only deepened her isolation.[5] "Madame and the Comtesse d'Artois," wrote Madame de Chastenay, "are unlikeable and not very beautiful. Treated coldly by the queen and nearly abandoned by their husbands, they did not console each other with their friendship; they would not even share their solitude."[6]

Madame's lethargy was overturned by Anne de Caumont-La Force, who was everything she was not: "of a never-ending happiness and loved by everyone."[7] In a breach of etiquette that appalled the court, Madame offered her protégé the title of Lady of the Wardrobe without the knowledge or consent of its current holder. Despite the ensuing scandal, the Comtesse de Balbi assumed her new position, but viewed it merely as a means to another end and soon established herself as Monsieur's acknowledged mistress.

Montreuil

In March 1781, hoping to escape an indifferent court, Madame purchased a modest country seat at

The Comtesse and Comte de Provence in portraits drawn by Madame Élisabeth Vigée-Lebrun in 1777. The Royal Collection, London.

Montreuil, on the outskirts of Versailles, and began renovations.[8] The property was considerably enlarged by a series of land purchases, for Madame was determined to rival the queen's gardens at Trianon. Jean-François-Thérèse Chalgrin, Monsieur's First Architect, who had studied with Boullée and apprenticed with Servandoni,[9] both encouraged and supervised the ambitious program; within a few years a cadre of gardeners and workmen, sporting gold-buttoned livery, had planted more than ten thousand trees on a plot of forty acres, including mature specimens that arrived by barge and horse-drawn sledge from across Europe.

The backbone of any English-style garden in France was a poetically meandering watercourse, and at Montreuil this river flowed from a rockwork to wander through the grounds,[10] interrupted by several low waterfalls and two small islands featuring follies—a thatched hermitage stood on the first and a rustic wooden rotunda on the second. The river emptied into a lake containing a third island, the destination for Madame's boating parties—two whimsical barges were ordered—where she spent entire days fishing, to the despair of her ladies-in-waiting.

A large lawn separated the river from the Hameau, a dozen small farm buildings modeled on Marie Antoinette's celebrated village. The compound was dominated by an artificial mountain concealing an ice cellar, and upon its summit, some twenty feet high, stood a thatched belvedere and a rustic log tower. The grounds also featured an unusual octagonal Chinese Pavilion built of freestone, whose ground floor served as a hothouse, surmounted by a salon.

Chalgrin's Music Pavilion was the finest building erected on Madame's estate, though it has been altered substantially over time, having acquired side wings that disfigure its proportions and a balustrade that obscures an enlarged attic story. Begun in 1783 and completed the following year, the pavilion is situated on a long rectangular lot appended to the gardens and fronts upon the avenue de Paris. Unlike the deliberate ornamentality of the garden's other follies or the vernacular architecture of the manor house, the Music Pavilion displays a rigorous, adamant classicism, reinforced by sharp geometries, severe detailing, and crisp rustication. Its plan, a central circular salon inscribed within an elaboration on the Latin cross, is a sophisticated visual counterpoint to Gabriel's French Pavilion at Trianon.

Raised upon a stone base, the Music Pavilion is entered by a flight of steps that leads to an open loggia sheltered behind a Palladian arch. A vestibule opens into a skylit central salon, among the most beautiful trompe-l'œil rooms in France: a painted balustrade and eight Ionic columns evoke the interior of a classical rotunda set amid lush gardens—an illusion heightened by abundant natural light and a marble floor—creating the most successful winter garden of the period. Though Madame's village could not compare with the queen's Hameau, her Music Pavilion rivaled Mique's Belvedere at Trianon in beauty and surpassed it in comfort, and even may have helped, during her twilight guitar serenades, to make her somehow beautiful.

The entrance facade of the Music Pavilion at Montreuil in a watercolor attributed to Jean-François-Thérèse Chalgrin, its architect. Musée Lambinet, Versailles.

THE BALBI GARDENS

Her house was adorned with a multitude
of little marvels, models of the sort
of baubles so fashionable under the reign
of the late king Louis XVI.
—The Baronne d'Oberkirch,
in her *Mémoires.*[11]

WHILE MADAME WAS ARRANGING her estate at
Montreuil, Monsieur ordered Chalgrin to plan a second English-style garden for the Comtesse de Balbi
on a plot of land adjoining the kitchen gardens of

*T*he Belvedere in
the Balbi Gardens. Built circa *1787*
by Jean-François-Thérèse Chalgrin.
The Belvedere is perched atop
an enormous grotto and can be reached
by a tiny bridge (authors' rendering).

Versailles. The couple designed a one-story pavilion
that rambled along the southern edge of the property;
its plan lacks any discernable hierarchy, but a few elegantly planned rooms are embedded in its sprawl—
undoubtedly the work of Chalgrin, providing designs
beyond the abilities of Monsieur and his mistress.[12]
Monsieur visited the countess in the house morning
and evening and readily confessed to finding her
company superior to all other pleasures in the
world.[13] The couple hosted frequent suppers in the
pavilion; an invitation to one of these evenings was
considered a great honor, though Monsieur, with his
haughty manner and cruel wit, and the countess, with

The Comtesse de Balbi in a miniature by Lefrançois dated 1788. Musée des arts décoratifs, Bordeaux.

The plan of the Balbi Gardens, with the Balbi Pavilion at lower right and the couple's residence at lower left. Bibliothèque municipale de Versailles, Versailles.

scape it overlooks. Unlike the English-style gardens of the period—which are essentially a series of evocative landscape scenes—the mannered, pastoral landscape of the Balbi Gardens is dominated by its dramatically overscaled grotto, a sublime gesture that presages the sensibility of the Romantic Age.

In October 1789, only three years after the Balbi Gardens had been completed, the Revolution swept the court from Versailles and Monsieur and Madame followed the king and queen to Paris. They fled quietly, swiftly, and successfully on the night of the royal family's failed flight, with the countess following them into exile soon after. The Revolutionary government declared both women emigrants and their estates were confiscated; Montreuil's derelict gardens were eventually partitioned and developed by builders, while the Balbi Gardens were looted and the property sold to repay debts. The countess' house has been destroyed but her Belvedere survives in the reconstructed gardens, one of the overlooked beauties of Versailles.

her effervescence and devastating remarks, must have been terrifying hosts. The parties often ended at dawn, in no small part because no one was willing to be the first guest to leave the room.

The house, completed in 1786, faced a landscape garden richly planted with exotic trees. An extensive grotto was built into an artificial hill at the garden's eastern end; immeasurably grander than Madame's rockwork and larger than Hubert Robert's grotto at Versailles, it was constructed of boulders dragged from a quarry near Fontainebleau, and its theatrical interior, replete with narrow passages and dimly lit tunnels, contains a cave with a waterfall, today fallen into disuse, that once fed the lake before it. Steep paths and uneven steps lead to a small bridge at the grotto's summit, site of the diminutive Belvedere, which offers views of the park and lake below, the king's kitchen garden, and the château of Versailles.

The pavilion, square in plan and with three semicircular apses, is built of wood painted in trompe-l'œil to represent brick walls and a stone base and quoins, and contains a salon of white faux marble where the countess' entourage gathered for refreshments. In its use of an austere vernacular, the Belvedere's architecture anticipates the coming century, as does the land-

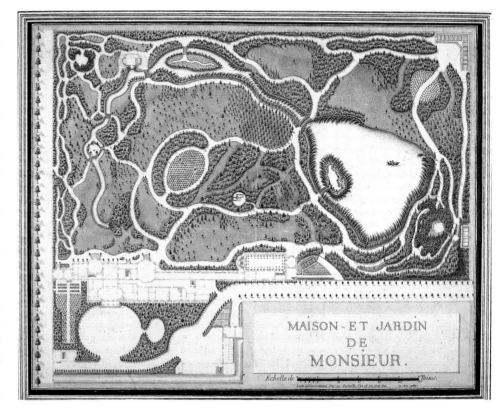

MAISON ET JARDIN DE MONSIEUR.

"NOTHING EXCLUDED EXCEPT NATURE":
PARC MONCEAU

It is not a garden. It is taste without judgment.
—The Prince de Ligne,
Coup d'œil sur Belœil

PARADOXICALLY, A MAN WHO was universally loathed would create the beloved Parc Monceau. The Folie de Chartres began as a pleasure pavilion built in 1769, the year of the Duc de Chartres' marriage;[1] erected just outside Paris near the village of Monceau, it became an infamous setting for the duke's gambling parties, occult seances, and secret Masonic rites. The corrosive combination of enormous wealth and lifelong leisure quickly defeated him; he once wagered the Comte de Genlis, whose wife was for a time his mistress, that he could perforate a piece of paper with a half-million pinpricks before the count could ride to Fontainebleau and return; the duke lost the gamble, but history does not record how many holes he made.[2]

The parterres surrounding his folly formed the nucleus of a grand scheme conceived in 1773, when the duke became intrigued by the idea of building an Anglo-Chinese garden and began purchasing lots that would enlarge the park to nearly fifty acres.

The royal family's English-style hunts in the Bois de Boulogne: The Duc d'Orléans and his son the Duc de Chartres at a hunting party in 1788 *by Carl Vernet. Musée Condé, Chantilly.*

The Dutch Windmill in the Parc Monceau. Built circa *1776 by Carmontelle. The windmill, long destroyed, sat atop a rockwork grotto and housed a pumping mechanism (authors' rendering).*

A Land of Illusions

The duke instinctively turned to Louis Carrogis, known as Carmontelle, to design the garden. Carmontelle had proven his abilities by staging the duke's theatricals and entertainments and also served as his reader and social secretary, but is known today as an artist and portraitist and the author of several comedies. The duke's choice was a prescient one, for Carmontelle not only understood his patron's indiscriminate hunger for novelty but also possessed the skills necessary to turn the duke's desires into reality.

Carmontelle was uninterested in creating a garden that emulated nature and dismissed the Rousseau-inspired movement as a sentimental fad promulgated by the Marquis de Girardin and the garden designer and theoretician Jean-Marie Morel. Instead, he promoted ideas formed during his theatrical and artistic labors, as he explained in the introduction to an album of engraved plates of Monceau: "It was hardly an English garden that one was hoping to create at Monceau, but exactly what it was being criticized for, the uniting in one garden of all times and places. It is a simple fantasy, the desire to have an extraordinary garden, a pure amusement. . . . If one can transform a picturesque garden into a land of illusions, why not do so, since only illusions amuse . . . we should bring the changing scenes of opera into our gardens, letting us see, in reality, what the most accomplished painters offer on canvas—all periods and places."[3]

Of all the gardens of the period, the Folie de Chartres most resembled a modern amusement park, to such an extent that its clear masonic undercurrents were overwhelmed by an unabashed pursuit of pleasure.

The Dutch Windmill, whose sails pivoted to catch the wind. Detail of an engraving by Michault after Carmontelle. B.N.F., Paris.

Several dozen attractions were scattered across a landscape that featured the obligatory meandering stream; appropriately costumed servants stood in attendance at each folly, and incredibly, if Carmontelle's own description is to be believed, no more than two hours were required to view the gardens.

The Dutch Windmill, long since destroyed, was a scenic pastiche typical of Monceau's amusing opera sets and sat atop a rockwork grotto at a rise in the grounds; its mechanism drove the pump for the cascade beneath and its balcony afforded views of the gardens. The folly perfectly illustrates how the era's craving for the picturesque eventually encompassed the mundane artifacts of rural life—for nothing could have been more common to the eighteenth-century eye than a windmill—and transformed them into æsthetically charged objects.

Though his remarks were published in 1808, Comte Alexandre de Laborde echoed contemporary opinion in detecting nothing but hypocrisy in such pretense: "While praising the pure country air, one rose at two o'clock in the afternoon after gambling until four o'clock in the morning, and while professing the deepest attachment to rural life, women wore makeup and beauty marks, and corsets under their dresses."[4] The Prince de Ligne was equally harsh in his assessment of Carmontelle's work: "The greatest misfortune for garden designers is not to have an overall plan before beginning their work. . . . Arrangements are made that, more than anything else, derange. Buildings take precedence over plantings, and what plantings exist are seen at a disadvantage. An open plain is no place to establish viewpoints, especially when the visitor is exposed on all sides. The owner thinks he has a garden but has everything but that. This happened to the Duc de Chartres."[5] The prince could muster only faint praise for Carmontelle's follies: "These are mere scenes, but of such liveliness and truth that one only wishes the ensemble had been composed with a surer hand than his," and recommended revisions be made to Monceau, declaring,

"Millions have been spent on it, yet it has neither enough water nor enough walks."

In 1781, barely two years after Monceau's completion, the duke called upon Thomas Blaikie to simplify the gardens. The begrudging Scot found little to admire: "the whole was a small confusion of many things joined together without any great natural plan, the walks winding and turning without reason, which is the fault of most of these gardens done without taste; I changed most of the gardens and destroyed most of the walks, which I thought unnecessary and unnatural."[6] Such were the diametrically opposed conceptions of French and English landscape gardens that where Ligne found far too few paths at Monceau, Blaikie found far too much of everything.

A "simple fantasy" conceived as a stage set for a prince's amusement. Carmontelle presenting the Duc de Chartres with the keys to Parc Monceau by Carmontelle. Musée Carnavalet, Paris.

After his father's death in 1785, the Duc de Chartres inherited the title of Duc d'Orléans, becoming head of the cadet branch of the Bourbon family, though to posterity he remains the treacherous Philippe-Égalité, who cast the deciding vote that condemned his cousin, Louis XVI, and who was guillotined in turn ten months later.

Monceau was confiscated during these upheavals, then returned to the Orléans family under the Restoration, and reverted to the state in 1852. A large portion of the park was sold during the Second Empire; the remainder was redesigned by Adolphe Alphand in what was then considered the English style. The Pyramid, the Colonnade, and some minor follies are all that remain of Carmontelle's "land of illusion."

THE DÉSERT DE RETZ

I went with His Majesty to the Désert,
which is charming. M. de Monville showed us what
money and good taste can achieve when allied with the
wildest of Nature.
—Baron Gustaf Mauritz Armfelt, gentleman to
Gustav III of Sweden, in his *Journal*

A MAGNIFICENT LOVER, A RICH young widower, and very handsome, noble, and romantic—but not a member of the court,"[1] was Madame de Genlis' admiring description of François Racine de Monville, creator of the Désert de Monville, today known as the Désert de Retz. An excellent amateur musician and harpist, a gifted sportsman who "shot an arrow better than a savage,"[2] an early lover of Madame Du Barry, and a companion of the Duc de Chartres, de Monville was blessed with all the advantages of wealth, nature, and position and made his way effortlessly through society and life—a man who inspired both admiration and jealousy. To Thomas Blaikie, de Monville was "a would-be connoisseur in everything," and he scoffed that the Désert was "a labyrinth of

Above: section through the Ruined Column. The Royal Library, Stockholm.

The Ruined Column at the Désert de Retz. Built in the late 1770s by François Racine de Monville as the center of an extraordinary folly-park (authors' rendering).

narrow, crooked walks" and its Ruined Column a perplexing homage to the tower of Babel; however, he acknowledged that its builder was "tolerably admired"[3] by society—a brash understatement, given that Queen Marie Antoinette, the American ambassadors Franklin and Jefferson, and King Gustav III of Sweden would each make pilgrimages to meet de Monville and view his extraordinary folly park.

The Désert was begun in 1774 and, more than any other park of its time, was a creation of profound imaginative power; its physical and symbolic center was the enormously overscaled Ruined Column, set into a gently rolling hillside, suggesting the remnant of an incomprehensibly vast ancient monument. Its interior contained three floors of apartments arranged about a central spiral stair; rooms on the fourth floor were lit through a clerestory hidden behind the column's broken parapet and by jagged, glazed cracks in the facade. In contrast to the illusion of its crumbling exterior, the column's interior was richly decorated with pale grey boiseries and *toile de Jouy* hand-printed with Indian patterns; mirrors were placed throughout the rooms to capture and multiply both light and views, and, in concert with the idiosyncratic plans, must have generated curiosity and confusion in equal measure. The column's floorplans are masterpieces of refined geometries and use *poché*—the residual mass between geometrically shaped rooms—to great effect, sculpting from it wardrobes, passageways, and cabinets. Thomas Jefferson exclaimed: "How grand the idea excited by the remains of such a column!" and its plan would inform his own design for the library-rotunda of the University of Virginia.[4]

The Follies

The Ruined Column was de Monville's second residence at the Désert, built in the early 1780s; his original home and favored retreat was the Chinese House, a two-story, teak pavilion built in 1777–1778 beside a small lake. The building's exterior featured faux-bamboo columns and intricately carved latticework panels and was animated by life-sized chinoiserie mannequins standing in niches and leaning over the upper balustrade; the pagoda was lauded by the Prince de Ligne as an excellent example of an authentic Chinese structure, but Alexandre de Laborde, appraising it some two decades later, judged it a tasteless patchwork.

Surrounding the Ruined Column, and disposed much like the spokes of a wheel, were the garden's secondary follies—seventeen in all, their styles an admixture of historical periods and widely divergent cultures. Masonic symbols predominated, and included the

The Pyramid at Retz. Built in the late 1770s by François Racine de Monville, the Pyramid shelters an icehouse (authors' rendering).

A contemporary view of the Désert de Monville, whose name meant "de Monville's Wilderness." Watercolor by Carmontelle. Nationalmuseum, Stockholm.

Ruined Column itself, a hermitage, a grotto-entry similar to the entrance to the Pyramid of Mauperthuis, a Tomb, and a Pyramid built atop an icehouse, as well as the authentic ruins of a small Gothic church which de Monville had incorporated into the park. Much as the Duc de Richelieu had achieved with his combined rotunda and icehouse at Gennevilliers, de Monville found in necessity the opportunity to embellish his estate, and the Pyramid's carefully studied proportions and evident expense reveal that he took great pleasure in conceiving and constructing a monument where a functional structure would have sufficed.

The garden also featured a Temple to the God Pan—today in partial ruin—and a Tartar Tent on a small island in a wooded glade which has recently

been reconstructed. The tent, more an eye-catcher than a usable folly, is sheathed with metal sheets painted in trompe-l'œil to represent striped canvas; its entrance is framed with illusionistic swags and a central skylight illuminates a rather uninviting interior. After his visit in 1784, Gustav III requested documentation of the Désert,[5] and wrote to de Monville upon receiving it: "I believe that anyone with taste cannot but applaud the whole and the details of your plan";[6] the drawings of the Tartar Tent would directly inspire the Chinese Tent in his gardens at Haga.

The Revolution ended de Monville's charmed existence; he sold the estate to an Englishman in 1792, was briefly imprisoned for his allegiance to Philippe-Égalité,[7] and died in 1797. The estate remained in the

The Tartar Tent at Retz.
Built in the late 1770s by François Racine
de Monville. Destroyed and rebuilt,
and set upon a small island in a
wooded glade (authors' rendering).

possession of a single family for most of the nineteenth century, and for much of our own it has been left to neglect and abandonment. Colette would write poetically of its decay: "I shudder to think of it altered, deprived of its excrescences, affronted by the glamour of its own renewal,"[8] and for her lifetime and beyond her wish was granted. In 1950, she wrote of the Chinese House "subsiding into the center of the lake like moist sugar . . . yielding to the pressure of the dog-rose and elder." The Chinese House was indeed lost, but the current restoration program at the Désert de Retz is a testament to the impassioned dedication of the architect Olivier Choppin de Janvry, who with Jean-Marc Heftler has worked tirelessly for decades to preserve the estate.

MODERN PHILOSOPHY:
THE GARDENS OF ERMENONVILLE

Inscriptions at almost every step—
a veritable tyranny over the mind.
—Madame Vigée-Lebrun, describing the park
of Ermenonville

The Temple of Modern
Philosophy at Ermenonville.
Built circa *1775 by the Marquis*
de Girardin and modeled upon
the Temple of Vesta at Tivoli
(authors' rendering).

LOUIS-RENÉ, MARQUIS DE GIRARDIN, after distinguishing himself in the Seven Years' War, became captain of the guards at the court of Stanislas Leczinski at Lunéville, where he had ample opportunity during his service to observe the garden *Wunderkammer* of the exiled Polish king. He traveled extensively throughout Europe to view gardens and was particularly impressed with that of the English poet William Shenstone, which seized his imagina-

tion and revealed Lunéville's rococo gardens as hopelessly outdated.

Upon Leczinski's death in 1766, Girardin embarked upon a decade-long program to construct his own English-style park at Ermenonville, a nearly nine-hundred-hectare estate to the northeast of Paris that he had inherited some years before. He began renovations to the château, called in Scottish gardeners to create emerald lawns, and employed Jean-Marie Morel to advise him in the park's design. Their task was enormous; Morel described an estate riddled with mires and springs, "nothing more than impassable swampland, showing a most repellent aspect."[1] Hubert Robert has also been credited with advising the marquis on the park's design, but scant proof exists of this consultancy, and his influence upon English-style gardens seems to have been as pervasive as that of Le Nôtre in the previous century. Nonetheless, it is clear that Girardin controlled the estate's design, for he was acknowledged as its author by his contemporaries and had also written a gardening treatise entitled *On the Composition of Landscapes*,[2] which became a bible for his followers upon its publication.

The volume testifies to Girardin's belief that painting and literature were the primary sources of inspiration for gardens: the landscapes of Nicolas Poussin, Claude Lorraine, and the Dutch school were influential, but it was Jean-Jacques Rousseau's *La Nouvelle Héloïse* that most deeply affected him—so much so that he reimagined and recreated the novel's settings in Ermenonville's gardens. He was so successful that the Prince de Ligne would write, "I returned to Ermenonville, thinking only of Julie."[3] Girardin was not alone in his fascination with Rousseau: the phrase *à la Rousseau* was then quite in vogue and was applied to anything contrived to appear rustic and picturesque;[4] one could build a *jardin à la Rousseau,* stage a country outing *à la Rousseau,* and so forth, and the

garden's greatest faults were the result of Girardin's breathless pursuit of the fashionable.

The marquis dedicated a chapter of his book to garden structures, elaborating commonsense principles to follow to ensure the appropriate folly is built on the appropriate site; for example, he recommends canvas mock-ups to judge a building's massing and its effect upon the landscape. He obviously implemented his own guidelines: contemporary plans detail as many as fifty points of interest in Ermenonville's park, from an Altar to Revery to an Indian Tepee, though most of the garden's follies were small, ephemeral structures. Although the site was exploited to best advantage to produce secluded, tranquil vistas, many of these incidental ornaments added little to an appreciation of the park, and invariably the marquis ensured that each was inscribed with literary and philosophical quotations.

Girardin presented himself as a man of acute sensitivity—a chapter of his treatise is entitled, "Of the power of Landscapes upon our senses, and therefore upon our souls"—but his ubiquitous quotations engendered a chorus of complaint. The marquis doubtless believed that an inscription would transform a few stacked rocks or a stone bench into an object of great import through the alchemy of literary allusion, but Madame Vigée-Lebrun described their effect as intellectual tyranny, and Ligne dismissed them as "trivial, pedantic, unfortunate, innumerable, or ill-sited inscriptions, none of which is able to satisfy the demands of its beautiful setting."[5]

Nonetheless, the largest of Ermenonville's follies successfully shouldered the burden pretension had placed upon them: the crenellated bastion of the Tower of Gabrielle, dedicated to Henri IV's mistress, Gabrielle d'Estrées, inspired Marie Antoinette to commission the Marlborough Tower at the Hameau, and the Temple of Modern Philosophy, situated on a hillside overlooking Ermenonville's placid lake, is just sublime enough to mask its clever conceit. A virtual copy of the iconic, ruined Temple of Vesta at Tivoli recorded by artists from Claude Lorraine to Fragonard—Hubert Robert adopted it as a subject

numerous times, and many suggest he is the folly's true author—the temple is dedicated to the pursuit of knowledge, symbolized by its unfinished state. Inevitably, it carries numerous inscriptions: that upon the lintel quotes Virgil, *Rerum cognoscere causas*, To understand the true nature of things, and the interior bore a dedication to Montaigne, "who said everything." The names of Newton, Descartes, Voltaire, Penn, Montesquieu, and Rousseau are inscribed upon the six erect columns, and those lying before the temple are the metaphorical equivalents of future luminaries, which prompted Mérigot the Younger to quip: "It is much easier to obtain a seat in the Académie than to merit a column at the Temple at Ermenonville."[6]

Hermits and Hermitages

In Mérigot's *Promenade,* the author states approvingly that the Hermitage at Ermenonville was not cluttered with the usual hermit's accessories—an hourglass, staff, and a skull—and in keeping with its character, was simply furnished. Horace Walpole ridiculed hermitages as corners to which one retired to be melancholy,[7] but they were popular with less jaundiced contemporaries, who looked upon them as *tableaux vivants* vaguely suggestive of Saints John or Jerome in the desert. The hermitage at Le Lydieu, a compound in the gardens of Gaillon, was among the earliest recorded hermitages in France, first mentioned in 1508 as being sited near a chapel in a secluded garden.[8] The Hermitage at Betz, built nearly three centuries later, consisted of a small log cabin that was the hermit's residence and an attached oratory combining a chapel and an elaborate *rocaille* grotto.

The Hermitage at Ermenonville. Built circa *1775 by the Marquis de Girardin. The watercolor is based upon Georges-Louis Le Rouge's engraving, but as is often the case with Le Rouge, reality has been discarded and an idealized structure presented. Nonetheless, the small stone-and-thatch building is representative of the many hermit's huts that appeared in the gardens of the period (authors' rendering).*

Despite undeniable architectural whimsy, a hermitage's main attraction was its inhabitant; little is known of Ermenonville's hermit, but it is known that the occupant at Betz had been recruited by an agent specially employed to locate potential hermits.

The Princesse de Monaco, the owner of Betz, had composed detailed rules of conduct for her hermit: he was to dress in sackcloth and clean his hut, but could not leave his immediate surroundings except to attend Mass, and he was not permitted to have contact with the peasants or break his silence. However, he could grow vegetables beside his hut, keep pigeons, and collect firewood. Most importantly, he was to show curious visitors the chapel and his little garden and politely ensure that no one disturbed anything. As compensation for his splendid isolation, he received one hundred *livres* per annum and was allowed to accept donations. This hermit must have found his lot a comfortable one, for he remained in his hut when the princess left for exile and, all but forgotten, abided by her regulations until his death at the age of seventy-nine in 1811.[9]

Ermenonville achieved great fame in its time and René de Girardin played host to many eminent figures of his day; however, the most honored guest was undoubtedly Jean-Jacques Rousseau, aged and impoverished, who spent six weeks in a pavilion beside the château, where he died of apoplexy in July 1778, aged sixty-six. He was interred in a sarcophagus on a small island ringed by poplars at the far end of the lake fronting the château, fittingly becoming the most renowned folly of all in the park that was dedicated to his writings.[10]

A MONUMENT TO EXILE:
THE PAGODA OF CHANTELOUP

Étienne François, duc de Choiseul, touched by the displays of friendship, kindness, and care with which he was honored by numerous visitors during his exile, has erected this monument to immortalize his gratitude.
—The commemorative inscription in the Pagoda of Chanteloup

THE DUC DE CHOISEUL-STAINVILLE was a man of exceptional ability and position: for twelve years during the reign of Louis XV he was Minister of Foreign Affairs, of War, of the Navy, and of the

The Duc de Choiseul at the height of power in 1765; portrait by Louis-Michel Van Loo. Musée de Versailles, Versailles.

The Pagoda at Chanteloup. Built 1775–1778 by Louis-Denis Le Camus. In a curious twist of fate, the Château de Chanteloup was destroyed but its folly survives (authors' rendering).

Post.[1] In many ways, he was the government of France, and his spectacular fall from power resulted from an equally spectacular misreading of a subject in which he seemed to be expert: love affairs, specifically that of Madame Du Barry and the king.

Louis XV's dreaded *lettre de cachet* was delivered at ten o'clock in the morning of Christmas Eve 1770;[2] no one at Versailles ever missed the occasion of another's public disgrace, and a buoyant, glittering rabble had gathered to witness the event. The duke appeared punctually, aloof and impeccably dressed. Choiseul was not handsome: rather short and unfortunately

Chanteloup
in the years before Choiseul's exile.
The château and the terrace
facing Amboise. These miniature
views (left and facing page) were painted
on vellum by Louis Nicolas
van Blarenberghe and mounted in gold
for a snuffbox. The Metropolitan
Museum of Art, New York. Gift of
Mr. and Mrs. Charles Wrightsman.

stout, his round face was ringed by reddish curls almost always tucked under a powdered wig. His button nose, double chin, and dark, animated eyes led the king in better days to call him teasingly *Mon Cochon*, My Piglet, also a wordplay on his role as *le cocher de l'Europe,* the coachman of Europe.[3] Acquaintances invariably found him charming and expansive, with a sharp wit and a brilliant intelligence overlaid with a seductive *"laideur piquante,"* a powerful man's charm.[4]

The duke was a well-known womanizer who had achieved a subsidiary fame for his conquests, and so it is remarkable that he so badly misjudged the status of the Comtesse Du Barry. Choiseul's clique had spread vicious rumors concerning her unsavory past, and once installed in power, she wasted no time exacting vengeance. After enduring a momentous, twenty-month struggle between the council chamber and the bedchamber, and furious at having been maneuvered into opposition to England when he could ill afford

war, the king finally sacrificed his minister for the sake of domestic peace.

Custom allowed Choiseul two hours to leave Versailles: the king had no wish to see the stricken faces of the exiled, and it was mainly due to the popularity of Choiseul's wife that they were allowed to retire to Chanteloup.[5] The duke accepted the news with outward calm, but the people of Paris, sensing an opportunity to spite the king, responded with a hero's farewell, and cheering crowds mobbed the departing carriage. The couple's good friend and society fixture, the Marquise du Deffand, hyperbolized: "Never had a disgrace won so much glory; there is no comparable example in ancient or modern history."[6]

"The Most Magnificent Establishment in Europe" [7]

Choiseul's meteoric rise had included governorship of Touraine, where in 1761 he had acquired Chanteloup, in the heart of the province. But his happiness was not complete; it seemed that another four thousand hectares were needed to provide a gracious setting for a country gentleman, and it was Madame de Pompadour who resolved his dilemma: Choiseul would purchase her marquisate and offer it to the king in exchange for neighboring Amboise, the royal estate he coveted. Louis XV turned a blind eye to their machinations and Choiseul's daring was rewarded: Pompadour was again bestowed on its marquise, along with a handsome profit and Choiseul's gratitude.

Choiseul chose Le Camus de Mézières to create an estate worthy of his rank; the architect had earlier renovated Choiseul's Paris residence and is remembered for the Halle aux Blés and the Hôtel de Beauvau, today housing the Ministry of the Interior. Chanteloup was then an unassuming château designed by Robert de Cotte, and Le Camus' most notable additions were a pair of colonnades connecting the château's main block with two-story pavilions, creating a transparent facade both elegant and imposing.

As at Versailles, the estate of Chanteloup was composed of a small park with terraces, lawns, parterres, and fountains surrounding the château, and a great park with tree-lined avenues cut through the adjoining forest. The main axis of the château was dominated by a cascade, beyond which was a semicircular reflecting basin extended by a canal. Water was the eternal bane of French gardens, and Le Camus persuaded the duke to build an enormously expensive subterranean system, thirteen kilometers in length, to replenish the basins and the canal. His additions and alterations were carried out in the 1760s, and when the exiled duke arrived he found a perfectly kept and newly outdated estate. The oriental influence unleashed by William Chambers' writings on China had swept through Europe,[8] rendering the whole of French gardening as formulated by Le Nôtre obsolete: nature was to be romanticized, not regimented.

This was a serious setback for as fashionable a man as Choiseul, who after years of obsessive building at Chanteloup, found himself deeply in debt: not only had his own fortune been spent on the grounds, but much of his wife's as well. In 1772, the duke auctioned a third of his nearly four hundred paintings—eventually selling off the entire collection, including three Rembrandts now in the Louvre—the land surrounding his townhouse, and finally the hôtel itself. A grant from the new king, four million *livres* given on behalf of Marie Antoinette in 1774,[9] melted like snow in the sun. With these massive infusions of money, building continued, and portions of the park were transformed into an Anglo-Chinese garden with irregular springs and picturesque monuments.

A Splendid Exile

Chanteloup housed Choiseul and the duchess; the duke's sister, the overbearing Duchesse de Gramont; and, much to his wife's chagrin, his mistress the Comtesse de Brionne. "The greatest liberty sets the tone of the house," wrote Madame du Deffand,[10] alluding to what some contemporaries termed the duke's seraglio. A generous host, Choiseul entertained

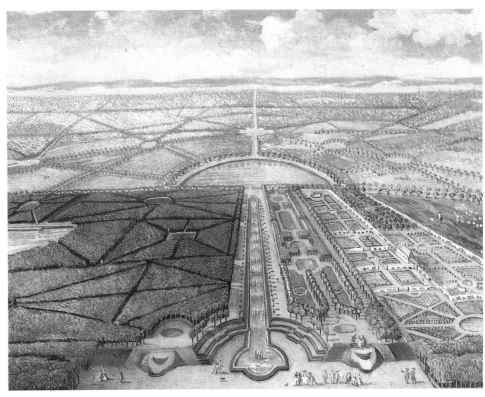

The gardens spreading out beyond the Château de Chanteloup. The cascade was later replaced with a greensward, and its far end was the site of the Pagoda. The Metropolitan Museum of Art, New York. Gift of Mr. and Mrs. Charles Wrightsman.

a constant tide of courtiers and was delighted both by the irritation this was sure to cause in Versailles and by the opportunities it afforded him to meddle in affairs of state. He held forth brilliantly on politics, and the king's constant refrain was, "What does one say at Chanteloup?"[11]

Indeed, Chanteloup echoed Versailles both in splendor and tedium. During the afternoons, the little court, surrounded by *abbés*, blackamoors, and dogs, walked the ever-changing gardens. Afterwards, guests parted to rest, read, or write letters reporting the doings at the château, issuing an amusing stream of gossip to courts throughout Europe. In summer, entertainments were held in the gardens; particularly memorable was an evening in July 1773 when the grand basin above the cascade was lit with torches, and a small frigate ablaze with lights sailed the canal as an orchestra played through the night. The Duchesse de Lauzun, the Princesse de Poix and Madame de Vaudreuil had been persuaded to aban-

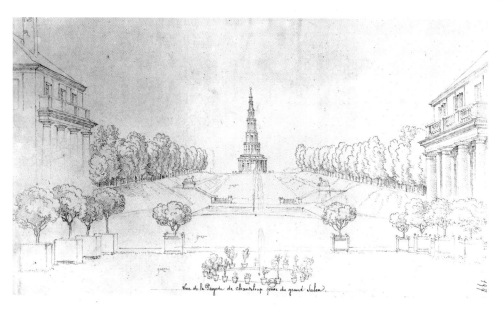

shrugged off."[13] The tower, the work of Le Camus de Mezières' protégé, Louis-Denis Le Camus, is a strange amalgam of French classicism and unorthodox massing vaguely reminiscent of William Chambers' pagoda at Kew. The ground floor, a rotunda of sixteen Doric columns, echoes the Temple of Vesta; the second floor was used as a salon, and dinners would be held with a light orchestra playing on the floor above. A marble plaque bearing an inscription thanking friends for their constancy, along with plaques bearing their names in gilt, were mounted on the walls. A delicate, spiral staircase with a creaking wooden railing winds gracefully to the tiny room at the building's summit, affording panoramic views. Acanthus leaves, fir cones, and laurel wreaths recur as carved decorative motifs, and the only overt allusion to the Orient appears in the fretwork patterns of the iron railings on the pagoda's many balconies.

don all pretense of noble rank and to perform as the Three Graces, and sang impromptu invitations to the dance.

"A Style of Chinese Obelisk" [12]

Choiseul, reduced from the pinnacle of power to gentleman farmer, plotted his return to favor amid these glittering diversions, and though Louis XVI rescinded his exile in 1774, the duke was not recalled to government service. Forced to accept his fate, he busied himself with pig farming and his memoirs and later published a tract on cultivating silkworms. To refurbish his gardens, the duke replaced the outmoded cascade of the grand axis with a simple greensward. Between this lawn and the semicircle of the grand basin, he decided to erect a pagoda as a monument to his friends' loyalty during his exile; the foundation stone was laid in 1775 on the site of the Three Graces' radiant performance.

The pagoda was conceived as a simple structure, but the duke was soon swept up in its planning. Dufort de Cheverny avowed: "This building, which the duke had regarded as a bauble of a thousand *louis*, finally cost him forty thousand *écus*, an amount he

The great exclamation mark of the Pagoda, as viewed from the château's cour d'honneur in an anonymous drawing. B.N.F., Paris.

A bankrupt in all but name, Choiseul celebrated the pagoda's completion in April 1778 with the expected panache, and the great exclamation mark became as much a monument to his own audacity as to those he wished to honor. Versailles emptied to attend, and courtiers pored over the marble plaques in search of their names. Construction then came to an abrupt halt, though the duke would continue to entertain until his death in 1785. The following year, Chanteloup was sold to the Duc de Penthièvre for an enormous sum that recovered only a fraction of Choiseul's debt, and his wife would spend the rest of her life repaying his creditors, represented by their solicitor, the ubiquitous oracle of revolution, Pierre Caron de Beaumarchais.

Chanteloup was confiscated during the Revolution, and after a succession of owners the estate fell into the hands of speculators. In 1823, the abandoned château was demolished, and today the idiosyncratic pagoda stands aloof and defiant, much as Choiseul himself had done in an earlier age.

The Duc de Choiseul's intimates:
La Duchesse de Gramont, Madame de Stainville,
Monsieur le Comte de Biron, *watercolor by*
Carmontelle. Musée Condé, Chantilly.

A PAGODA BY THE LAKE

A little palace in an extraordinary style, and the perfect place to pass the time on a summer's day
— André Félibien, writing of the Trianon de Porcelaine

Gardens are driven by curiosity; a great garden does not reveal itself at once, but instead unfolds slowly, enticing with vistas of an almost magnetic attraction. In the great formal French gardens, water is the animating force: the distant roll of falling spray, a sun-struck jet shimmering white in a clearing, draw visitors down lengthy *allées*, and a garden such as that at Versailles is only half a garden when seen without its fountains at play. In Anglo-Chinese gardens, follies serve much the same circulatory purpose:

The exception that proves the rule: the Carousel, built beside the Petit Trianon. Though water was some distance away, the Carousel fulfilled all the requirements of chinoiserie follies. Detail from a painting by Claude-Louis Châtelet. Biblioteca Estense, Modena.

The Chinese Pavilion at Cassan. Built circa 1787 and unattributed. The only structure completed for a vast folly-garden thwarted by the Revolution (authors' rendering, detail).

dotted about the landscape, connected by winding paths and watercourses, they offer, one after another, the novelty of fresh mysteries and discoveries, and no single element is more characteristic of these picturesque gardens than a chinoiserie pavilion—a summerhouse pagoda set invariably beside a lake.

The development of the pagoda as a garden structure is inseparable from that of the Anglo-Chinese garden itself, for the one could not have been conceived without the inspiration of other. Both are at once outgrowths and the most fully conceived examples of the decorative style of chinoiserie, an enduring wellspring of creativity inspired by the idea of the Orient and an extraordinary testament to Europe's collective imagination.

The Trianon de Porcelaine

Louis XIV commissioned the first chinoiserie building in Europe in 1670 from Louis Le Vau. The Trianon de Porcelaine, an extravagant garden compound created at Versailles for the king's mistress, Madame de Montespan, had little in its outward appearance to suggest the East, but nevertheless set a precedent for chinoiserie structures to follow: it was enormously expensive; it was fleeting, lasting a mere seventeen years; and it was a richly embellished pleasure dome.[1] Located at the end of the northern arm of the Grand Canal, the Trianon was dedicated to love and the pleasures of the senses, a spirit which found its expression in exuberant ornamentation: polychromed faience tiled the walls of the forecourts, urns and cupids crowded the pavilions' balustrades, and roof ridges featured porcelain vases interspersed with naturalistically painted sculptures of birds. The legend that the Trianon's roofs were shingled in porcelain tile is undoubtedly apocryphal,[2] but does reveal the impact the building had upon the popular

Above: The Chinese Dance *by François Boucher; the canvas was once in the collection of Pierre Jacques de Bergeret, owner of Cassan. Musée des Beaux-Arts et d'Archéologie, Besançon.*

The Trianon de Porcelaine. Built in 1670 by Louis Le Vau for Louis XIV. The contemporary engraving perfectly captures the naïve orientalism of the first chinoiserie building in Europe. Authors' collection.

imagination, and there can be no doubt that the small retreat was an unparalleled sight, for the Trianon was, relative to its size, among the most expensive buildings ever erected in France.

This first Trianon established a pattern that would endure as chinoiserie developed: a familiar structure was overlaid with rich, fantastic ornament, with the intention of creating an exotic caprice, not a serious essay in a foreign style. Likewise, it is significant that the idea of the Orient, so wrapped in enticing mystery and fabulous half-truths, served as the inspiration for the king's retreat: tales of divine Emperors and golden pagodas from Mandeville's fictitious *Travels*[3] had combined with a trickle of trade in the luxuries of silks, spices, and porcelains to create in the European mind a vision of an Orient of incalculable wealth and unfathomable strangeness. This fantastic image, which barely altered as China became better understood, in time was recognized as the perfect means to express "the naïve joy of the eighteenth century in colorful curiosities and playthings with the charm of the useless."[4]

Chinoiserie in France would develop in interior decor over the following decades,[5] but it was not until a Turkish kiosk was built in the provincial court of Lunéville in 1738, followed shortly by the Trèfle—a pagoda with a cloverleaf plan—that other chinoiserie structures would appear. These buildings had little impact elsewhere in France, however, and it was the

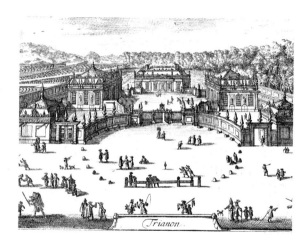

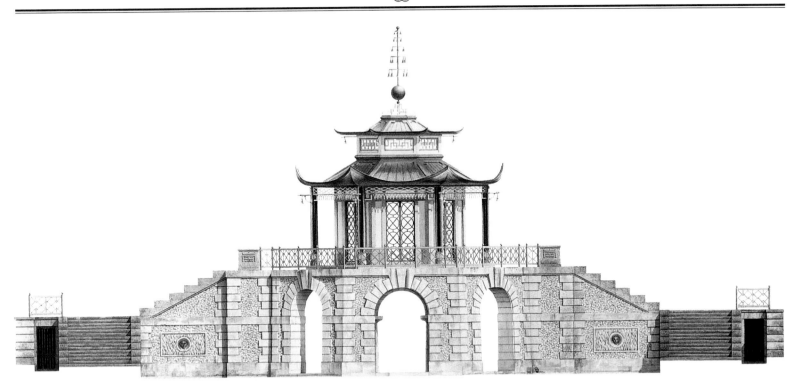

English, who had been building small chinoiserie pavilions in their parks since the late 1730s, who would exert a decisive influence upon French gardens once the legacy of Le Nôtre was finally exhausted.

France in turn adapted English forms to its own ends; there was never any serious attempt to replicate the gentle sweep of open landscapes punctuated with distant eye-catchers, and the elements used to compose English-style parks, or rather a caricature of them, resulted in gardens that were essentially decorative in spirit, in their own manner as rigorously artificial as the formal gardens that preceded them. Within confined plots a fraction of the size of their English models, these new gardens were furnished like rooms, with an eclectic mix of follies meant both to be visited and enjoyed. Georges-Louis Le Rouge entitled several of his celebrated portfolios of documentary engravings *Détail des nouveaux jardins à la mode*,[6] and his use of the terminology of fashion underscored the essentially decorative nature and appeal of these gardens.

The Chinese Pavilion at Cassan. Built circa 1787 and unattributed (authors' rendering, full view).

The Chinese Pavilion at Cassan

The pagoda at Cassan is located in what is today a town just beyond the grasp of the northern suburbs of Paris.[7] The building's history remains obscure, but it may have been commissioned by Pierre Jacques Bergeret, the scion of a family of tax farmers. A dedicated though overbearing art patron, he and his son traveled through Italy in 1773–1774 accompanied by a miserable Fragonard and his wife, and local tradition holds that the temperamental artist was the building's author. A more plausible commissioner is Bergeret's son, who purchased the domain that was later to become Cassan in 1778 and inherited his father's estate after its settlement in 1788–1789. The pagoda was probably erected following the death of the father in 1785, when the son, confident of a vast inheritance, may have conceived of constructing an ambitious English-inspired estate designed around an artificial lake.

The Chinese Pavilion, which incorporates a dam and spillway in its substructure, was the first, essential phase of this work, and would have stood just to the

P̃ierre Jacques Bergeret, the imposing art patron and putative commissioner of the Chinese Pavilion at Cassan. Portrait by François-André Vincent. Musée des Beaux-Arts et d'Archéologie, Besançon.

Ãn anonymous plan of the estate of Cassan, l'Isle-Adam, projecting a vast landscape park of visionary grandeur. The Chinese Pavilion is at far right, center. Musée d'Aquitaine, Bordeaux.

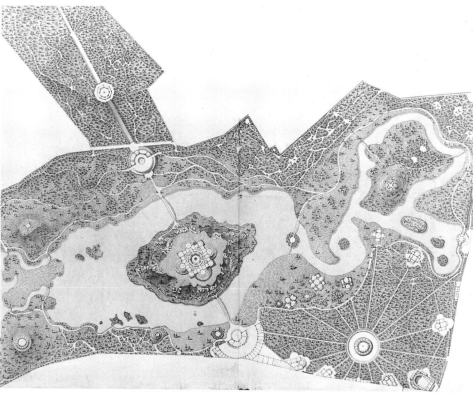

north of the projected Grove of Apollo, a great ring of eleven pavilions encircling a rotunda—a design in its essentials reminiscent of the layout of the Désert de Retz. Considering the beauty of the Chinese Pavilion and the scale of Bergeret's undertaking, it is regrettable this work was never realized, for Cassan would have ranked among the most impressive late English-style gardens in France.

The pavilion in fact comprises two structures—a monumental stone plinth upon which stands the wooden pagoda—and is typical of the period's practice of pairing dissimilar architectural elements to create picturesque effects. The base is notable for its sophisticated planning and vigorous ornamentation; both a stairway and a plinth, it also shelters a vaulted grotto in its octagonal substructure featuring a central pool ringed by eight Greek Doric columns.

The Chinese Pavilion was strongly influenced by the designs of William Chambers, and its free-standing columns and large glazed doors create a building of remarkable transparency that masks its great structural strength; aside from a miniature kiosk, it is the only wooden pagoda of the period remaining in France.[8] The Chinese Pavilion has endured Revolution, neglect, air raids, and vandals, a remarkable survivor standing beside a greatly reduced lake, today encroached by suburban development.

Rambouillet and Bonnelles

The Pagoda at Rambouillet was commissioned by the Duc de Penthièvre before 1784, as part of the great park's transformation into an English-style landscape garden and, as with the Chaumière a few yards distant, was probably built for the amusement of his widowed daughter-in-law, the Princesse de Lamballe. The pagoda straddled a rockwork grotto that still divides a watercourse, and its access stairs served as the bridge for a major garden path.

The pagoda was a simple frame structure with large wooden panels that could be propped open to admit light and air, similar to a chinoiserie pavilion today preserved at Boughton House in England.

*T*he Pagoda at Rambouillet. Built circa *1780*
and attributed to Jean-Augustin Renard. The pagoda has been destroyed but the grotto
survives; its color scheme is based upon period chinoiserie designs (authors' rendering).

*T*he Pagoda at Bonnelles.
Built circa 1780 and unattributed.
Destroyed (authors' rendering).

$\mathcal{T}$he Pagoda
at Rambouillet as it appears on the cover
sheet of the eleventh portfolio
of Georges-Louis Le Rouge's engravings
of Anglo-Chinese gardens.
B.N.F., Paris.

$\mathcal{T}$he whimsical Pagoda
at Bonnelles, reached by arching
bridges, and a small
island with its Philosopher's Pavilion.
Engraving by Georges-Louis Le Rouge.
B.N.F., Paris.

The dragons at the corners of the roof were a free interpretation of traditional Chinese decorations—as was the crowning chattra, a series of graded hoops with bells—testifying to a desire for greater authenticity in later chinoiserie follies. The architect is unknown, but may have been the Inspector of the King's Buildings, Jean-Augustin Renard, the architect who designed the Duc de Penthièvre's folly garden at Armainvilliers; however, pagodas such as these were considered minor garden structures and little documentary trace of them remains. Local legend records that the pavilion burned in the portentious year of 1792 after having been struck by lightning, serving as a pyre for a pair of hapless lovers who had sought shelter within.[9]

The Duc d'Uzès, a descendant of Claude de Bullion, commissioned the Pagoda at Bonnelles in approximately 1780. The tiny structure, square in plan and with large circular windows, featured detached corner columns inscribed with fanciful Chinese inscriptions. The belevedere stood atop a large artificial rockwork in the park's central lake and was reached by a series of rustic, arching footbridges, the last of which sprung from a small island featuring a hermit's hut. Le Rouge's engraving perfectly captures the ingennous charm of the arrangement while evoking earlier views of Chinese landscape gardens.

$\mathcal{L}$e Rouge's spirited
but often inaccurate engravings afford
the only visual records of the pagodas at
Rambouillet and Bonnelles. At the same time,
the two pagodas are among the best-
documented of these lost structures by virtue
of having been drawn at all.
The elevations (left and page 159) present
conjectural details and color schemes based
upon contemporary precedents, and have
been included for their undeniable
charm and whimsy. It is our hope that these
watercolors serve to spark further
investigation that will lead to a finer
understanding of the appearance of both pagodas.

*T*he Pyramid
at Mauperthuis. Built circa *1780*
by Alexandre-Théodore Brongniart as
the entry to the Élysée, a landscape
garden informed by Masonic principles
(authors' rendering).

ENTRY TO ELYSIUM:
THE PYRAMID AT MAUPERTHUIS

*At Mauperthuis one truly finds the image
of Elysium so praised by poets. At Mauperthuis,
everything speaks to the senses: the eye
is enchanted, the soul is moved. Its grounds
are imposing, its details charming;
at Mauperthuis, Nature is astir.*
—Pierre Villiers, *Manuel du voyageur
aux environs de Paris . . .*

*The Marquis
de Montesquiou, who claimed direct
descent from the legendary King Clovis.
Engraving by Charles François
Le Tellier after Charles Toussaint
Labadye. B.N.F., Paris.*

MAUPERTHUIS WAS THE HOME of one of the most liberal noblemen of the Enlightenment, a country manor and an extensive park dedicated to a life of sophisticated pleasures, but the estate and its complex history were ablated by the Revolution, then obscured by centuries of indifference. With renewed interest in the architecture of the French Enlightenment, attention turned to Mauperthuis, site of Claude Nicolas Ledoux's early work, but with few physical remains and an indistinct past, the estate has vexed researchers.[1] Some scholars have even suggested that Ledoux's château was an entirely utopian concoction, but the existence of Mauperthuis' Pyramid has never seriously been disputed: though somewhat dilap-

idated, it still stands, a ruined ruin, the emblem of an age defined both by the fragile spirit of Reason and the restless search for meaning.

Deeply divided beliefs made its owner, Anne-Pierre, Marquis de Montesquiou, the embodiment of the contradictions of his time. Though he was among the most progressive and free-thinking of aristocrats, a radical mind for whom membership in a masonic lodge was a matter of course, the marquis was also fiercely proud of having been named Gentleman of the Dauphin's Sleeve. As holder of the title, he was one of three gentlemen-in-waiting permitted to guide the king's firstborn son by the sleeve; however, the marquis was forbidden to take his charge by the hand, which would have been an unspeakable breach of etiquette—that privilege was reserved for yet another member of the Dauphin's entourage. Like the Duc de Saint-Simon and René de Longueil before him, Montesquiou was obsessed by his own genealogy and was unrelenting in his efforts to prove a lineage more ancient and distinguished than the king's—a presumption which earned him only mockery at court.[2] Yet this same man would, at the outbreak of the Revolution, ally himself with the Third Estate and later fight as a general in the Revolutionary armies.

The Estate

The marquis began work at Mauperthuis *circa* 1761, when he was but twenty-three years old. Ledoux, three years Montesquiou's senior, came to his attention through the marquis' marriage in 1760; the architect had already received several commissions from the bride's family, but later considered Mauperthuis to be his most important and challenging early work.[3] The château is known primarily through Ledoux's own, highly suspect, engravings: the architect extensively reworked his early designs for publication late in his career, aggrandizing the estate until it became unrecognizable, while Charles-Louis Châtelet's oil painting, some crude sketches, and a number of vague and occasionally conflicting descriptions by contemporaries only add to the general confusion. In any event, the marquis had room enough to entertain on a grand scale. In her *Mémoires*, Madame Vigée-Lebrun remarked that "the château could easily accomodate thirty or forty noble guests, all lodged in perfect comfort, an endless stream of society" animating the hinterlands.[4]

The Château de Mauperthuis stood on a bluff amid formal parterres that descended in steps to a large octagonal basin fed by the river Aubetin; to one side was a large kitchen garden,[5] and wedged between these areas was an informal garden whose meandering paths led to a Chinese pagoda built upon stilts, an early precedent for the Chinese Tent later constructed at Bagatelle. The pagoda, overlooking the river, served as an exotic backdrop for Montesquiou's birthday festivities in 1771, when he appeared as a mandarin, properly attired for the occasion in an embroidered silk robe.

The pagoda and its small Anglo-Chinese garden were the work of Alexandre-Théodore Brongniart; Ledoux's association with Mauperthuis had come to an obscure end in approximately 1767, when neither the château nor its gardens had been completed.

*T*he architect
of the Château de Mauperthuis, Claude Nicolas Ledoux, and his elder daughter Adélaïde in a portrait attributed to Antoine Vestier. Musée Carnavalet, Paris.

*T*he architect
of the Élysée, Alexandre-Théodore Brongniart, in a lithograph by Béranger after Gérard and Arnoult. B.N.F., Paris.

Brongniart was a student of Blondel and a protégé of Boullée: having been taught by the great theorist of the French classical tradition, he would emulate one of the visionaries who was to overturn it. He began his remarkable career by designing the Hôtel de Montesson for the mistress of the Duc d'Orléans and was also a member of the marquis' masonic lodge—an excellent place to encounter potential clients, for many aristocrats had abandoned Catholicism and secretly practised masonic rites. The link Brongniart exploited between freemasonry and gardens was a fertile one, as many of these men were to commission the great English-style gardens of the period.[6] Significantly, Ledoux was a fervent mason as well.

The Élysée and the Masonic Garden

Though much of masonic ritual has remained successfully shrouded in mystery, it is clear that freemasonry is fundamental to understanding the gardens of Mauperthuis. Masonic initiation ceremonies "entailed ritual journeys—that is, a succession of specific moves corresponding to the 'ordeals' which symbolize the essential moral and spiritual evolution of the future initiate. The space of a garden lends itself ideally to this sort of symbolic circuit, to almost ritual perambulations, in which the *fabriques* [follies] become compulsory stages . . ."[7] A garden's layout could thus bear masonic meaning, as could individual follies, which fall into clear categories: those structures symbolizing philosophical ideas, such as Elysium, Friendship, Wisdom, and Virtue, as well as the houses of hermits and sages; medieval towers and fortresses evoking the Knights Templar, the legendary ancestors of freemasons; those structures relating to Egypt; and grottoes and windowless buildings where seances and alchemy were performed.[8]

The formal gardens in the immediate vicinity of the château were laid out during Montesquiou's youth; surviving plans reveal ambition but little innovation. The separate garden of the Élysée, however, occupied Montesquiou in his maturity and was developed during the 1770s and 1780s in conjunction with Brongniart.[9]

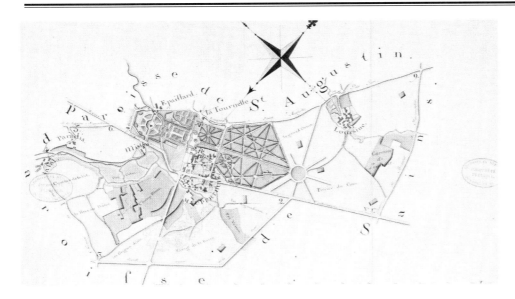

The Pyramid was conceived as the entrance to this once-famed garden, a strip of informal landscape running beside the Aubetin that was separated from the château's grounds by a roadway. "The park of Mauperthuis, before its destruction during the Revolution, was one of the places most celebrated for its beauty in France," remarked Alexandre de Laborde. "It featured an enchanted valley named the Élysée, which seemed to owe all its beauty to nature, even though it was the result of art. Monsieur de Montesquiou himself laid out its lines and overcame many difficulties with the site, reworking and replanting the entire hill, at the foot of which run a small river and several springs which form the area's chief ornaments."[10]

The most striking feature of Mauperthuis was its absolute physical division, which mirrored the divided allegiances of its owner to a remarkable degree. The old estate with its formal gardens was the embodiment of the received wisdom of the *ancien régime,* while the picturesque landscape of the Élysée presented an alternate world influenced by masonic ideas—its very name was charged with masonic reference. These two gardens and worlds were linked by an underground passage: "One enters by an audacious and imposing cavern that leads under the road. At the end of it is an ancient pyramid, built in a semi-

The plan

of Mauperthuis before construction of the Élysée, illustrating the formal gardens surrounding the château. The Élysée would occupy the curling strip of land at left center, with old and new gardens linked by the Pyramid. Archives départementales de Seine-et-Marne.

The Pyramid

in a view painted by Claude-Louis Châtelet; Admiral Coligny's tomb is at left and Ledoux's disputed château in the distance (overleaf). Private collection, Paris.

ruinous state, which contains a grotto, and from there the eye discovers a pleasant landscape."[11] The pastoral landscape of this Elysium, a landscape carefully transformed, is entirely composed of paths meandering between a network of streams—a dense web of literal and symbolic "ritual perambulations."

The follies placed about the garden were above all masonic symbols, and often functioned, as did the Pyramid and its grotto-tunnel, as bridges linking the garden's physical and metaphorical planes.[12] The garden also featured a thatched hut set in a grove, suggesting secluded seers in contemplation.

Death in the Bosquets

The marquis also discovered the profoundly symbolic remains of Admiral Coligny—a prominent Protestant whose murder presaged the infamous Saint Bartholomew's Day massacre in 1572—and placed them in a tomb erected beside the Pyramid.[13] Laborde's moving observations are well worth repeating: "This use of tombs in gardens dates from the last years before the Revolution. A long prosperity seemed to have inured us to pleasant images. One needed drama, theater, death in the bosquets. Real suffering has only sharpened our appreciation of the true, and one is no longer tempted to play with unhappiness, to place a tomb on the roadside for the amusement of passers-by, containing remains that humanity has deprived of a grave." [14]

But this is a judgment formed in hindsight; unhappiness was a rare guest in these gardens, moments of reflection rarer still. As an example, a grand reception was held before the pyramid in 1785, attended by Louis XVI's brother, the Comte de Provence. A thunderstorm brought the evening's entertainments to an abrupt halt, but the rain eventually stopped; though it was after midnight, the count—as jaded and blasé a nobleman as Versailles had ever produced—left the château to inspect the gardens by torchlight. To Montesquiou's enormous relief, he enjoyed the Élysée immensely, particularly a boating party that had been hurriedly staged before the illuminated Pyramid.

BETZ: A TEMPLE TO FRIENDSHIP

A L'AMITIÉ

The Temple of Friendship at Betz. Built circa 1784 by Jean-François Leroy (authors' rendering).

The most beautiful English garden in France . . .
where Genius and Art scattered miracles
amid untamed Nature, simply to please the Princess.
—Joseph-Antoine-Joachim Cérrutti,
Les Jardins de Betz

I AM FINALLY MISTRESS OF BETZ,"[1] Marie-Catherine de Brignole, Princesse de Monaco, wrote in 1780 of her new estate, "not too far from and not too close" to Paris. However, her triumphant letter failed to mention a more important consideration: Betz's proximity to Chantilly, the seat of Louis-Joseph de Bourbon, Prince de Condé, her lover and mentor. The widowed prince, though not always faithful—he excused himself by blaming God for having given him too sensitive and too tender a heart[2]—was, with her cherished estate, the center of the princess' life, and it was at Betz that she enjoyed a decade of happiness before the outbreak of revolution.

She was nearly universally admired: Madame de La Ferté-Imbault described the princess as charming,

even-tempered, and "one of the most beautiful women of her time"[3] and Condé himself compared his mistress to the dawn of a beautiful day. Goethe encountered her in exile in 1792, when she was fifty-three years old, and left this description: "The Princesse de Monaco, declared mistress of the Prince de Condé and the ornament of Chantilly in better days, is spirited and charming. It would be impossible to find anyone more gracious. . . . I was very surprised to find her so vivacious and full of joy."[4]

"Betz, a hundred times visited,
still not entirely seen!" [5]

The gardens at Betz were conceived as a testament to love, for the work was guided from its inception with the intense involvement of the princess and Condé, who fostered a productive collaboration

between Hubert Robert and the Duc d'Harcourt. The duke, the governor of Normandy and, more prestigiously, governor of the Dauphin, Marie Antoinette's son, was author of a witty, prescient gardening treatise, today nearly forgotten.[6] The duke offered sound advice for designing a proper landscape garden, warning against indiscriminately cluttering one's grounds and attempting to create grand effects with paltry means. Having both "studied and directed nature, being at once her slave as well as her master,"[7] the duke observed that to appreciate the elaborate, simplicity is a necessary foil, just as repose informs effort. Following such maxims, he created his gardens in Normandy, which Condé greatly admired, prompting his invitation to oversee the gardens at Betz.

Known to posterity as a painter of architectural ruins without equal, Hubert Robert was also much in demand as a garden consultant, though his direct involvement is often difficult to trace.[8] That a painter would design gardens was at the time considered natural; contemporary treatises[9] stressed the importance of creating a series of "pictures" within a garden, and drew an explicit link between artists' and poets' compositional devices and those gardeners should employ. One strove for "picturesque effects," a phrase strongly connoting artistic composition that had not yet fallen into the banality of formula.[10]

The Gardens

With the Duc d'Harcourt encouraging the princess' enthusiasms, the gardens at Betz became a curio cabinet of follies, holding a Gothic Turret, an Oriental Kiosk, a Chinese Bridge, a Druid's Temple, a Valley of Tombs, a Pavilion of Repose, a ruined Roman Bath, a Hermitage, Tancred's Column, and an Obelisk commemorating American Independence— all skillfully wedged into a few walled acres. Hubert Robert, master of the melancholy prank, authored a grandiose feudal ruin and its ficticious history, so convincingly executed that it soon found its way into guidebooks and histories.

*T*he Gothic Ruin *at Betz, in a view that captures its eclectic inspirations, from Piranesi to the cult of the Valois kings. Engraving by Massard after Constant Bourgeois. B.N.F., Paris.*

The Temple of Friendship is handsomely sited against a background of Weymouth pines, named for Lord Weymouth, whose country seat was their source; with their ruddy trunks and twisted silhouettes, they were highly sought-after plantings for picturesque gardens. Laborde remarked: "On the summit of a hill one can see a facade of the Ionic order, of simple architecture, set agreeably against

*H*ubert Robert,
*a painter without peer of architectural
ruins and equally sought-after as
a garden designer. Portrait by Madame
Élisabeth Vigée-Lebrun.
Musée du Louvre, Paris.*

*T*he Temple
*of Friendship, its white stone portico set
dramatically against a backdrop
of greenery. Engraving by Massard after
Constant Bourgeois. B.N.F., Paris.*

the mass of surrounding trees."[11] Jean-François Leroy, Condé's architect at Chantilly, received the commission for the "small Parthenon to Love,"[12] which was constructed in the early 1780s. Statues of *Castor* and *Pollux*, inseparable companions of Greek mythology, stand in niches framing the entry. The temple's neoclassical interior anticipated the spare elegance of Marie Antoinette's Dairy at Rambouillet and features a rectangular room screened by columns alternating with fluted column-pedestals.[13] A skylight at the apex of the vaulted, coffered ceiling illuminates an altar, and opposite the entry is an apse displaying a copy of Jean-Baptiste Pigalle's statue of *Love and Friendship*.[14]

Once the temple was completed, a dispute erupted over the appropriate interior furnishings and the Abbé de Barthélemy was consulted. To general surprise, the *abbé* stated that the Greeks prayed either standing or on their knees—witness the lack of furniture in their temples—and proposed that one should look instead to Roman precedents, particularly sena-

tors' chairs and thrones. "Finally," he added anticlimactically, "I agree with Monsieur Cérrutti that, considering Friendship as an eternal goddess, one can furnish [the temple] however one wants."[15] A circular daybed was finally chosen, from which one could read the statue's inscription:

*Sage Friendship! Love seeks your presence;
Intrigued by your sweetness,
Infatuated by your fidelity,
She comes begging you to enrich her bonds
With all your sacred virtues.*

The princess' bond of love and friendship lasted until her death; her architectural commissions, though, were short-lived. By 1808, Comte de Laborde remarked, "Nothing more remains of Betz than a ruined château, traces of the follies, and some admirable vegetation."[16] For some decades the estate has been the property of His Majesty King Hassan II of Morocco; the Temple of Friendship is one of the few follies to have survived.

ANCIENT ECHOES:
THE NYMPHÆUM OF CHATOU

*An architect whose sage and virile taste
stood firm against that of his century,
corrupted by the capricious and the bizarre.*
—La Font de Saint-Yenne, praising Soufflot

T HE MOST REMARKABLE FRENCH GROTTO of the eighteenth century is the strangely marvelous Nymphæum built for the minister Henri-Léonard Bertin at Chatou. A neglected masterpiece by Jacques-Germain Soufflot which both anticipates the immense utopian schemes of Revolutionary-era architects and reprises the anachronistic grandeur of the Age of Louis XIV, the grotto was among the architect's last commissions—a project that gave him considerable pleasure amid the grief consuming his

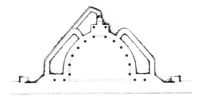

*The plan of the Nymphæum,
its semicircular basin ringed by an arcade
of columns and its farthest reaches accessed
by tunnels. B.N.F., Paris.*

*The Nymphæum of Chatou. Built
1774–1777 by Germain Soufflot. The
massive shell-like vault shelters a
semicircular basin (authors' rendering, top).*

ambitions for the church of Sainte-Geneviève in Paris, today the Panthéon.

Henri-Léonard Bertin, a competent administrator and dedicated agronomist under two monarchs, was one of the few ministers of the *ancien régime* whose career did not end in disgrace or exile; instead, he resigned his offices and retired to his country estate at Chatou. On a rise above the Seine with a commanding view toward Paris, Chatou was Bertin's favorite residence, and he spent his time there improving his extensive kitchen gardens and collecting oriental objects that he displayed in a chinoiserie pavilion designed by the idiosyncratic architect Jean-Jacques Lequeu.[1]

Bertin first met Soufflot in the 1750s, while the minister was Intendant of Lyon, where the architect had settled after his second trip to Italy.[2] Madame de Pompadour had chosen Soufflot as artistic preceptor for her brother, the future Marquis de Marigny, during the latter's formative Italian journey, and upon their return Soufflot was assured a place as one of France's premier architects. Soufflot built numerous châteaux in the countryside surrounding Lyon, among them La Rivette, where Bertin may have seen the diminutive grotto set in a rustic retaining wall; though unimpressive, its alternating bands of stone and volcanic tufa anticipate the decorative scheme of the Nymphæum.[3]

After purchasing Chatou in 1761, Bertin commissioned Soufflot to design a new château and remodel the existing residence to accomodate guests, servants, and a pair of spinster sisters. Despite grandiose plans, Soufflot built a simple country manor to house the retired bachelor and his collections, and it is clear that all Bertin's interest lay with his gardens.

The Nymphæum

Chatou's impressive kitchen garden was acclaimed for the geometric beauty of its beds, but the Nymphæum was the hidden centerpiece of the estate and is the largest surviving grotto in France. It is ingeniously sited: its great arch opens toward the Seine, and the entire structure acts as a retaining wall. No trace of it could be seen from the château, and even upon reaching the last of several terraces stepping down toward the river, visitors had no idea that the grotto lay beneath them. The Nymphæum's parapet appears to be the balustrade of a retaining wall; beyond is a panoramic view of river and countryside. Two steep flights of steps bracket the structure, and only after descending them does the grotto come fully into view, opening like an immense shell, the underside of its great vault dancing with the reflected light of the water in the basin beneath.

The Nymphæum was commissioned in 1774, and its daring structure required the expertise of the engineer Jean-Baptiste Rondelet, who had collaborated earlier with Soufflot on the design of Sainte-Geneviève.

*H*enri-Léonard Bertin.
Engraved by Dupin after a portrait by Alexandre Roslin. B.N.F., Paris.

*T*he architect
Jacques-Germain Soufflot in a portrait by Louis-Michel Van Loo. Musée du Louvre, Paris.

Rondelet, who avowed that the Nymphæum could not have been completed without his aid, invented a cement that included metal filings, gravel, and iron, thereby ensuring the stability of a span of nearly forty-five feet. Bertin himself provided material for the polychromed stonework: what appear to be tufa and lapis are actually slag and colored gravel, residue from smelting operations at Bertin's metal forges near Perigueux.

The Nymphæum's polychrome decoration is indebted to grottoes of the previous century, but the spirit of the ruins Soufflot studied in Italy is also evident, particularly in the use of stout, baseless Doric columns and tufa rustication. Other details, such as the witty string of keystones above the arch and the lapis-blue mosaic panels lining the gallery beneath the vault, are evidence of a knowing and spirited play upon the antique. From the great shell itself to the small shell fountain at its heart, the Nymphæum is a work of monumentality, simplicity, and conceptual unity.

In April 1777, the wedding of Bertin's nephew to the daughter of the last governor of the Bastille inaugurated the Nymphæum; the bride's father was to become the first victim of the Revolution. Bertin had planned the alliance for years and hosted a memorable reception; commemorative lapis-blue hearts had been worked into the Nymphæum's panels, and as evening fell the grotto blazed with torchlight. French horns echoed through the spring night, and a fireworks display ordered from China burst over the Seine at the evening's end. Nothing similar was ever repeated at Chatou; at the outbreak of the Revolution, Bertin wisely sold the estate and emigrated to Germany. He died in 1792, taking the waters in Spa.

An evening fete inaugurated the Nymphæum and celebrated the marriage of Bertin's nephew. The Ball at Saint-Cloud, a drawing by Augustin Saint-Aubin. Musée du Louvre, Paris.

ARMAINVILLIERS AND
THE DUC DE PENTHIÈVRE

This land has everything necessary for
the seat of a great nobleman.
—Piganiol de La Force

With spring-fed lakes and woodlands rich with game, the ancient estate of Armainvilliers, some twenty miles southeast of Paris, had been prized since the time of the Carolingian Empire.[1] In 1609, it was acquired by the de Beringhen family, the king's equerries,[2] who built a handsome, moated château and laid out extensive gardens. However, their fortunes had waned by the mid-eighteenth century and Armainvilliers, which had settled into rural, timeworn "magnificence and good taste,"[3] was sold to Louis XV in 1762. The king exchanged the estate with the Comte d'Eu, who owned the principality of Dombes which the king coveted, and upon d'Eu's death in 1775 Armainvilliers passed to his cousin, the Duc de Penthièvre.

Born in 1725, Louis-Jean-Marie de Bourbon, Duc de Penthièvre, was the only son of the Comte de Toulouse, the legitimized son of Louis XIV and Madame de Montespan. The duke would unite through inheritance his own family's wealth with the fortune bestowed upon the Comte de Toulouse's brother, the Duc du Maine, also legitimized.

The Turkish Pavilion
at Armainvilliers. Built circa 1785 and
attributed to Jean-Augustin Renard.
Destroyed (authors' rendering,
preceding page).

The venerable,
moated Château of Armainvilliers.
Detail of an anonymous French drawing.
Archives départementales
de Seine-et-Marne.

Du Maine's own two sons—including the Comte d'Eu—had died without offspring; as the Comte d'Eu's universal heir, Penthièvre, who already owned numerous estates, among them Rambouillet, Anet, Crécy, and Châteauneuf, also became lord of Sceaux, Gisors, and Armainvilliers. His extensive landholdings, solid finances, and numerous high offices combined to make him, for practical purposes, the richest man in France.

The duke was a man of outstanding integrity and goodwill and, through the example he set, became the most respected and honored nobleman of his time. He was a trusted friend of Louis XV, and like the king was prone to melancholy and shunned public display; but where Louis XV sought relief in fleeting amusements and debauchery, the duke found refuge in his faith and in good works. A widower at twenty-nine, he refused to remarry and sought consolation in the company of his children. His son, the Prince de Lamballe, was an enormous disappointment: after a dissolute life, he died at the age of twenty, leaving a young widow and no heirs. The duke's daughter married the Duc de Chartres, the Orléans prince who was to perfect every vice the duke so loathed; yet Penthièvre encouraged the alliance, hoping to remove the stain of his family's illegitimacy.

No documentary evidence explains why, at nearly sixty years of age, a pious widower should embark on an English-style folly garden in an obscure corner of the Île-de-France, but the duke previously had commissioned a number of follies at Rambouillet to amuse his widowed daughter-in-law, the Princesse de Lamballe, in the decade preceding the purchase of the estate by Louis XVI in 1783. Construction at Armainvilliers coincided with this sale, and in all probability the duke commissioned the folly garden to console the high-strung princess for the loss of Rambouillet.

Armainvilliers afforded a perfect stage for the careworn duke and his tremulous charge to act out a life of melancholy: the moated château held the venerable air of *Le Grand Siècle* and its garden preserved a dignified formality that predated Le Nôtre, more Renaissance

than baroque, grown to a well-groomed maturity. Dezallier d'Argenville[4] and Piganiol de La Force, both writing in the late 1760s, detail a garden composed of topiary rooms, green bowers, and leafy cloisters, offering "delicious promenades"[5] under clipped trees trained into *tournelles*, arcaded *allées* that ran beside canals and encircled a large lake—descriptions reminiscent of gardens in the age of Henri IV.[6]

Nostalgia would influence many of the follies built in France during the reign of Louis XVI; in particular, neo-Gothic ruins and pavilions attested to a newfound interest in the Middle Ages. As the ancient pillars of French society were undermined by the fierce intellectual inquiry of the Enlightenment, past centuries came to be imbued with a hierarchical order and social stability that the present sorely lacked. At the same time, the rise of the English-style garden encouraged the abandonment of the classical architectural vocabulary for the design of garden structures, leaving a *tabula rasa* upon which the architect could trace the wildest fantasies, unconstrained by any but the barest demands for utility. The resulting follies, a gaudy spectrum of designs, attempted to fill a profound void with the emblems of meaning, not meaning itself.

The Follies

The Bathing Pavilion at Armainvilliers perfectly embodied this confluence of nostalgia and fantasy: a small, foursquare Gothic tower, turreted and crenellated, sat incongruously astride a vaulted grotto and housed a bathing salon on its ground floor and a gaming room above. The miniature toy-fortress and Gothic follies like it offer the first, amusing precedents for Eugène Viollet-le-Duc's Gothic essays, and their influence can be traced to the muddled Romanticism Ludwig II of Bavaria later would embrace at Neuschwanstein.

*T*he Gothic Bathing Pavilion. Built circa
1785 and attributed to Jean-Augustin Renard. Destroyed.
The pavilion stood atop an arched grotto and was
outfitted with baths and a gaming salon (authors' rendering).

Coupe sur AB.

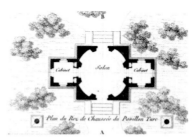

Plan du Rez de Chaussée du Pavillon Turc.

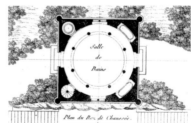

Plan du Rez de Chaussée.

Jean-Augustin Renard, Inspector of the King's Buildings, designed two Chinese pagodas and a Turkish bridge for Armainvilliers, handsome but unremarkable. The Turkish Mosque, however, was a truly unusual building, simply massed but richly adorned with bands of intricately diapered stuccowork, tufa rubble, and brick. Ostensibly a pavilion in which to enjoy coffee, tea, or chocolate, the mosque featured a cylindrical, domed and skylit rotunda flanked by small cubic cabinets profusely decorated in a fantastic Turkish style; though the building is best understood as a flamboyant eye-catcher inspired by William Chambers' mosque at Kew Gardens. The Prince de Ligne also claimed to have constructed a mosque at his estate of Baudour, and his remarks illuminate the practical ends devised for the poetically useless: "The two minarets serve as dovecotes. One knows that they are a type of column, or tower, from which the Muslim crier calls the faithful to prayer."[7] The mosque, with Armainvilliers' gardens and the dilapidated château, were destroyed by a succession of owners in the course of the nineteenth century.

Left: the section through the Turkish Mosque, and below: its plan. Engravings by Boulay after Krafft. B.N.F., Paris.

Above, the foursquare plan of the Bathing Pavilion, and right: its section, revealing a basement grotto, baths, and gaming rooms above. Engravings by Boulay after Krafft. B.N.F., Paris.

The Princesse de Lamballe had only a few years to enjoy Armainvilliers: she fled homeward to Turin during the Revolution, but returned to be with Marie Antoinette in her adversity. Her loyalty led to one of the most inhuman acts of the Revolution: during the massacres of September 1792, the mob stormed the prison where she was held and she was raped and mutilated, then decapitated. Her head and breasts were paraded on pikes before the queen's window at the Temple, and her body was dragged through the streets before being thrown into a mass grave.[8]

The Duc de Penthièvre remained in France throughout the Revolution; loyal to king and country, he watched in horror as the nation crumbled. The respect he inspired was such that neither he nor his lands were threatened by the mob or by revolutionaries, and he died in March 1793, shortly after Louis XVI was beheaded.

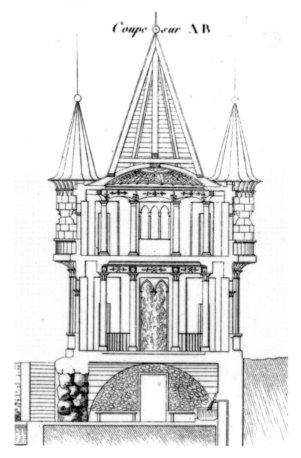

Coupe sur AB

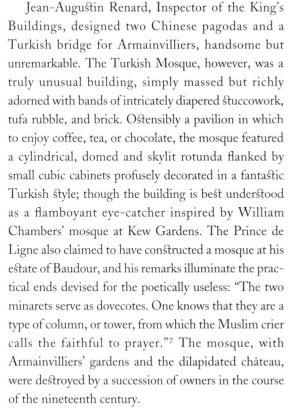

VISITOR'S GUIDE

Many of the pavilions presented in this book have been destroyed, and several are privately owned. However, a number of buildings are open to the public, and those listed below are well worth visiting; often they sit amid parks and gardens of rare beauty and great historical interest.

To aid the reader, the sites listed below follow the order of their presentation in the text. Access rules and dates vary widely, and many sites are closed from noon to two o'clock in the afternoon; telephone before visiting for current information.

LUXEMBOURG GROTTO
Jardin du Luxembourg
Entrances: rue de Médicis, rue de Vaugirard
75006 Paris
tel. 42 34 20 00
Today a popular Parisian park, site also of the Palais du Luxembourg, now the French Senate. Open daily, dawn to dusk.

GROTTO AT RICHELIEU
Château de Richelieu
37520 Richelieu
tel. 47 58 10 09
The grotto and a remaining pavilion of the château may be visited daily from the first week of June to the first week of September.

GROTTO AT MAISONS
Château de Maisons
78600 Maisons-Lafitte
tel. 39 62 01 49
Guided visits through the château are offered. Open daily from April to October, closed holidays and Saturdays during winter months.

MARLY
Musée Promenade de Marly-le-Roi-Louveciennes
Parc de Marly
78430 Louveciennes
tel. 39 69 06 26
Though Marly's major structures are destroyed, the outlines of its park have been preserved as a haunting monument, open daily from sunrise to sunset. The Musée Promenade (open Wednesday to Sunday afternoons, excluding holidays) offers concise exhibits of Marly and Madame Du Barry's Music Pavilion at Louveciennes.

AURORA PAVILION AT SCEAUX
Musée de l'Île-de-France, Château de Sceaux
92330 Sceaux
tel. 46 61 06 71
The park is open daily, dawn to dusk; the museum is open Wednesday to Sunday, excepting holidays; and the Cascade runs daily in the summer months. Permission to visit the interior of the Aurora Pavilion must be obtained in advance by writing the Conservateur of the Museum. The site of the Menagerie Pavilion—and its entrance columns—have also been preserved.

THE BUTARD HUNTING PAVILION
Entrance: route des Puits, off highway N307
La Celle Saint Cloud
Butard may only be seen from the exterior, though it is used periodically for art exhibitions.

CRÉCY
Association de Sauvegarde de l'Ancien Domaine de Crécy
Résidence Dreux Panoramic
28100 Dreux
tel. 37 46 48 64
Crécy-Couvé is today a small village around the outlines of the ancient domain, of which little remains. It is highly recommended that one contact the Association to view the site; much of it is now private property.

BAGATELLE
Parc de Bagatelle
Route de Sèvres à Neuilly
Bois de Boulogne
75016 Paris
tel. 40 71 75 23
The extensive landscape park of Bagatelle is open daily, sunrise to sunset. Guided tours of the Château de Bagatelle are offered from April to October, in the afternoons on Saturday, Sunday, and public holidays.

FOLLY SAINT-JAMES
Lycée La Folie Saint-James
32–34, Avenue de Madrid
Neuilly sur Seine
Today a school, the Folly Saint-James and the Grand Grotto on its grounds may be visited in tours organized by the Caisse National des Monuments Historiques, periodically announced in Parisian newspapers and weekly city guides.

MUSIC PAVILION AT MONTREUIL
Avenue de Paris
78000 Versailles
Private property
Though it cannot be visited, the exterior of the Music Pavilion is easily viewed from the sidewalk, incongruously set amid a Victorian housing development.

BELVEDERE IN THE BALBI GARDENS
Parc de Balbi
Rue du Maréchal Joffre
78000 Versailles
tel. 39 50 36 22
The park abuts the Potager du Roi (The King's Kitchen Garden), itself worthy of a visit. Open year-round in the afternoons, except Monday and Tuesday. The Belvedere's interior is closed to the public.

PARC MONCEAU
Boulevard de Courcelles
75008 Paris
tel. 42 94 08 08
Open daily, dawn to dusk. Though most of its follies have been lost, the Parc Monceau, set in an elegant neighborhood, is a well-manicured garden oasis. Note the surviving pyramid, Colonnade, Grotto, and the Pavillon de Chartres, a tempietto by Ledoux.

DÉSERT DE RETZ
78240 Chambourcy
tel. 39 76 90 37
*Visits the fourth Saturday of the month from March to October at 2:30 and 4 p.m. by appointment. For more information, contact:
Société Civile du Désert de Retz
La Maison de Joséphine
6, bis Grande Rue
78290 Croissy-sur-Seine
tel. 39 76 90 37*

ERMENONVILLE
Parc Jean-Jacques Rousseau
1, rue René de Girardin
60950 Ermenonville
tel. 44 54 01 58
The extensive park is open daily, afternoons from May to September, excepting Tuesdays. In winter months, telephone in advance for opening times.

PAGODA OF CHANTELOUP
1 km south of Amboise on highway D31
Private property.
Open daily, Palm Sunday to 30 September. The guard pavilions and the pagoda are all that remain of the domain of Chanteloup. The latter is an extraordinary and affecting monument, easily integrated into a tour of the Loire valley châteaux.

CHINESE PAVILION AT CASSAN
Rue de Beaumont
95290 L'Isle-Adam
tel. 34 08 19 19
Situated in a small public park at the outskirts of the town of L'Isle-Adam, open daily, dawn to dusk. The interior of the pavilion is closed to the public.

RAMBOUILLET
Domaine National de Rambouillet
78120 Rambouillet
tel. 34 83 02 49
Though the Pagoda at Rambouillet is destroyed, the park boasts several fascinating follies, including Marie-Antoinette's Dairy and the Shell Pavilion, a simple thatched cottage with a breathtaking shellwork interior. The park is open daily from dawn to dusk; the pavilions are visited by guided tour, closed Tuesday and Wednesday. The château is a residence of the President of France and may not always be visited; hours vary.

VERSAILLES AND TRIANON
Domaine National de Versailles et de Trianon
78000 Versailles
tel. 60 66 97 09
The courts and gardens of Versailles and the Trianon are open from dawn to dusk daily; admission is charged when the fountains run, accompanied by period music—Sundays from May to early October—and for periodic special events. The Château de Versailles and the Grand and Petit Trianons are open daily, excepting Mondays and official holidays; a variety of guided and unguided tours are offered.
The Bosquet of Fame or Bosquet des Dômes and the Grotto of the Baths of Apollo may only be viewed on Sundays when the fountains play. The buildings at Trianon, including the Hameau, have unrestricted access, though their interiors are closed to the public. The gardens are best savored in the late afternoon and early evening, when crowds have vanished and a magical twilight slowly descends.

All foreign language quotations have been translated by the authors unless otherwise stated in these notes. Several period memoirs are widely reprinted; therefore dates of composition and/or page numbers have been cited to aid reference.

INTRODUCTION

Introductory quotation: Friar Claude Buffier, quoted in Prince de Ligne, "Introduction," *Coup d'œil sur Beloeil et sur une grande partie des jardins de l'Europe*, Basil Guy, trans. and ed. (Berkeley: University of California Press, 1991) [Beloeil: Ligne, 1781], p. 73. All quotations of the Prince de Ligne appear in this edition.

PART I
LOUIS XIII AND THE REIGN OF THE CARDINALS:
A *COUP D'ŒIL* AT ITALY

Introductory quotation: Cardinal Mazarin on his deathbed, 9 March 1661, quoted in Brienne Le Jeune, *Mémoires*, vol. II, appearing in Paul Guth, *Mazarin* (Paris: Flammarion, 1972), p. 768.

CHAPTER 1
THE MEDICI LEGACY

Introductory quotation: Marie de Medici, letter of 6 October 1611 from Fontainebleau. (Florence: Uffizi, Archivio Mediceo, 5935; 6c; 27/28).

1 Voltaire, *Le Siècle de Louis XIV, Oeuvres Complètes* (Geneva: Institut et Musée Voltaire, 1969), vol. XVI, p. 174. Unless otherwise stated, all quotations of Voltaire appear in this edition.

2 Gédéon Tallemant des Réaux, *Les Historiettes*, 2nd ed., M. Monmerqué, ed. (Paris: Delloye, 1840), vol. I, p. 83. Though anachronistic, since banknotes were not yet in use, this translation of "votre grosse banquière" best captures Madame de Verneuil's spiteful double entendre, addressed to Henri IV.

3 Thomas Francini's son François would later be instrumental in creating the fountains of Versailles, and the family would hold royal positions involving fountains until the Revolution. For a lucid discussion of this ubiquitous family's activities, see Kenneth Woodbridge, *Princely Gardens* (New York: Rizzoli, 1986), p. 124.

4 Marc Fumaroli, "Introduction," in Pierre Rosenberg, *France in the Golden Age* (New York: Metropolitan Museum of Art, 1982), p. 5.

5 The queen built the palace very near the town home of her acquaintances the Gondi family; these financiers were bankrupted by their services to the crown, and Marie de Medici bought the Hôtel Gondi to make amends, offering it as yet another ineffectual bribe to the Prince de Condé. Bourbons would also buy Saint-Cloud and the land for Versailles from the family. See: Alfred Marie, *Naissance de Versailles* (Paris: Vincent, Fréal & Cie., 1968).

6 Antoine-Nicolas Dézallier d'Argenville, *Vie des fameux architectes* (Paris: Buré l'Aîné, 1787), vol. I, p. 327. Salomon de Brosse was the son of the architect to Henri IV's first queen and Marie de Medici's own engineer since her arrival in France.

7 Marie-Noëlle Badouin-Matuszek, *Marie de Médicis et le Palais du Luxembourg* (Paris: Ville de Paris, 1991), p. 190.

8 The Queen Mother urged Louis XIII to appoint the cardinal a counselor in 1624; Richelieu quickly achieved independent stature and formulated policy in opposition to the Queen Mother. In 1629 he allowed passage of an edict construed as promoting religious liberty—abhorrent to Marie de Medici, a *dévote*. She also believed Richelieu had turned France against Catholic Spain while slighting domestic programs, and blindly forced an ultimatum—mother or minister—upon her son, who saw the future through Richelieu's eyes, forcing her banishment.

9 An anonymous early plan, annotated in Italian, in the Cabinet des Estampes at the Bibliothèque Nationale (Est. Va. 419J, fol. 13), indicates a grotto projected just beyond the hemicycle that ends the axis, though this Grotto of Demogorgon was never built.

10 The current statues date from 1862, when the grotto was moved to its present location. An engraving by Jean Marot depicts three vases atop the arched pediment, but in view of the inaccuracy of many period engravings and the queen's exile before the grotto was completed, it is doubtful they were ever executed.

11 In gratitude, the queen granted Thomas Francini a pension of twelve hundred *livres* and half the water his project brought to her gardens—itself a lucrative reward which the ingenious engineer ran across the Pont Neuf to feed a fountain on the Right Bank. Document of 11 November 1628 (Paris. Archives Nationales, o¹-1595, pièce 13). See also: Albert Mousset, "Les Francine . . .", in *Mémoires de la Société de l'histoire de Paris et de l'Île-de-France*, vol. LI (Paris, 1930).

12 Alexandre Francini, *Livre d'Architecture, contenant plusieurs portiques . . .* (Paris, 1631).

13 A dispute over the accuracy of its common name, the Luxembourg Grotto, serves to focus attention upon two of the various forms of grottoes in the period. Some, such as those at Saint-Germain-en-Laye, Fontainebleau, and Meudon were arcaded substructures and an integral part of the architecture siting the château. Others at Wideville and Luxembourg stood at a distance from the château and, flanked by walls, featured compact, highly decorative facades that served to terminate garden axes. The celebrated grotto at Vaux-le-Vicomte, designed by André Le Nôtre later in the century, was a hybrid form (a long, bayed structure removed from the château without an interior) which in reality is a highly embellished retaining wall.

CHAPTER 2
SOURCES OF WEALTH:
THE NYMPHÆUM AT WIDEVILLE

Introductory quotation: *Fortis Superenatat Undas*.

1 Tallemant des Réaux, *Les Historiettes*, vol. II, p. 197.

2 Revenues were tightly proscribed: the First Estate (the Catholic Church), the largest landowner, offered a gift of a fraction of its income, but was exempt from taxation, as was the Second Estate (the nobility). Much of the king's revenues passed to the nobility in the form of hereditary offices and royal gifts, in exchange for fealty and wartime service. The Third Estate (the bourgeoisie and the peasantry) bore the main financial burden of the kingdom.

3 Claude Fregnac, *Châteaux de l'Île-de-France* (Paris: Hachette, 1963), p. 175. Louis d'or—gold coins bearing the king's likeness—were first minted under Bullion's administration.

4 Nicolas Fouquet was a Finance Minister installed by Mazarin. His arrogance, daring, and lust for power—he expected to rule France as First Minister—lead Louis XIV to arrest him on charges of treason and embezzlement shortly after inaugurating Vaux-le-Vicomte with a splendid fete in August 1661. After a celebrated but indecisive trial, Fouquet was banished for life by the king.

5 For a further discussion, see: Vincent Scully, *Architecture: The Natural and the Man-Made* (New York: Saint Martin's Press, 1991).

6 Marguerite Charageat, "Le Nymphée de Wideville et la Grotte du Luxembourg," *Bulletin de la Société de l'Histoire de l'Art Français* (Paris, 1934), pp. 16–31.

7 The invention of Philibert Delorme. See: Charageat, op. cit.

8 The Gondi had built elaborate grottoes at their estates at Saint-Cloud and Noisy-le-Sec.

9 Anthony Blunt, *Art and Architecture in France: 1500 to 1700*, 2nd ed. (Baltimore: Penguin Books, 1970), p. 188.

10 Vicomtesse de Galard, "Wideville," *Versailles Illustré*, no. 86 (Versailles, May 1903), pp. 13–19.

11 Louis XIII, letter of 23 December 1640, quoted in Vicomtesse de Galard, *Lettres de Louis XIII à Richelieu* (Paris: Société des Bibliophiles Français, 1903), mélanges 2, p. 27.

CHAPTER 3
"WHAT GOES ON THERE?"
THE GROTTOES AT RICHELIEU AND RUEIL

Introductory quotation: Voltaire, vol. LXXXV, p. 111.

1 Gédéon Tallemant des Réaux, *Le Cardinal de Richelieu* (Paris: Éditions Bossard, 1920), p. 52.

2 Mademoiselle de Montpensier, *Mémoires* (Paris: Librairie Fontaine, 1985), p. 32.

3 And following citation, Tallemant des Réaux, *Richelieu* , pp. 65–66.

4 Montpensier, op. cit., pp. 31–32.

5 Jean de La Fontaine, letter of 5 September 1663, *Lettres de Jean de La Fontaine à sa femme* (Paris: Hachette, 1892), vol. IX, p. 254; and following, letter of 12 September 1663, p. 262.

6 Voltaire, letter of 25 October 1721 to Claude Thiériot, vol. LXXXV, p. 111.

7 John Evelyn, entry of 27 February 1644, *Diary, from 1641 to 1705–1706*, William Bray, ed. (London: W.W. Gibbings, 1890), p. 50.

8 Tallemant des Réaux, *Les Historiettes*, vol. II, p. 206.

9 Richelieu was referring to Fleury-en-Brière, a château where he often stayed during Louis XIII's summer voyages to Fontainebleau. Quoted in Alfred Cramail, *Le Château de Rueil et ses jardins* (Fontainebleau: Éditions Bourges, 1888), p. 10.

10 Peter Heylyn, *The Voyage of France* (London: Leake, 1673).

11 Tallemant des Réaux, *Le Cardinal de Richelieu*, p. 123.

12 _____, *Les Historiettes*, vol. IV, p. 186.

13 Heylyn, op. cit.

14 Cramail, op. cit., p. 9.

15 Woodbridge, op. cit., p. 151.

16 Père Papin de la Société de Jesus, *Les jardins, poème en quatre chants*, S.M. Gazon Dourxigné, trans. (Paris: Cailleau, 1773), chant III, p. 174. Away from these impressive set-pieces along the Grande Allée were two large ponds: the first was secluded amid groves of trees and featured an artificial island where exotic waterbirds nested; the second formed a water parterre before the manor.

17 Jean-Marie Pérouse de Montclos, ed., *Le Guide du Patrimoine: l'Île-de-France*, (Paris: Hachette, 1992), p. 558. Bernard Chevalier in this guide credits Jean Séjourné with building the grotto in 1608.

18 Louis Huygens, quoted in Henri L. Brugmans, "Châteaux et jardins d'Île-de-France d'après un journal de voyage de 1655," *Gazette des Beaux-Arts*, fifth series, vol. XVIII (Paris, September 1937), pp. 93–114. The original manuscript is held at the Royal Academy of Sciences, Amsterdam.

19 Elias Brackenhoffer, *Voyage de Paris en Italie, 1644–46*, Henri Lehr, trans. (Strasbourg: Berger-Levraut, 1927),
p. 39. (After the manuscript held at the Musée Historique de Strasbourg.)

20 Woodbridge op. cit., p. 151.

21 Duchesse d'Aiguillon, quoted in Cramail op. cit., p. 27.

22 Brackenhoffer op. cit., p. 40.

CHAPTER 4
THE TEMPLE OF TASTE: THE GROTTO AT MAISONS

Introductory quotation: Charles Perrault, *Les Hommes illustres* (Paris: A. Dézallier, 1701), vol. I, p. 87.

1 Georges Poisson, *De Maisons-sur-Seine à Maisons-Lafitte*, 3rd ed. (Maisons-Lafitte: Association de Sauvegarde de Maisons-Lafitte, 1993), p. 29. This volume is recommended as a comprehensive history of the estate of Maisons.

2 Ibid., p. 30.

3 Anonymous, "La Mansarade," *Archives de l'Art Français*, 2nd series, 1862, vol. II, p. 246.

4 The Parlement of Paris was a regional judicial body, not a legislature, and its most important legal role was to register royal edicts. Since their titles derived solely from their judicial offices, *parlementaires* were known as the Nobility of the Robe, as opposed to the Nobility of the Sword—the ancient landed families who composed the court and the highest echelons of French society.

5 Longueil traced his ancestry to a certain Adam de Longueil who had distinguished himself in the Battle of Hastings in 1066. Saint-Simon, an extremely conscientious pedant concerning rank and precedence, fiercely disputed Longueil's claim, remarking that the family "descended recently from a wayward hussar from the village of Longueil, in Normandy, which is filled with nonsense titles." Duc de Saint-Simon, *Mémoires*, A. de Boisisle, ed. (Paris: Hachette, 1879), vol. XXVI, p. 20. All quotations of Saint-Simon appear in this edition.

6 Guy Patin, letter CCXVIII, *Lettres* (Paris: Éditions Réveille-Parise, 1846), vol. II, p. 21.

7 Jean Loret, letter of 23 April 1651, *La Muse Historique* (Paris: P. Jannet, 1857–1878), vol. I, book II, p. 111.

8 Voltaire, vol. XIV, p. 26.

9 Poisson, op. cit., p. 48.

10 Voltaire, "Le Temple du goût," vol. VIII, p. 561.

Simple en état la noble architecture
Chaque ornement à sa place arrêté,
Y semblait mis par la nécessité;
L'art s'y cachait sous l'air de la nature,
L'œil satisfait apercevait sa structure,
Jamais surpris et toujours enchanté.

11 Denis Diderot, quoted in Cyril Connolly and Jerome Zerbe, *Les Pavillons* (New York: Macmillan, 1962), p. 22. All quotations of Connolly appear in this edition.

PART II
LOUIS XIV: AN AGE OF MAGNIFICENCE

Introductory quotation: Louis XIV as quoted in Jean Racine, "Fragments Historiques," *Œuvres Complètes*, 2nd ed., l'Aîné-Martin, ed. (Paris: Lefêvre, 1822), vol. V, p. 300.

CHAPTER 5
"QUELQUE CHOSE DE PLUS MAGNIFIQUE": THE GROTTO OF THÉTIS AND THE BOSQUET OF FAME AT VERSAILLES

Introductory quotation: *Instructions au duc d'Anjou*, quoted in Michel Déon, *Louis XIV par lui-même* (Paris: Gallimard, 1991), p. 95.

1 The sons of Thomas Francini; their family name was modified to the French *de Francine*. See: A. Mousset, op. cit.

2 Charles Perrault, *Mémoires de ma vie*, P. Bonnefon, ed. (Paris: Macula, 1993), p. 208.

3 A. Marie, op. cit., vol. I, pp. 65–80.

4 André Félibien, *Description de la grotte de Versailles* (Paris: J. Desprez, 1676), p. 2, and following, p. 7.

5 Mademoiselle de Scudéry, *La Promenade de Versailles . . .* (Paris: Barbin, 1669), p. 77. All quotations of Mademoiselle de Scudéry appear in this edition.

6 Félibien, op. cit., p. 1.

7 *La Gazette de France*, (Paris, 11 August 1669).

8 P. Bourget and G. Cattaui, *Jules Hardouin-Mansart* (Paris: Vincent, Fréal & Cie., 1960), p. 11.

9 Saint-Simon, vol. XVI, p. 40.

10 Cf. Giovanni Battista Falda, *Le fontane de Roma . . .* (Rome: C.G. de Rossi, c. 1674–1682). A note [appearing in Jean-Baptiste Colbert, *Lettres, Instructions et Mémoires* (Paris: Imprimerie Impériale, 1861–1882), vol. V, letter 140, p. 382, citing *Travaux*

Hydrauliques de Versailles by M. Le Roi] states that: "In 1676 Louis XIV also ordered built, to Le Brun's drawings, a new basin given the name of Fame, due to the principal figure which was a Fame proclaiming to all the earth the king's glory. . . ."

11 Thomas Hedlin, *Gaspard and Balthazar Marsy* (Columbia: University of Missouri Press, 1983), p. 202.

12 Robert Berger, *In the Garden of the Sun King* (Washington, D.C.: Dumbarton Oaks, 1985), p. 13.

13 Colbert's contract of 24 August 1679 with the metalworker Ladoireau offers a fascinating insight into the scope of just one portion of the work and illustrates the minister's outstanding managerial talents: "[To render] bespoke panels, to provide the plaster forms, the polish wax, the materials, the moldings; to do the gilding and to provide the gold necessary for the mentioned work and to achieve the vermeil color of the bronze, to polish and to put [the finished plaques] in place, and in general to provide all the expenses necessary to deliver the work as good and perfect as the baluster at the staircase of Versailles." (Paris: Archives Nationales, 0I 1790–1).

14 Marquis de Dangeau, entry of 15 May 1685, *Journal*, Soulié, Dussieux, de Chennevières, eds. (Paris: Firmin Didot Frères, 1854–1860). All quotations of the Marquis de Dangeau appear in this edition.

15 Ibid., entry of 7 July 1684.

CHAPTER 6
A KING'S INDULGENCE: THE PAVILIONS AT THE VERSAILLES MENAGERIE

Introductory quotation: An inscription from an engraving by Nicolas de Fer, 1705.

1 Louis XIV, letter of 4 November 1696 to Madame de Maintenon, quoted in Déon, p. 306.

2 Madame, letter of 1 October 1687 to the Duchesse de Hanovre, Ernest Jaegle, ed., *Correspondance de Madame, duchesse d'Orléans* (Paris: Emile Bouillon Librarie, 1890), vol. I, p. 59. Unless otherwise noted, all quotations of Madame appear in this edition.

3 Trictrac is a French variant of backgammon. See: Abbé S***, *Le Grand Trictrac*, 2nd ed. (Avignon: Alexandre Giroud, 1756).

4 Madame de Maintenon, quoted in Voltaire, vol. XIV, p. 473.

5 Saint-Simon, vol. XXII, p. 282.

6 Madame, letter of 31 March 1701, vol. I, p. 236.

7 Madame de Noyer, *Lettres Historiques et Galantes* (Amsterdam: P. Brunel, 1720), vol. I, letter 26, p. 261.

8 Dangeau, entry of 19 May 1698, and following citation, entry of 25 May 1698.

9 Duchesse de Bourgogne, letter of 2 July 1698, Princess Maria della Rocca, ed., *Correspondance inédite de la duchesse de Bourgogne et de la Reine d'Espagne* (Paris: Michel Levy Frères, 1865), p. 26.

10 For a thorough description of the Versailles Menagerie, see Gérard Mabille, "La Ménagerie de Versailles," in *Gazette des Beaux-Arts*, vol. I (Paris, January 1974), pp. 5–36.

11 Beneath the salon was a sunken grotto whose remains could still be seen at the turn of the century. Vaulted, with richly patterned walls, it was encrusted throughout with shellwork and shards of colored stones. A fountain splashed in an octagonal basin and water shot from holes in the floor, creating the illusion of thousands of rain drops. Pipes also ran to the ceiling, and it is doubtful whether every visitor was delighted with the fontainiers' ingenuity. See Georges-Louis Le Rouge, *Les curiositez de Paris, de Versailles, de Marly, . . .* (Paris: Saugrain Père, 1733), vol. II, pp. 206–208.

12 Scudéry, p. 95.

13 Fiske Kimball, "Le décor du Château de la Ménagerie," in *Gazette des Beaux-Arts* (Paris, 1936), vol. II, pp. 245–256.

14 Louis XIV, letter of 10 September 1699 to Jules Hardouin-Mansart from Fontainebleau, quoted in Fiske Kimball, op. cit., p. 252.

15 See: J. J. Marquet de Vasselot, *La Ménagerie du Château de Versailles, la Grotte et les Pavillons* (Versailles: Léon Bernard, 1899).

16 Dangeau, entry of 23 July 1705.

17 Saint-Simon, vol. XXII, p. 283.

18 Duc de Luynes, entry of 23 August 1750, *Mémoires sur la cour de Louis XV*, L. Dussieux and E. Soulis, eds. (Paris: Firmin Didot Frères, 1860–1865). All quotations of the Duc de Luynes appear in this edition.

CHAPTER 7
MARLY

Introductory quotation: Racine, *Oeuvres Complètes*, 2nd ed., vol. VI, p. 202.

1 And following, Saint-Simon, vol. XXVIII, p. 170.

2 Cronström, letter of 1699 to Nicodemus Tessin, quoted in Ian Dunlop, *Royal Palaces of France* (New York: W.W. Norton, 1985), p. 160.

3 Saint-Simon, vol. XXXI, p. 59.

4 Madame Campan, *Mémoires sur la vie privée de Marie Antoinette* (Paris: Ramsay Image, 1979), p. 113. All quotations of Madame Campan appear in this edition.

5 Abbé Jacques Delille, *Les Jardins . . .* (Paris: Didot l'Aîné, 1782), chant I, p. 29.

6 At Cardinal Richelieu's estate of Rueil, a famed trompe-l'œil wall painting of a Roman triumphal arch in false perspective abutted one end of the Orangerie. At Marly, on a blank wall directly on the cross axis with the King's Pavilion, a large trompe-l'œil painting of a peristyle by Jacques Rousseau hid offices and gave the building its name, The Perspective.

7 The series of Le Brun's gouaches are held in the collection of the Musée des Arts Décoratifs, Paris. Preliminary sketches of facades are held in the Département des Arts Graphiques in the Louvre.

8 Both paintings are in the collection of the Musée de Versailles, inv. nos. 741 and 762.

9 These watercolored elevations are held in the Cabinet des Estampes at the Bibliothèque Nationale.

10 The Salle des Hoquetons at Versailles was decorated in 1672 with a trompe-l'œil interior that is strikingly similar to the facades of Marly.

11 Diderot, letter of 10 May 1759 to Mlle. Volland, *Œuvres Complètes*, J. Assézat, ed. (Paris: Garnier Frères, 1875), vol. XVIII, p. 23. All quotations of Diderot to follow appear in this edition.

12 For a thorough discussion of the genesis of the decorative schemes for the Courtiers' Pavilions and Le Brun's involvement in Marly's design, see Robert W. Berger, "On the Origins of Marly," *Zeitschrift für Kunstgesichte*, vol. 56, no. 4 (Deutscher Kunstverlag, 1993), pp. 534–543.

13 Madame, letter of 2 August 1705 to Raugräfin Louise, vol. II, p. 31.

14 Diderot, letter of 23 September 1762 to Mlle. Volland, vol. XIX, p. 135.

15 Madame de Maintenon, letter of 25 November 1700 to the Cardinal de Noailles, quoted in *Mémoires et lettres de Madame de Maintenon* (Maestricht: J.E. Doufour and P. Roux, 1778), vol. IV, letter CLXVI, p. 227.

16 Madame, letter of 6 July 1702 to the Duchesse de Hanovre, vol. I, p. 269.

17 Louis XIV, quoted in M. Déon, p. 267.

18 We are indebted to Georges Gibault's informative and amusing essay, "Les Carpes de Marly," in *Le Vieux Marly* (Marly, 1932–1940), vol. I, pp. 209–214.

19 Verse appearing in Sautreau de Marsy, *Le Nouveau Siècle de Louis XIV* (Paris: F. Buisson, 1793), vol. IV, p. 336.

A Marly paroit un courier
Que l'on devoit expédier,
Mais l'huissier qui garde la porte
Lui dit: "Retirez-vous d'ici!
La carpe favorite est morte,
On ne reçoit personne aujourd'hui!"

20 Marly has inspired many architects, most prominently Thomas Jefferson and his design for the University of Virginia. Schloss Clemenswerth near Sögel in northern Germany is the most complete and evocative surviving interpretation of Marly in Europe.

CHAPTER 8
FIDELITY AND INTRIGUE:
THE AURORA AND
MENAGERIE PAVILIONS
AT SCEAUX

Introductory quotation: Perrault, *Les Hommes illustres*, vol. I, p. 83.

1 Ines Murat, *Colbert* (Paris: Fayard, 1984). We are indebted to this excellent biography for details of Colbert's private life and the description of the evening fête of 1677.

2 Chamfort, *Oeuvres Complètes de Chamfort* (Paris: Colnet, 1803), vol. II, p. 173. For more information on (the lack of) hygiene at Versailles, see *Le Temps: Versailles au Siècle de Louis XIV* (Paris: Réunion des Musées Nationaux, 1993).

3 Quoted in Murat, p. 358.

4 *Mercure gallant* (Paris, July 1685).

5 Letter of Louis XIV of 18 May 1674, "Encamped before Besançon," quoted in M. Déon, p. 80.

6 Saint-Simon, vol. XXVIII, p. 162.

7 Letters of Louis XIV, May 1674 and 29 September 1673, quoted in Murat, p. 327.

8 F. Hamilton Hazlehurst, *Gardens of Illusion* (Nashville: Vanderbilt University Press, 1980), p. 233.

9 *Mercure galant* (Paris, July 1685).

10 Hazlehurst, op. cit., p. 246.

11 Georges Poisson, *Le Pavillon de l'Aurore* (Sceaux: Musée de l'Île-de-France, n.d.), p. 2.

12 Jean Mariette, *Architecture françoise*, 4 vols. (Paris: Mariette, 1727).

13 Mademoiselle de Nantes, quoted in G. Rousset-Charny, *Guide du Patrimoine*, p. 622.

14 Madame de Sévigné, letter of 1 December 1690, *Lettres de Madame de Sévigné*, M. Monmerqué, ed. (Paris: Hachette, 1925), vol. IX, p. 589.

15 Saint-Simon, vol. XV, p. 19, and following, p. 21.

16 Madame, letter of 11 October 1718, *Correspondance Complète de Madame Duchesse d'Orléans* (Paris: Charpentier, 1857), vol. II, p. 13.

17 Antoine-Nicolas Dezallier d'Argenville, *Voyage pittoresque des environs de Paris . . .*, 4th ed. (Paris: Buré l'Aîné, 1779), part II, p. 221.

18 Unattributed, quoted by Poisson, p. 9.

19 A. Panthier, "La Vie au Château de Sceaux," *Bulletin: "Amis de Sceaux"* 2nd year (Sceaux 1926), p. 26

20 C.F. Gaignat de l'Aunay, *Promenade de Sceaux-Penthièvre . . .* (Amsterdam and Paris: P. Fr. Gueffier, 1778), p. 63.

21 Voltaire, quoted in G. Rousset-Charny, op. cit., p. 622.

PART III
LOUIS XV AND MADAME
DE POMPADOUR:
THE AGE OF INTIMACY

Introductory quotation: *Lettres de Madame de Pompadour* (London: Owen, 1774), vol. II, letter 56, pp. 40–41.

1 Connolly and Zerbe, p. 3.

2 Louis XV, quoted in André Castelot, *Madame Du Barry* (Paris: Perrin, 1989), p. 96.

CHAPTER 9
L'ART DE VIVRE:
THE PAVILION FOR THE
DAUPHIN, THE FRENCH
PAVILION, AND
THE PETIT TRIANON
AT VERSAILLES

Introductory quotation: Abel Dechêne, *Le Dauphin, Fils de Louis XV* (Paris: Librairie Dauphin, 1931), p. 23.

1 Ibid, p. 36.

2 Anonymous, *Manuscrit de la Mairie de Montdidier* (Montdidier, 21 July 1739).

3 Anonymous, "La Chanson de Pommard," in *Bulletin du Syndicat d'Initiative et de Tourisme de Dijon et de la Côte d'Or*, no. 55 (July–August 1959).

4 Jean-Aymar Piganiol de La Force, *Description de Versailles . . .*, 7th ed. (Paris: G. Desprez, 1738), vol. II, pp. 187–191.

5 Millet, known as Francisque le fils, quoted in Pierre de Nolhac, *Histoire du Château de Versailles: Versailles au XVIIIᵉ siècle* (Paris: Emile-Paul Frères, 1918), vol. III, p. 157.

6 Jacques-François Blondel, *Architecture Françoise* (Paris: Jombert, 1756), vol. IV, p. 104.

7 Duc de Croÿ, entry of 18 January 1754, *Journal inédit du duc de Croÿ 1718–1784* (Paris: Grouchy & Cotton, 1906–1907), vol. I. All quotations of the Duc de Croÿ appear in this edition.

8 Ibid., entry of 1–2 January 1751.

9 Margaret Trouncer, *The Pompadour* (London: Hutchinson, 1956), p. 215.

10 A notable example of this move to geometric figuration was Germain Soufflot's church of Sainte-Geneviève, begun in 1756, seven years after Gabriel's French Pavilion, whose plan was also based upon a Greek cross.

11 Christopher Tadgell, *Ange-Jacques Gabriel* (London: Zwemmer, 1978), p. 41.

12 Bernini's plan is illustrated in Allan Braham and Peter Smith, *François Mansart* (London: Zwemmer, 1973), vol. II, plate 450.

13 Comte de Fels, *Ange-Jacques Gabriel, premier architecte du roi* (Paris: Émile-Paul Frères, 1912), p. 154.

14 Allan Braham, *The Architecture of the French Enlightenment* (Berkeley: University of California Press, 1980), p. 39.

15 These "flying tables" were to descend from the dining room and the buffet to the basement kitchens, and the resulting holes were to be covered by radial metal lenses, but the work seems never to have been executed—despite a persistent legend grown around them—due to the ever-precarious state of the royal finances. A model was exhibited in 1769 and Pierre de Nolhac (*Le Trianon de Marie Antoinette*, Paris: Levy, 1927, pp. 66–68) writes confidently of their use and states that the remains of counterweights were then to be seen in the basement of the Petit Trianon. However, the Marquis de Marigny, Controller of the King's Buildings, authorized Loriot to be paid for his design in March 1772, writing "circumstances seem, Monsieur, not to be able to permit for some time the execution of the mechanical tables that

you invented for the new Trianon" (Paris: Archives Nationales, O1 1883). Tadgell (*Gabriel*, p. 126) believes the tables never were installed, and Christian Baulez, Conservateur at Versailles, has confirmed this in correspondence. An inevitable conclusion, given the monarchy's financial disarray and Louis XV's death little more than two years after Marigny's letter.

16 Pierre de Nolhac, *Le Trianon de Marie Antoinette*, p. 55.

CHAPTER 10
LA CHASSE:
THE HERMITAGES
OF MADAME
DE POMPADOUR

Introductory quotation: Madame de Pompadour, *Letters* (London: Owen, 1774), vol. III, p. 20.

1 Nancy Mitford, *Madame de Pompadour* (New York: Harper & Row, 1968), p. 179.

2 Pompadour, letter of 12 January 1753 to her father, *Correspondance de Madame de Pompadour* (Paris: J. Baur, 1878), p. 19. Unless otherwise noted, all quotations of Madame de Pompadour appear in this edition.

3 Ibid., letter of 25 September 1758 to the Duc d'Aiguillon, p. 137.

4 Ibid., letter of 12 January 1753 to her father, p. 19.

5 Ibid., letter of 27 February 1749 to Madame de Lutzelbourg, p. 102.

6 Croÿ, entry of 1–2 January 1751.

7 Luynes, entry of 8 October 1749.

8 All authorities writing on Gabriel have different opinions; like paintings produced in an atelier, the work of a major architect owes a great debt to many, often anonymous, hands. For a lucid discussion of the duties of the First Architect to the King, see: C. Tadgell.

9 Tadgell, op. cit., p. 140.

10 And following, Campan, p. 17.

11 Duc de Richelieu, *Nouveaux Mémoires du maréchal duc de Richelieu*, A. M. de Lescure, ed. (Paris: E. Dentu, 1869), vol. IV, "Gennevilliers."

12 Edward Christen, "Le Butard," *Revue de l'histoire de Versailles et de Seine-et-Oise* (1926), pp. 7–30. We are indebted to this essay for details of the royal hunt.

13 Claude Saint-André, *Madame Du Barry* (Paris: Émile-Paul Frères, 1909), p. 124.

14 Plans of these hunting pavilions are preserved in the Archives Nationales in

Paris. The existence of the house in Versailles was signaled by Jean Bastien in conversation.

15 As originally built, the room to the right of the entry was a kitchen, while to the left was a small bathroom and a staircase which led to a bed and dressing room above and cellars below.

16 The aristocracy, it should be recalled, was still a warrior class; though badly out of practice, noblemen commanded the armies and fought and often died in battle, and Louis XV and the Dauphin were nearly overrun at the notorious battle of Fontenoy in 1745.

17 The plan of the compound is reproduced in Ingrid Dennerlein, *Die Gartenkunst der Regence und des Rokoko in Frankreich* (Worms: Werner'sche Verlagsgesellschaft, 1981), pp. 139–147. We are indebted to the author for much of this discussion of Compiègne's successive hermitages.

18 Jean-Nicolas Dufort, *Comte de Cheverny, Mémoires sur les règnes des Louis XV et XVI*, R. de Crèvecoeur, ed. (Paris: Plon, 1886), vol. I., pp. 117–119. All quotations of the Comte de Cheverny appear in this edition.

19 Jean Bastien, "Les Hermitages," in *Madame de Pompadour et la Floraison des Arts* (Montreal: David M. Stewart Museum, 1987), p. 100.

CHAPTER 11
CRÉCY

Introductory quotation: Pompadour, *Correspondence*, p. 10.

1 We are deeply indebted to Madame Sabine and Monsieur Jean Bastien for their extraordinary help in sharing their vast knowledge of Crécy. As President of the Association de Sauvegarde de l'Ancien Domaine de Crécy, M. Bastien has graciously made his own findings available to us, explaining the estate *in situ*, and much that follows is informed by his excellent essay, "Le Roi chez madame de Pompadour," in *Madame de Pompadour et la Floraison des Arts*, op. cit. Crécy, at its height, absorbed a full third of the marquise's income.

2 Luynes, entry of 2 May 1746.

3 Pompadour, *Letters*, letter of 1748 to the Comtesse de Brézé (Owen), vol. I, p. 98. The same logic would confound Louis XV. Attempting to make economies after the disastrous Seven Years' War, he dismissed nearly a hundred royal gardeners, but when he was informed that these men had no

other work and dependant families that would starve, the king, thoroughly flustered, rehired them.

4 Kathleen Marie Russo, *Lassurance-the-Younger: Architect to Madame de Pompadour*, dissertation (Florida State University, 1976).

5 Luynes, entry of 29 May 1753.

6 Pompadour, quoted in J. Bastien, p. 89.

CHAPTER 12
SON EXCELLENCE
AT GENNEVILLIERS

Introductory quotation: Marquis d'Argenson, *Journal et Mémoires* (Paris: Veuve J. Renouard, 1859–1867), vol. VII, p. 283.

1 Olga Wormser, *Amours et Intrigues du Maréchal de Richelieu* (Paris: Le Club Français du Livre, 1955), p. 49.

2 Louis XVI as Dauphin, quoted in Hubert Cole, *First Gentleman of the Bedchamber* (London: Heinemann, 1965), p. 255.

3 *Mémoires du président Hénault*, François Rousseau, ed. (Paris: Hachette, 1911), p. 124.

4 Horace Walpole, letter of 5 December 1765 to Henry Seymour Conway, *The Yale Edition of Horace Walpole's Correspondence* (New Haven: Yale University Press, 1937–1938), vol. XXXIX, p. 35.

5 G. Imbert, Métra, et al. letter of 3 December 1778, *Correspondance secrète, politique et littéraire, ou Mémoires pour servir à l'Histoire des Cours, ses Sociétés et de la Littérature en France, depuis la Mort de Louis XV*, 7 vols. (London, 1787–1790), vol. VII, p. 154.

6 Richelieu, as quoted in Comte d'Allonville, *Mémoires Secrets, de 1770 à 1830* (Paris: Werdet, 1838–1845) vol. I, p. 178.

7 And following excerpt, Richelieu, op. cit.

8 A plan in the Bibliothèque Nationale (Rés. 6e D2484), drawn while the Duc d'Orléans owned Gennevilliers (1787–1789), presents a slightly modified—and probably more accurate—layout of the gardens than Labrière's plan (dated 1785), reproduced in Le Rouge's cahiers.

9 Richelieu, op. cit. Roque de Fillol visited a ruinous Gennevilliers in 1888, and noted that the pavilion's interior decor featured Venus and Love triumphant: four doves pulled their chariot, one pair driven by Cupid's mother, the other two with Mercury acting as postilion. Their reins were

flower garlands; diverse allegorical subjects intermingling with representations of the seasons completed the decor. See Roque de Fillol, *Histoire de la presqu'île de Gennevilliers et du Mont Valérien* (Asnières: Du Progrès, 1889).

CHAPTER 13
THE ORANGERIE AT COUBERT

Introductory quotation: Nancy Mitford, *The Sun King* (New York: Harper & Row, 1966) p. 20.

1 Suzy Rose, *Or, Oranges, Orangeries* (Paris: Ipomée-Albin Michel, 1993).

2 Salomon de Caus, *Hortus Palatinus* (Paris, 1620).

3 Jean de la Quintinie, *L'Instruction pour les jardins Fruitiers et Potagers* (Amsterdam, 1692).

4 Bernard's invitation was nothing more than a desperate attempt by Louis XIV to fund the War of the Spanish Succession: after Bernard's tour of the gardens, personally narrated by the king, the royal treasury magically filled.

5 G. Joudiou, "Coubert," *Cent Jardins à Paris et en Île-de-France* (Paris: Délégation à l'Action Artistique de la Ville de Paris, 1991), p. 112.

CHAPTER 14
MADAME DU BARRY AND LOUVECIENNES

Introductory quotation: Louis XV, quoted in Claude Nicolas Ledoux, *L'Architecture considérée sous le raport de l'art . . .* (Paris, 1804), p. 27.

1 Duc d'Harcourt, letter of 18 January 1779 to the Marquis d'Héricy, quoted in Ernest de Ganay, ed., *Traité de la decoration des dehors, des jardins et des parcs par feu Monseignieur le duc d'Harcourt* (Paris: Émile-Paul Frères, 1919), p. 10.

2 Comte d'Espinchal, *Journal d'émigration*, Ernest d'Hauterive, ed. (Paris: Perrin, 1912), p. 151.

3 René de Belleval, *Souvenirs d'un chevau-léger* (Paris: A. Aubry, 1866), p. 131.

4 Moufle d'Angerville, *Vie privée de Louis XV . . .* (London: J. P. Lyton, 1781), vol. IV, p. 266. Later disputed by the Marquis de Ségur, *Silhouettes Historiques* (Paris: Calmann Levy, 1911).

5 And following, William Beckford, quoted in J.W. Olivier, *The Life of William Beckford* (London, 1932), pp. 171–182.

6 Anathema in our day, in the eighteenth century an exotic young blackamoor

dressed in silk was considered an integral part of a noblewoman's entourage. Zamore had the Comte de la Marche, a Prince of the Blood, for a godfather and Madame Du Barry as his godmother, and the king had notoriously named him Governor of the Château and Pavilion of Louveciennes with a salary of six hundred livres a year. He later betrayed his godmother during the Revolution; his denunciations helped to pave Madame Du Barry's way to the scaffold.

PART IV
LOUIS XVI AND MARIE ANTOINETTE: THE RAGE FOR EXOTICISM

Introductory quotation: Marie Antoinette, quoted by Comte de Mercy-Argenteau in a letter to Empress Maria Theresa, 19 November 1777, Arneth and Geffroy, eds. *Correspondance secrète entre Marie-Thérèse et le Comte Mercy-Argenteau . . .* (Paris: Firmin-Didot Frères, 1874), vol. III, p. 132. Unless otherwise noted, all quotations of the Comte de Mercy-Argenteau appear in this edition.

1 Comtesse de Boigne, *Mémoires* (Paris: Mercure de France, 1971), vol. I, pp. 45–47. All quotations of the Comtesse de Boigne appear in this edition.

2 Ligne, p. 113.

CHAPTER 15
A ROYAL REFUGE: THE HAMEAU AT TRIANON

Introductory quotation: Comte de Calonne, quoted in Boigne, vol. I, p. 43.

1 Mercy-Argenteau, letter of 2 July 1774, vol. II, p. 193.

2 Ligne, p. 206. The financial reforms attempted by Turgot, Louis XVI's first Finance Minister, offered the monarchy its last and best opportunity for achieving equitability and solvency, but the minister's fiscal austerity thwarted the queen until his dismissal in 1776. A series of pliant finance ministers followed, leaving the queen free to pursue her diversions, but Marie Antoinette also faced an atmosphere of unspoken enmity at court and in turn neglected her public responsibilites by withdrawing, with a closed circle of friends, to a world of her own devising at Trianon.

3 For more information regarding the Carousel at the Trianon, see Annick

Heitzmann, "Un jeu de bague sous l'Empire à Trianon," *Gazette des Beaux-Arts* (Paris, March 1988), pp. 203–212.

4 M. de Fontanieu, quoted in Nolhac, *Le Trianon de Marie Antoinette*, p. 126.

5 Campan, p. 95.

6 Baronne d'Oberkirch, entry of 6 June 1782, *Mémoires* (Paris: Mercure de France, 1989), p. 194. All quotations of the Baronne d'Oberkirch appear in this edition.

7 Felix, Comte d'Hezecques, *Souvenirs d'un Page de la Cour de Louis XVI* (Paris: Didier, 1873), p. 245.

8 The working dairy, which stood opposite the Queen's Dairy, has been destroyed. See Gustave Desjardins, *Le Petit Trianon, histoire et description* (Versailles: L. Bernard, 1885).

9 Baron de Besenval, *Mémoires* (Paris: Mercure de France, 1987), p. 420.

CHAPTER 16
A ROYAL WAGER: BAGATELLE AND ITS GARDENS

Introductory quotation: Mercy-Argenteau, vol. III, p. 135.

1 Boigne, vol. I, p. 44.

2 Louis Petit de Bachaumont, et al., letter of 22 October 1777, Matthieu-François Pidansat de Mairobert, ed., *Mémoires secrets pour servir à l'histoire de la République des lettres en France . . . ou Journal d'un observateur* (London: Adamson, 1780–1784), vol. X, p. 259.

3 Hubert Robert's decorative canvases, repainted by the artist soon after their installation to remedy moisture damage, are now in the Metropolitan Museum of Art in Manhattan. See Joseph Baillio, "Hubert Robert's Decorations for the Château de Bagatelle," *Metropolitan Museum Journal*, no. 27 (New York, 1992), pp. 149–182.

4 Proposed by Jean Stern, *A l'ombre de Sophie Arnould: François-Joseph Bélanger* (Paris: Plon, 1930), vol. I, pp. 4–6.

5 Thomas Blaikie, *The Diary of a Scotch Gardener at the French Court* (London: George Routledge & Sons, 1931), p. 192. All quotations of Thomas Blaikie appear in this edition; his writings often border on incoherence, and so have been regularized throughout these pages.

6 And following, Jacques-A. Dulaure, *Nouvelle description des environs de Paris . . .* (Paris: Lajay, 1786), vol. I, pp. 19–20.

7 And following, ibid., p. 20.

8 Blaikie, p. 166, and following, p. 167.

9 Oberkirch, entry of 15 June 1784, p. 343.

10 Blaikie, p. 182.

CHAPTER 17
THE FOLLY OF SAINT-JAMES

Introductory quotation: Ligne, p. 197.

1 Louis XVI, quoted in Oberkirch, p. 479.

2 Élisabeth Vigée-Lebrun, *Souvenirs* (Paris: Féministe, 1984), vol. II, p. 312. All quotations of Madame Vigée-Lebrun appear in this edition.

3 M. Leroux-Cesbon, "Le baron de Saint-James et sa Folie de Neuilly," *Revue de Paris* (Paris, 1 January 1925).

4 Saint-James, quoted in J. Stern, vol. I, p. 135.

5 Artois, ibid., p. 135.

6 Blaikie, p. 181.

7 Horace Walpole, letter of 5 August 1771 to John Chute, quoted in *Horace Walpole, Gardenist*, Isabel Wakelin and Urban Chase, eds. (Princeton: Princeton University Press, 1943), p. 213.

8 Osvald Sirén, *China and the Gardens of Europe in the Eighteenth Century* (New York: Ronald Press, 1950), p. 149. This volume remains a solid introduction to exoticism in European gardens.

9 Jean-Charles Krafft published several monumental works documenting contemporary French architecture and gardens at the turn of the nineteenth century, including *Plans des plus beaux jardins pittoresques de France, d'Angleterre et d'Allemagne* (Paris: 1809–1810) and *Receuil d'architecture civile* (Paris: 1812). These two books provide the main visual documentation for the gardens of Saint-James and are the basis for the reconstructions presented here. All quotations of Krafft appear in the 1829 edition of the *Receuil* (Paris: Bance Ainé, 1829). This and the following citation, p. 20.

10 Ibid., p. 21.

11 "Plan des jardins du duc de Choiseul-Praslin," dated 1787, conserved at the Musée de l'Île-de-France, Sceaux.

12 In 1785, the French monarchy was rocked by this unseemly scandal, which involved an unwitting Marie Antoinette, the disappearance of a fabulously expensive diamond necklace, a thoroughly duped Cardinal de Rohan, a calculating countess named Madame de la Motte, and a disastrous public trial that did little to clarify what illegal actions had occurred and failed to identify and punish the guilty. Instead, by exposing

the gullibility and extravagance rife in the highest levels of government and the nobility, the trial prepared the ground for the Revolution.

13 Oberkirch, p. 479.

14 The Folie Saint-James was sold at auction to the Duc de Choiseul-Praslin for two hundred thousand *livres* on 12 June 1787.

15 Krafft, p. 22.

CHAPTER 18
FOR WIFE AND MISTRESS: THE PAVILIONS OF THE COMTE DE PROVENCE AT MONTREUIL AND BALBI

Introductory quotation: Hezecques, p. 58.

1 Louis XV as quoted by Charles Dupêchez, *La Reine Velue* (Paris: Grasset, 1993), p. 27.

2 Mercy-Argenteau, letter of 22 June 1771, vol. I, p. 173.

3 Jacqueline and Roger Zimmermann, *Le Jardin de Madame: La Comtesse de Provence à Montreuil-les-Versailles* (Versailles, 1989), p. 36.

4 Dupêchez, p. 29.

5 Opinion is divided as to why Savoy was so inexplicably favored as a source for royal wives; some historians believe it was due to Louis XV's fondness for his mother, Marie-Adélaïde de Savoie, and others point out that there were simply no other suitable princesses available. For a thorough biography of Madame, see Vicomte de Reiset, *Joséphine de Savoie, Comtesse de Provence* (Paris: Émile-Paul Frères, 1913).

6 Madame de Chastenay, *Mémoires* (Paris: Plon, 1896), vol. I, p. 92.

7 Oberkirch, entry of 9 June 1784, p. 329.

8 J. Robiquet, "La Propriété de la Comtesse de Balbi et du Comte de Provence," *Revue de l'histoire de Versailles* (Versailles, 1921), pp. 1–14.

9 After Servandoni's death, Chalgrin continued his master's work at Saint Sulpice; in 1775 he was named Monsieur's First Architect.

10 For more information concerning Madame's estate at Montreuil, see: Zimmermann, op. cit.

11 Oberkirch, entry of 9 June 1784, p. 329.

12 The pavilion had several other fascinating rooms, among them a gallery named the Winter Garden— probably inspired by the Duc de Chartres' *jardin d'hiver* at Monceau, which was painted in trompe-l'œil with flowers, trees, and treillage—connecting the main house with the celebrated

library. With a basilican plan and vaulted and coffered ceiling, it was a veritable temple to books, and exhibited Chalgrin's incisive clarity of design.

13 Philip Mansel, *Louis XVIII* (Paris: Pygmalion, 1982), p. 38.

CHAPTER 19
"NOTHING EXCLUDED EXCEPT NATURE": PARC MONCEAU

Chapter title: "Nothing excluded except nature" is a contemporary's disparaging summation of the English-style gardens surrounding Monsieur Du Barry's house in Toulouse, but is equally applicable to the Parc Monceau. Arthur Young, its author, also wrote, "As to the garden, it is beneath all contempt, except as an object to make a man stare at the efforts to which folly can arrive." *Arthur Young, Travels in France during the Years 1787, 1788 & 1789* (London: J. Bell & Sons, 1889), p. 33.

Introductory quotation: Ligne, p. 197.

1 For more information regarding the pavilion, see the exhibition catalogues *De Bagatelle à Monceau, 1778–1978* (Paris: Musée Carnavalet, 1978) and *Jardins en France, 1760–1820. Pays d'illusion, Terre d'experience* (Paris: Hôtel de Sully, 1977).

2 Vincent Cronin, *Ludwig XVI und Marie Antoinette* (Düsseldorf: Claassen, 1975), p. 226.

3 Carmontelle, *Jardin de Monceau près de Paris . . .* (Paris: Delafosse, 1779), p. 4.

4 Comte Alexandre de Laborde, *Description des nouveaux jardins de la France et ses anciens châteaux . . .* (Paris: Delance, 1808), p. 41. All quotations of de Laborde appear in this edition.

5 Ligne, p. 195.

6 Blaikie, p. 179.

CHAPTER 20
THE DÉSERT DE RETZ

Introductory quotation: Baron Gustav Mauritz Armfelt, journal entry of 14 July 1784 (Helsinki: National Archives, Aminne Papers).

1 Madame de Genlis, *Mémoires* (Paris: L'advocat, 1825), vol. I, p. 104.

2 Cheverny, vol. I, p. 55.

3 Blaikie, pp. 210–211.

4 Thomas Jefferson, quoted in Olivier Choppin de Janvry, *Le Désert de Retz* (Croissy-sur-Seine, 1988), item 64.

5 The plans are preserved in the Royal Library and National museum of Sweden in Stockholm.

6 Gustav III, King of Sweden, draft of a letter to de Monville, undated (Stockholm: National Archives, Kabinettet for Utrikes Brevvaxling. B1 â 1785, vol. III).

7 Philippe Égalité was the former Duc de Chartres, later Duc d'Orléans.

8 Colette, "Le Désert de Retz," *Un Pays Inconnu* (Paris: Fayard, 1986), pp. 16–20.

CHAPTER 21
MODERN PHILOSOPHY: THE GARDENS OF ERMENONVILLE

Introductory quotation: Vigée-Lebrun, vol. I, p. 119.

1 Jean-Marie Morel, *Théorie des jardins* (Paris: Pissot, 1776), p. 241.

2 René, Marquis de Girardin, *De la composition des paysages* (Geneva: Delaguette, 1777).

3 Ligne, p. 187.

4 J.-H. Volbertal, *Ermenonville* (Senlis, 1923), p. 13.

5 Ligne, p. 187.

6 J. Mérigot the Younger, *Promenade, ou itinéraire des jardins d'Ermenonville* (Paris: Mérigot Père, 1811), p. 154. Ernest de Ganay, *Bibliographie de l'Art des Jardins* (Paris: Bibliothèque des Arts Décoratifs, 1989), p. 31, has attributed the authorship of this volume to Comte Stanislas-Xavier de Girardin, the Marquis de Girardin's son.

7 Walpole, Wakelin and Chase, eds., op. cit., p. 34.

8 See: Woodbridge, op. cit., pp. 46–47.

9 Gustave Macon, *Les Jardins de Betz* (Senlis: Dufresne, 1908), p. 81.

10 Rousseau's body was later removed to the Panthéon.

CHAPTER 22
A MONUMENT TO EXILE: THE PAGODA OF CHANTELOUP

Introductory quotation: The plaque was composed at the duke's request by the Abbé de Barthélemy and remains *in situ*.

1 We are indebted to the following volumes for much of the biographical information on Choiseul and his family: Gaston Maugras, *Le duc et la duchesse de Choiseul* (Paris: Plon, 1902); _____, *La disgrace du duc et de la duchesse de Choiseul* (Paris: Plon, 1903).

2 The letter reads: "I order my cousin to deliver his resignation as Secretary of State for Foreign Affairs and Superintendent of the Post into the

hands of the Duc de la Vrillière and to retire to Chanteloup until further orders from me. Louis." Maugras, *La Disgrace*, p. 1.

3 Edouard André and Roland Engerand, *Chanteloup* (Chanteloup, n.d.), p. 81.

4 Adélaïde Labille-Guiard, quoted in Baron Roger de Portalis, "Adélaïde Labille-Guiard," *Gazette des Beaux-Arts* (Paris, February 1902), pp. 100–118.

5 In 1750, Choiseul had married Louise-Honorine du Chatel-Crozat, heiress to a great fortune and sister to one of his former lovers, the Duchesse de Gontaut, who had arranged their marriage on her deathbed. The bride was twelve at the time and Choiseul thirty-one. She was universally liked and survived the Revolution in Paris, but later died in poverty.

6 Madame du Deffand, letter of 27 February 1771 to Voltaire, *Correspondance complète de la Marquise du Deffand avec ses amis . . .* (Geneva: de Lescure, 1971), vol. II, p. 143. All quotations of Madame du Deffand appear in this edition.

7 Louis Dutens, *Mémoires d'un voyageur qui se repose* (Paris: Bossange, 1806), vol. II, p. 107.

8 Sir William Chambers wrote several influential volumes: *Designs of Chinese Buildings, Furniture, Dresses, Machines . . .* (London, 1757); *Plans, Elevations, Sections and Perspective Views of The Gardens and Buildings at Kew in Surrey* (London, 1763); and *A Dissertation on Oriental Gardening* (London, 1772).

9 Marie Antoinette was profoundly grateful to Choiseul for having arranged her marriage with Louis XVI, but did not want to interfere in state affairs so early in his reign, and requested the payment be made in recognition of her feelings.

10 Deffand, letter of 16 June 1772 to Horace Walpole, vol. II, p. 262.

11 Louis XV, quoted in L. Dutens, op. cit., vol. II, p. 105.

12 Cheverny, op. cit., vol. I, p. 417.

13 Ibid., p. 417.

CHAPTER 23
A PAGODA BY THE LAKE

Introductory quotation: André Félibien, *Description sommaire du château de Versailles . . .* (Paris: G. Desprez, 1674), p. 109.

1 For more information regarding the Trianon de Porcelaine, see Robert

Danis, *La Première Maison Royale de Trianon* (Paris: Morancé, 1927).

2 Related by Annick Heitzmann in conversation; see also her article "Trianon" in *Châteaux de Faïence* (Louveciennes: Musée-Promenade de Marly-le-Roi-Louveciennes, 1993), pp. 79–84.

3 For more information regarding literary influences upon the development of chinoiserie and upon the *Travels*, see Patrick Conner, *Oriental Architecture in the West* (London: Thames and Hudson, 1979).

4 Eleanor von Erdberg, *Chinese Influence on European Garden Structures* (Cambridge: Harvard University Press, 1936), p. 43.

5 For more information about the history of chinoiserie, see Dawn Jacobson, *Chinoiserie* (London: Phaidon, 1993).

6 Georges-Louis Le Rouge, *Détail des nouveaux jardins à la mode* (Paris: 1774–1789) Ten of the twenty volumes are entitled *Jardins Anglo-Chinois*.

7 The Pagoda was the subject of an exemplary restoration supervised by the architect Olivier Choppin de Janvry in the early 1970s. See Olivier Choppin de Janvry, "Le Pavillon chinois de Cassan à l'Isle-Adam," in *La Revue Française* (Paris, 1975).

8 The second structure is the Kiosk of Canon at Mézidon in Normandy.

9 Guy Nicot, *Le Château de Rambouillet* (Paris: Art et Tourisme, 1993), p. 25.

CHAPTER 24
ENTRY TO ELYSIUM:
THE PYRAMID
OF MAUPERTHUIS

Introductory quotation: Pierre Villiers, *Manuel du voyageur aux environs de Paris . . .* (Paris: Faure, l'An X [1802]), vol. II, p. 58.

1 All serious scholarship on Mauperthuis has been conducted in France. See, among others: Clery Rivière, *Un Village de Brie au XVIIIᵉ siècle: Mauperthuis* (Paris: Picard, 1939); Michel Gallet, *Ledoux* (Paris: Picard, 1980); and Pierre Dosque and Yves Richard, *Au Cœur de Brie*, Mauperthuis (1982).

2 Jean-Paul Denef, *Mauperthuis, un parc au siècle des Lumières* (Dax: Denef, 1992), pp. 60–62.

3 The site of the old manor, a sloping bluff above a small river named the Aubetin, was covered with large boulders which Ledoux cleverly integrated into an elegant

design for a circular ramp leading to the château's *cour d'honneur*.

4 Vigée-Lebrun, vol. I, p. 121.

5 The marquis in part planned Mauperthuis as a model agrarian estate; the village was laid out under his supervision and a fish hatchery contemplated for the octagonal basin; a grand pheasant house and a bizarre, spherical sheepfold was envisioned by Ledoux.

6 See Monique Mosser's incisive essay, "Paradox in the Garden: A Brief Account of Fabriques," in *The Architecture of Western Gardens*, Monique Mosser, ed. (Cambridge: MIT Press, 1992) pp. 263–279

7 Ibid. p. 274

8 Helmut Reinhardt, cited by Mosser, pp. 273–274

9 For further information on Brongniart and his work at Mauperthuis, see the exhibition catalogue of the Musée Carnavalet, *Alexandre-Théodore Brongniart 1739–1813* (Paris: Musées de la Ville de Paris, 1986).

10 Laborde, p. 156.

11 *Almanach de Meaux* (Meaux, 1786).

12 The Keeper's Lodge, another entrance to the Élysée, is one of these doubled bridges—a square, crenellated tower with a rustic addition that stood beside the access bridge crossing the river. Greatly modified, it still stands. The Tower of d'Artagnan, a crenellated medieval keep and drawbridge which was built circa 1782–1783 to reunite the Élysée after an access road to an adjoining property had been cut through the garden, is yet another of these doubled bridges. It is best understood as a picturesque homage to the Knights Templar and the recurrent nostalgia for Henri IV—not, as has been inexplicably suggested, as the sly mockery of a sterile line of musketeers who had once owned Mauperthuis, though its name nods to that history.

13 Some date the tomb to 1781, others to 1786, when the marquis is reported to have discovered the poor admiral's remains at Chatillon.

14 Laborde, p. 157.

CHAPTER 25
BETZ: A TEMPLE
TO FRIENDSHIP

Introductory quotation: Joseph-Antoine-Joachim Cérrutti, *Les Jardins de Betz* (Paris: Everat, n.d.), p. 1.

1 The Princesse de Monaco, as quoted in Pierre-Marie, Marquis de Ségur, *La Dernière Condé* (Paris: Calmann Lévy, 1899), p. 241.

2 André Hallay, *Autour de Paris* (Paris: Perrin, 1911), p. 222.

3 Madame de La Ferté-Imbault, *Souvenirs*, quoted in Ségur, p. 182.

4 Johann Wolfgang von Goethe, *Sämtliche Werke* (Stuttgart: J.G. Cotta'Scher Verlag, 1851), vol. XX, p. 3.

5 Cérrutti, p. 2.

6 Duc d'Harcourt, *Traité de la decoration des dehors, des jardins et des parcs*, Ernest de Ganay, ed. (Paris: Émile-Paul Frères, 1919).

7 Cérrutti, p. 9.

8 Hubert Robert authored both the grotto for the Baths of Apollo at Versailles, and more tenuously, the Temple to Modern Philosophy at Ermenonville. Robert worked with Jacques-Jean Thévenin in designing the grotto, resulting in his being named Designer of the King's Gardens in 1778—a position vacant since Le Nôtre's death.

9 See: Ligne, Harcourt, Girardin, op. cit.

10 Marquis de Girardin, *De la composition des paysages*, Michael H. Conan, ed. (Seyssel: Champ Vallon, 1992), p. 17.

11 Laborde, p. 170.

12 Ernest de Ganay, *Beaux jardins de France* (Paris: Plon, 1950), p. 193.

13 These pedestals were intended to carry busts of men whose fame was inextricably linked to their loves. For more information on artisans involved in constructing the Temple, see: G. Macon, op. cit.

14 Dejoux took a cast from the original sculpture for the temple's apse: it remained at Betz until the beginning of this century, and is now in the collection of the Walters Art Gallery, Baltimore, Maryland. Pigalle's original is now at the Louvre.

15 Abbé de Barthélemy, quoted in A. Halley, p. 247.

16 Laborde, p. 171.

CHAPTER 26
ANCIENT ECHOES:
THE NYMPHÆUM OF
CHATOU

Introductory quotation: La Font de Saint-Yenne, quoted by Michel Gallet, *Soufflot et son Temps* (Paris: C.N.M.H.S., 1980), p. 15.

1 For further information concerning the Château de Chatou and the Chinese Pavilion, see Jacques Catinat, *Les Châteaux de Chatou et le Nymphée de Soufflot* (Paris: Editions S.O.S.P., 1974).

2 For further information concerning Soufflot and his work in Lyon, see: M. Gallet, *Soufflot et son Temps*.

3 Soufflot's second known grotto is *Piccola ma Garbata*, Small but Gracious, at Menars, the estate in the Loire valley that Marigny inherited from Madame de Pompadour. Its facade, again set into a retaining wall, owes a debt to Palladio, and its unassuming interior harbors a spring.

CHAPTER 27
ARMAINVILLIERS
AND THE DUC
DE PENTHIEVRE

Introductory quotation: Jean-Aymer Piganiol de La Force, *Description historique de la ville de Paris et de ses environs* (Paris: G. Desprez, 1765), vol. IX p. 11.

1 For further information concerning Armainvilliers, see: Baron Olivier de Lavigerie, *Le Château d'Armainvilliers* (Paris: Morel, 1890).

2 Antoine Jourdain, *Un petit village Briard: Gretz-Armainvilliers* (Paris: Société Historique de Villiers-sur-Marne et de la Brie Française, n. d.), pp. 9–10.

3 Piganiol de La Force, vol. IX, p. 11.

4 See: "Armainvilliers," in Antoine-Nicolas Dézallier d'Argenville, *Voyage pittoresque des environs de Paris . . .* 3rd ed. (Paris: Buré l'Aîné, 1768) p. 365.

5 Piganiol de La Force, vol. IX, p. 11.

6 This nostalgia was exacerbated by France's recurrent cycles of disillusionment with its aging kings and blind hope for the promise of change embodied by its Dauphins. Upon Louis XVI's accession to the throne, Parisians hung a sign upon the statue of Henri IV on the Pont Neuf which read *Resurrexit*.

7 Ligne, p. 79.

8 Madame Guénard, *Vie du duc de Penthièvre* (Paris: Dujardin, 1802), vol. II, pp. 171–180. By far the greatest indignity, in Madame Guénard's view, was that a wig maker darted out and cut off the princess' celebrated golden hair after the duke's agents had located her head in a mass grave.

ACKNOWLEDGMENTS

For their support and generosity, we are deeply indebted to
M. Hervé Aaron, the Honourable André Baeyens, Mme. and M. Bruno de Bayser,
Mr. Alfred Bush, Mr. Charles Ryskamp, Mr. Alan Salz and Mrs. Charles Wrightsman.
We wish to thank Mrs. Christian Aall, Mr. Joseph Baillio, Mr. Victor Barcimanto,
Mme. and M. Jean Bastien, M. Christian Baulez, Ms. Isabelle Bédard, Prof. Robert Berger,
M. Roland Bossard, Ms. Anne Brady, Mr. Charles Bricker, Jr., Mr. Thomas Burke,
M. Olivier Choppin de Janvry, M. Jean-Paul Denef, Mme. Marie-Amynthe Denis,
Ms. Cara Dennison, Mrs. Jill Dienst, Mrs. Nancy Druckman, Mme. Denyse Emery,
Mrs. and Mr. Meyer Feldman, Ms. Barbara Foss, Prof. J. François Gabriel, Mme. Annick Heitzman,
Mme. Simone Hoog, Mrs. Penelope Hunter-Stiebel, Ms. Laurie Kerr, Mrs. Evelyn Kraus,
M. Emmanuel Le Roy Ladurie, Mr. David Garrard Lowe, Ms. Marian McEvoy, M. François le Meignan,
Mme. Marianne de Meyenbourg, M. Roger Moreau, Dr. Peter F. Ohr, M. Gilbert Pillet,
Mr. João Marques Pinto, Ms. Alice Quinn, Mme. Marianne Roland-Michel, Ms. Betsy Rosasco,
Mme. Setton, Mrs. and Mr. Robert C. Smith, Mr. Garrick Stephenson, Ms. Suzanne Stephens,
Ms. Marilyn Symmes, Ms. Sophy Thompson, Mrs. Marie H. Trope-Podell,
Prof. Gerold Weber, and the late Ms. Eleanor White. Ms. Suzanne Tise and Ms. Diana Groven of
Flammarion have guided this book with creativity and aplomb, to our deep gratitude.

This book is dedicated to our parents.

The Authors

Bernd H. Dams is an architect and architectural historian educated at R.W.T.H.
Aachen and T.U. Munich. He has collaborated on several American architectural exhibitions and is a private
researcher on European architecture and garden history. He lives in New York and Paris.

Andrew Zega is an architectural illustrator, designer, and writer educated at Princeton University.
His paintings have illustrated several books and numerous
other publications, and are held in both public and private collections.

The authors' interest in the architectural history of seventeenth- and eighteenth-century Europe led
to the creation of the fifty watercolors illustrating this book, which were exhibited
at Didier Aaron, Inc. in New York in January 1994 and at the Galerie de Bayser in Paris in October 1995.

PICTURE CREDITS

(The figures refer to page numbers)

Typesetting by Octavo Editions, Paris
Origination by Graphic Color, Wasquehal
Printed and bound by Canale, Turin